PHILOSOPHY IN LITERATURE

PHILOSOPHY IN LITERATURE

Metaphysical Darkness and Ethical Light

Konstantin Kolenda
Carolyn and Fred McManis Professor of Philosophy
Rice University
Texas

BARNES & NOBLE BOOKS
TOTOWA, NEW JERSEY

First Published in the U.S.A. 1982 by
BARNES & NOBLE BOOKS
81, Adams Drive, Totowa,
New Jersey, 07512
ISBN 0-389-20224-X
Printed in Hong Kong

Library of Congress Cataloging in Publication Data

Kolenda, Konstantin.
 Philosophical ideas in literature.

 1. Philosophy in literature. 2. Literature, Modern—
History and criticism. I. Title.
PN49.K64   1981   809'.9338   81-7979
ISBN 0-389-20224-X   AACR2

TO RICE UNIVERSITY
ITS STUDENTS AND SCHOLARS,
PAST, PRESENT AND FUTURE

Contents

Introduction

'Winter completes an age / With its thorough levelling', says W. H. Auden about our times in *For the Time Being*. Auden is not the only one to see signs that our epoch is coming to a close. Many voices proclaim the demise of values that have dominated the West since the Renaissance. If we take science as the fulcrum of the Modern Age, then we cannot ignore the growing scepticism about the ability of science to provide an exhaustive framework and an adequate method for answering all the important questions we want to ask. We see many signs that the adequacy of modern science to supply such answers is being questioned. Increasingly we feel the pressure of the need to look around for alternative modes of thinking about ourselves and the world.

We need not take as definitive the recent vehement attacks on 'objective consciousness' by the student generation, nor the popularity of various forms of Eastern thought, nor the sympathetic turn to revivals of indigenous religion, nor the eager search for new, even chemically induced, forms of consciousness. But all of these phenomena, taken together and coupled with a great deal of disillusionment with the social and political arrangements now governing the world, call for a serious look at the basic foundations of our beliefs and values. If Auden is right in saying that these values are undergoing a serious levelling, given that one of the connotations of 'levelling' is demolition, destruction, then it is time to take stock and to examine where we have been and where we seem to be going.

In such a quest it would be desirable to explore all the available resources. Among such resources we have a variety of disciplines and studies: history, philosophy and various forms of social science. But we also have another form of thought: namely, literature. Less systematic and more intuitive than various depositories of organised knowledge, literature may nevertheless serve as an informal and yet highly accurate weathervane of our civilisation. Great writers are sensitive to the general climate of opinion and often manage to capture its crucial currents. In great works of art across the centuries of the Modern Age are scattered statements about the human condition that express our highest expectations and deepest fears.

In this study I should like to make use of literary works that seem to throw considerable light on the way we have tended to interpret our situation since the Renaissance. Although the selection is to some extent arbitrary and is but a sample from a larger body of available works, it was nevertheless chosen as representing a certain definite line of development. It can be traced through the centuries in which the modern ethos, initiated by the Renaissance and then perpetuated into the Enlightenment and its various offsprings throughout the nineteenth and twentieth centuries, has displayed itself. Since the spirit of literature as a commentary on life 'moveth where it listeth', and since the rate at which changes in insight occur differs significantly from author to author, it would be an error to expect a neat chronological progression. Nevertheless, there *is* a definite change in the self-perception of Western man as registered in the consciousness of successive generations of authors.

This change will be marked in our study by four parts: 'Noon', 'Twilight', 'Night' and 'Dawn'. The headings are not meant as hard and fast distinctions, but they do call attention to significant differences in the way gifted literary observers of the human scene have estimated its character. The change moves, roughly, from the heights of affirmation (Noon), through hesitation and doubt (Twilight), through despair and denial (Night), to a renewal of hope (Dawn). Again, it would be a mistake to see this development as absolutely linear and neat. At most one can point to trends, aspects of which are scattered through the entire consciousness and self-consciousness of the Modern Age, but these trends are nevertheless clearly visible in some specific works, and it is fitting and proper for us to ponder what they may portend.

In the short preface to each part section the basic themes of the works to be discussed are briefly sketched. Each work is discussed in two phases: section A presents an interpretation (which in the case of novels, short stories and plays includes some amount of interpetative narrative) and section B contains a broader commentary on that interpretation, concerned with emphasising special insights of the work in question. The reader familiar with the works themselves will obviously have an advantage in seeing connections and critically following the interpretation, but a previous acquaintance with the work in question is not an absolute prerequisite for understanding what is being said about it. Indeed, my hope is that this study will serve as an inducement to turn or to return to the original works. In my opinion, they repay reading and rereading. If this study stimulates its readers to ponder the themes and developments discussed in this collection of landmark literary works, it will have accomplished its main purpose.

This study deliberately blurs the borderline between literature and philosophy, or, more accurately, it moves within this *preexisting* territory without trying to violate its borderline character. To work merely with concepts developed strictly within the framework of systematic philosophy would be to do undue violence to what the authors have tried to say. On the other hand, it is a mistake to think that, because a writer does not present his views in a manner of a philosophical tract, he is therefore not capable of stimulating fruitful philosophical reflection. What distinguishes the writers represented here is precisely their ability to think deeply about questions that always have been also in the province of philosophy. Indeed, if this study is at all successful, it will contribute in a modest way toward diminishing the forbidding prestige of departmental fences – or at least it will suggest that it is a bit narrow-minded to keep those fences perfectly mended.

Whatever the setting in which great literature is read, formal or informal, it is possible and desirable to concentrate on the ideas it contains. These ideas may become a focus of reflection for students from various scholarly disciplines and for people from all walks of life who have not written off the possibility of connecting academic learning with everyday life. Literary classics have a life of their own and cannot be easily confined to a classroom. If this study is at all successful, it will show the injustice of such a confinement.

Many persons have contributed to eliciting thoughts examined in this study. Besides several generations of students in my course on philosophy in literature, some individuals have helped to make it better than it otherwise would have been. For reading either the whole or parts of this book and for making constructive suggestions for its improvement I wish to thank Jewel Spears Brooker, Terry Doody, Kathy Myers, Bill and Kay Piper, Regina Pappas Seale and Monroe Spears. I also wish to thank Margot and

Michael Hecher, in whose Carinthian mountain retreat the first two chapters of the book have been written. As the dedication indicates, I have a special affection for the institution of learning which made my years as student, teacher and scholar rewarding and fulfilling.

Part I
NOON

The three works to be discussed in this part have one thing in common: the conviction that human beings can be grand. There is grandeur in Faust's resolute striving, in Hamlet's pitting himself against the rotten morals of his time, in the multiple vitality of the Karamazov brothers. Although these works come from different centuries of the modern period and explore different sorts of circumstances, all three confidently set before their protagonists very difficult tasks, but they do so without doubting that the magnitude of those tasks can evoke a proper response.

The authors' expectations of their characters are high, and there is no antecedent sceptical wondering whether they are capable of meeting those expectations. Indeed, Faust's task, as Goethe describes it in the Prologue in Heaven, is to prove that God's attribution of essential goodness to man is correct. Shakespeare's Hamlet refutes those who would make much of human depravity and corruptibility; even though the whole society may be morally out of joint, there may arise in its midst a noble individual who pits himself, heroically and at tremendous cost to his psyche and his fortunes, against the cynicism and corruption around him. Dostoyevsky's characters show not only an insatiable appetite for life, they also take up its opportunities and challenges with great gusto; they throw themselves into the circumstances of their situation without reservation and without any nagging doubts whether their actions and decisions matter. The Karamazov family represents a whole spectrum of philosophical beliefs and moral attitudes, but in each case the characters not only try fully to live out the consequences of their convictions but also show a great capacity for moral and spiritual growth while wrestling with their problems.

In other words, the works with which we start represent the high noon of affirmation in response to the biblical question 'What is man that thou art mindful of him?' There is no question in the authors' minds that human beings are called upon to prove their mettle in their earthly careers. They have no antecedent qualms or misgivings about subjecting their characters to high-level, demanding tasks, simply on the grounds that they do not have it in them to rise to the occasion. Such misgivings will arise, and we shall follow them in other works, closer to our times, when the notion of modernity itself begins to lose its 'brand new world' look. But such negative or cynical thoughts are foreign to the creators of Faust, Hamlet or the Karamazov brothers. Altough these protagonists are not immune from error or evil, they manifest qualities of character, intellect and spirit that make us sit up and watch, if not always in admiration yet at all times with interest and attention. Not without reason have these fictional characters invaded our cultural consciousness; they are startling models of humanity, challenging us to measure up to at least some of the characteristics which they so vitally manifest.

1 Striving Glorified: Goethe's *Faust*

A

Goethe's *Faust* is the product of the author's lifelong reflection on the meaning of human life. Although Faust is an extraordinary person, with titanic aspirations, Goethe's hero is, nevertheless, everyman writ large. His questions and dissatisfactions are not foreign to anyone, even if his talents and ambitions are magnified by the dramatist to gigantic proportions. The barest outline of the story, to be filled out and interpreted as we go along, is this. Having reached a certain degree of knowledge and fame, and approaching old age, Faust experiences an acute disappointment with what life has to offer. His dissatisfaction is rather profound, engulfing him in a mood of despair and cynicism, which drives him to the brink of suicide. The sound of Easter bells distracts him from this drastic resolve, and, after mingling with simple peasants celebrating the holiday in the village square, he returns to his study, and to his melancholy state. Mephistopheles appears, offering Faust the satisfactions he desires in return for Faust's soul when he dies. Faust agrees to the proposal on one condition. The devil may have his soul only if he succeeds in providing him with an experience to which he will say, 'Remain with me forever, you are so wonderful'*. Mephistopheles agrees to this condition, and the contest begins.

The devil, with magical powers at his disposal, provides Faust with the means of experiencing anything he desires on all levels of human interest: love, power, achievement, fame. And so the drama moves from scene to scene in which the dreams of wildest imagination are transformed into reality. The catalogue of Faust's wishes to be realised is immense in scope. Mephistopheles's

---

* The translation is by B.Q. Morgan (New York: Liberal Arts Press, 1954).

5

magic provides all that Faust requests, but Faust remains the judge of the *value* of what he experiences. The devil is impressed, and annoyed, by Faust's voracious appetite for experience, but, bent on getting hold of Faust's soul, bears with him and works very hard to satisfy his every whim.

Toward the end of the play, the devil thinks he hears Faust say the words which would make Mephistopheles the winner in this long drawn-out contest. But, as it turns out, he is mistaken. The judge of the contest is, of course, God, who has been watching the development all along. Faust is pronounced the winner and worthy of salvation. In fact, the wager between Faust and Mephistopheles is preceded by a parallel wager between the devil and God in the Prologue in Heaven, in which the Lord gives his consent to Mephistopheles's scheme to conquer Faust's soul, expressing his confidence that Faust, a good man in God's eyes, will not lose. Not surprisingly perhaps, it turns out that God was right.

The big question is *why* God was right. Goethe gives the answer in his drama. Although he uses theological symbols both at the beginning of the play and at the end, Goethe does not use them in their traditional meanings. He finds them appropriate for capturing some essential concerns of human existence and uses them only allegorically. He falls back on the resources of religious imagery to call attention to some fundamental truths about human existence, without himself subscribing to or encouraging orthodox religious beliefs. The use of religious symbolism may seem surprising in the light of the fact that Goethe regarded himself, and was regarded by others, as a pagan. But it must be acknowledged from the outset that he understood and deeply appreciated the spiritual and cultural resources of Western civilisation, including those supplied by the Christian religion. His conviction was, however, that all deeper truths, wherever they can be found, should be encompassed in a larger vision, which would capture the purpose and meaning of human existence.

With this brief sketch and preliminary general comment behind us, let us turn to some details of the story. These details are presented selectively. The scope of this colossal poetic work precludes the possibility of treating it exhaustively. Goethe's *Faust* is one of the few truly inexhaustible works of literature. The author pursued in it more than one end and crammed into it literary, poetical, historical, political and philosophical insights of his entire life-span, finishing the gigantic work only shortly before his death in 1832 at the age of eighty-three. The selection of episodes in this study is guided by our objective: to extract the essential philosophical message Goethe tries to communicate in this work.

The famous opening lines of the drama, in which the aged Faust expresses his disillusionment with the limited scope of human knowledge and experience, call for an interpretation. It is not obvious what Faust's state of mind signifies. Is it boredom? ennui? exhaustion? inevitable consequence of old age? Or is it something else? The Prologue gives us a clue. It comes from two sources: Mephistopheles and God. Mephistopheles is annoyed by man's restlessness on earth. He finds man's insatiable curiosity and ceaseless activity pointless and obnoxious. Man sticks his nose into everything, disturbs the elements around him, piles up troubles for himself and for others. His special instrument of action is what he calls reason, says Mephistopheles, and in virtue of possessing it he claims superiority over other animals on earth, but in fact he is using it in order to be beastlier than any beast. All of this bustling does not get him anywhere in the end.

This, by the way, is the devil's general conviction about all creation. As he says later, everything deserves to perish, because nothing has really any worth. This fact makes the devil, in his opinion, the most realistic and useful being in the universe, because it is his business to help things out in the inevitable process of destruction and self-destruction. That is why he proudly refers to himself as the spirit that denies. What particularly annoys Mephistopheles is that in his ultimately pointless activity the human animal puts on airs and acts as if what he is up to were really important. But, in the devil's more experienced wisdom, it is not. Nothing is important. Therefore, he finds man's pretensions both obnoxious and comical at the same time. Mephistopheles laughs at them and remarks that God too would be prepared to laugh at this pride of his creation, had he not forsworn laughing.

This is Mephistopheles's point of view. What is God's? Somehow God is not ruffled by his adversary's carryings on. He admits that human life is full of error, but that in the end it does not add up to nothing. Faust is a good example. Although moved by obscure impulses which lead him into trouble, he has it in him to come into the light. In his own special way he furthers God's purposes, and therefore God calls him a good man.

When Mephistopheles scoffs at Faust's special standing in the eyes of God and boasts that he can reduce him to dust, God gives him permission to divert Faust's attention from his true calling. If Mephistopheles succeeds, he can have him as his own. Thus we have two pacts in force at the same time: one in heaven, another on earth. In one case the protagonist is God, in the other man, God's servant. The adversary in both cases is the devil.

It is important to keep in mind this early characterisation of contending forces. They provide vital clues to the understanding of what is to follow. In a way, if one takes the message of the Prologue seriously, one may be inclined to conclude that the whole game is given away at the very start. God and Faust are bound to win, and the devil is bound to lose. In fact, this is the drama's message, and in that sense there is no suspense in the plot. But this is not a detective story. It is an exploration of life as it is, as it is in essence known to every man. The biblical imagery is to be taken not literally but allegorically; it illustrates a deep truth about man's role and place in the universe. Mephistopheles too is a personification of familiar, all too familiar and not necessarily always unwelcome elements in human life. But to this point we shall turn by and by; it is time to return to our hero.

Faust's dissatisfaction has many levels. A student of most profound subjects—theology, philosophy, science—he has come to the point of seeing the inconclusiveness of them all. None of them leads up to big final truths, illuminating the core and the meaning of the universe. If there are superior beings, man, the earthly creature, cannot hope to measure up to their knowledge. The sphere of the earth alone is too varied, too protean, too complex to be grasped in one all-embracing vision. Practical application of knowledge, including such highly respectable fields as medicine, in most cases is pious fraud, pretending to help while in the long run hindering, pretending to heal while killing. Having seen too much failure and too many disappointed hopes, so glowing and fervent in his youth, Faust is now too weary to keep up the struggle and is inclined to put an end to it all. Indeed, the idea of suicide has an attraction of its own. For it constitutes the only act in which man is the complete master of his destiny: he can say a resolute no to all the powers that brought him into existence.

At this point in the play Goethe introduces one of his dramatic devices which, while carrying the action further, symbolise a universal insight. When Faust, almost in elation over his brave and defiant resolution of his inner conflict, raises a glass of deadly poison to his lips, he hears the sound of Easter bells. The sound not only distracts him: it also brings a wave of memories associated with Easter, celebration of spring, resurrection, renewal of life, joy and hope. Faust puts down the glass and joins the rejoicing crowds of villagers in the street. He comments on the remarkable power of life to refresh man's spirit, to form bonds of love and companionship, to invite the celebration of nature in rituals and games. His own spirit is lifted by the sight of the cheerful throng of simple folk, although even then he fleetingly recalls how these simple people put misplaced faith in him as a doctor and believe in his abilities while he himself is appalled by his fumbling ignorance. Nevertheless, the important thing has already happened.

The impulse to suicide was dispelled by the resurrecting manifestations of spring and life expressed in traditional rituals and celebrations. It is important to keep in mind the presence of such external forces impinging on individual human existence. For Goethe these external forces are manifestations of nature in its multicoloured and multipurposed garb. 'Nature', for Goethe, is a rich concept. It includes the physical and the biological aspects of the world, but it also includes human art and creations of the human spirit. Among such creations must be counted what we today may call cultural goods: traditions, societal arrangements, poetry, literature, religion. These goods have an existence that is independent of any individual's life, and they can impinge on that life at unexpected moments in healing, restoring ways. This is precisely what happened to Faust in his darkest moment when he contemplated suicide. He was saved by nature, by the life around him.

Not for long, however. Even as he is enjoying the afterglow of pleasant childhood memories, the countervailing forces are astir. Another temptation comes his way, in similarly unexpected fashion to his salvation from suicide. This time the spirit that denies enters while Faust is engaged in the translation of the first line of the Gospel of St John. The dramatic action of the encounter with the devil is complex and involves much poetry and symbolism. The long and the short of it is that Faust gets an opportunity to ally himself with the devil, who first comes disguised as a dog but then reveals his true identity. Here again the symbolism is in-

tended to communicate something universal. The exchanges between Mephistopheles and Faust cover a larger territory and
include pointed critical and ironic remarks on many subjects,
educational, political and philosophical, which, while not unre-
lated to the main drama, only enrich its essence. The crucial item
is the pact into which Faust enters with Mephistopheles. What
does it amount to and in what spirit is it transacted? The second
part of the question is just as important as the first. Faust is not
impressed by the devil. In fact, he treats him with contempt from
the very beginning. He plays games with him and teases him.
Nevertheless, the very presense of the devil reintroduces
melancholy thoughts into Faust's mind and he begins to curse
life. The devil chooses the moment to make his offer: he will be
Faust's servant and companion, enabling him to fulfil his desires.

It is important to note the spirit in which Faust enters into the
agreement. He *defies* the devil to do what he promises. He is not
eager to get something out of the bargain, if in the process he
loses his essential identity. Therefore, the terms which Mephistopheles proposes do not frighten him at all. The terms call for
Faust to find any one of the experiences to be provided with the
devil's help as ultimately satisfying. When Faust says to such an
experience, 'Stay with me forever!' he will lose the bet and forfeit
his soul to the devil. He is not afraid to enter into that sort of
compact, because he knows his own strength, and he literally
scoffs at his adversary's presumption that he will succumb. Says
Faust, 'Only have no fear of my breaking the contract. To strive
with all my might is precisely what I am promising.' Moreover, he
is not seeking mere enjoyment: he seeks experiences allotted to all
mankind in all their dimensions, joyful and painful. He wants to
be one with mankind.

It seems in a way surprising that Mephistopheles agrees to those
terms. This has reasons. In spite of all his superficial intelligence
and great magic power, the devil is stupid. He does not and can
never understand what Faust understands and seeks. Already at
this early stage the estimate and the prophecy of the Prologue in
Heaven get their confirmation – but how and in what way further
developments will show.

The first important and most famous of Faust's exploits with
Mephistopheles's help is the conquest of Gretchen. That episode
is the best known part of *Faust,* and it has been celebrated in
many art forms, including opera. It is a perennial story of seduc-

tion of an innocent young girl by a scheming male. Goethe's treatment of it has deeper dimensions. It is not surprising for an aging man to want to regain not only his youth but also to include in that recaptured bloom of emotional powers *the* perfect love relationship. Faust is no different. He sees a vision of a lovely girl during a witches' night obligingly arranged by Mephistopheles, and he wants her. Obediently and gladly, the devil complies. He is pleased to perform this assignment because he knows the power of sexual attraction. He hopes that Faust will quickly be caught in its bond and will want to remain in it, thus losing the bet. By means of magic transformations, in which Faust's age and appearance are adjusted accordingly, he is brought into the presence of the beautiful, sweet, innocent peasant girl Margaret, or, endearingly, Gretchen. It is of course love at first sight for Faust. Here at last is someone who is lovely, genuine, simple, and duly impressed by the nobility, manliness, wealth and wisdom of the suitor. Convinced that it is just a fleeting conquest for his master, Mephistopheles arranges convenient trysts, himself playing the role of a worthy suitor for Gretchen's chaperone—neighbour Martha. By means of gifts and flattery he soon creates a receptive atmosphere for Faust. Faust is received with the awe due such a highly placed gentleman, and soon conquers Gretchen's mind and body.

But somehow things do not work out as Mephistopheles hopes. Expecting Faust to get involved on the level of mere sensuality, he is annoyed and upset when he learns that Faust really falls in love with the girl. In the meantime things become even more complicated because, not knowing his real state of mind, Faust treats the relationship less seriously than it is and gets both Gretchen and himself in trouble. She becomes pregnant, and later is accused by pious villagers of drowning her illegitimate baby. Faust unwittingly is instrumental in the death of her brother Valentine, who, hearing about her disgrace, comes to defend her honour. With that much mess on this hands, even Mephistopheles cannot quite handle the situation, and he urges Faust that they should both leave the scene.

For Faust this is not an easy matter. He too expected no more than a pleasant, delicious fling, but, lo and behold, he finds himself genuinely and deeply in love. Instead of heeding Mephistopheles, who, as expected, makes light of Gretchen's misery, cynically commenting, 'she is not the first', Faust insists on visiting her in jail, where she is put as punishment for her sin. The scene in prison is heart-rending. By this time Gretchen is dimly aware that her lover has an ungodly ally. She still loves Heinrich (Faust's assumed name), for she has given herself fully, wholeheartedly, without reservations, and with complete trust. But she is deeply religious and her simple faith imposes on her an absolute demand to expiate her sin. When Faust urges her to leave with him, and he has everything arranged for the break, including horses shivering outside, she turns down his pleas, showing signs of having lost her mind under the pressure of the consciousness of her transgressions and of her illicit love. When Mephistopheles finally wrenches Faust away from his beloved, he says of her, 'She is doomed!' Yet at the same time a voice from above proclaims, 'She is saved!' This difference in verdicts will become important at the very end of the drama, where Gretchen plays an important role in Faust's salvation.

The Gretchen episode reveals an important contrast in perceptions on the part of the two partners–antagonists. As we already know, the devil has a rather low estimate of man's aspirations. It is incomprehensible to him how Faust could develop a genuine loving bond with Gretchen, a bond not limited to sexual exploitative attraction. He does not understand that part of human nature which Faust has and which God recognised when he called Faust a good man. A truly spiritual bond between persons is not something a devil can comprehend, and Faust tells him that much in their quarrels over the matter. Such arguments are bound to fall on deaf ears, because the devil *is* deaf and dumb on that score. No wonder he is upset and annoyed by Faust's behaviour and considers the whole affair bungled.

What about Faust's view of the matter? Goethe shows him genuinely distraught once he learns of Gretchen's plight. His impulse to help, to rescue her, is sincere. Moreover, he knows that he is guilty. This guilt increases after he leaves the prison, leaving Gretchen to her fate. Although Faust is conscious of this guilt, Goethe does not have him dwell on it. Unless the reader takes seriously Faust's expression of sorrow and suffering as he realises Gretchen's plight, he might be tempted to think of him as callous and cynical. Yet Goethe does not present him as such. This may be due to Goethe's own view about the proper way of dealing with guilt and remorse. He gives us an illustration of this view at the beginning of Part II.

At the opening of Part II Faust lies asleep under a tree. He is in a state of nervous and emotional exhaustion, brought about by the trials and disappointments experienced in connection with the Gretchen affair. The question is in what state he will wake up from his disturbed restless sleep. The spirits of nature hover around him, and, as he struggles uneasily in his sleep, the mere passing of time and the regenerating, peaceful course of nature return to him his calm and his zest for life. He wakes up strangely refreshed and renewed; his troubles and turmoils have fled from him as if in a dream. He gets up to face new opportunities and challenges of life.

What are we to make of this way of getting over one's shady past? It looks too easy, too cavalier, too casual. Does not Faust deserve to suffer the pangs of guilty conscience for a long time to come? Has he not inflicted enough suffering on others to deserve punishment? These are our normal reactions. We are uneasy with people who show no remorse. But Goethe seems to attribute little value to it. Perhaps he does so because he believes that to carry around a constant sense of guilt and self-condemnation is not really doing us as much good as we may think. Perhaps a full realisation and admission of one's wrongdoing should be genuine and honest, but it should not be drawn out to last indefinitely. Here again man has an ally in nature, represented in the play by benign spirits. They show compassion for what Faust has gone through. By allowing him to rest in sleep they are also helping to restore his physical strength and the resolve to return to future tasks with confidence and resoluteness. Time and nature can act as healers. This seems to have been Goethe's own philosophy.

When Faust resumes the search for experience, still in the company of and assisted by Mephistopheles, he does not dwell on the wrongs and mistakes he committed before. This does not mean, however, that he has not learned from them. Goethe does not show us Faust committing the same mistake and doing the same injustice twice. He does make new mistakes and commit further crimes. Man errs as long as he lives, observed the Lord in the Prologue. And Faust's objective is to plunge into as many experiences as he can. In every case he shows various degrees of ignorance or arrogance or criminal carelessness. He does not lose his vices all at once. Indeed, he does not lose them until he dies. But what seems important is that he enters each new experience with a real desire to do justice to its value, to achieve the satisfaction it promises, thus enriching his life. He is not actively pursuing moral knowledge, but he is not indifferent to the immorality of the unintended consequences of his actions. His acts often appear childishly irresponsible, but usually his moral blindness is due to his concentration on the positive objectives of his search. The reader would often wish him to be more careful, more foresightful, more cautious than he is, thus avoiding some foreseeable untoward consequences of his actions. But this would put into question the value of activism, to which he is centrally committed and of which the Lord himself expressed approval.

One other factor is not to be forgotten. Everything he does in the drama, Faust does with the assistance of the devil. This is bound to keep things more out of hand than they normally would be. The devil intensifies the risks and dangers, and, inasmuch as Faust willingly uses the devil's magic help, he is not helping himself morally. But the demythologising of the devil's role is still before us, so let us leave this line of inquiry until it becomes more centrally relevant.

Faust's exploits and adventures in Part II are incredibly bold and literally fantastic. Among other things, he gains power over kingdoms, becomes a medieval knight, marries Helen of Troy, and has a son by her. Through magic abolition of time and space barriers and of all or almost all physical limitations, he can explore the riches of experience stored up in the history and in the fantasies of mankind, or at least of those possibilities of human existence on which Goethe wanted to make a comment. In this work, the author manifests unsurpassed mastery of mythology and of classical and modern learning, often using his drama as a vehicle of contemporary criticism or satire. All these riches are reserved for careful students of this great work, but they are not needed for our limited purposes. As the drama nears completion, Goethe's conclusions about the meaning of Faust's wager become more evident, and he himself does not hesitate to spell them out.

Act V of Part II shows Faust, now quite old, nearing the completion or the termination of his pact with the devil. In this act we see him lording over a large territory which he wants to make usable for his people by an elaborate irrigation scheme. The objective is clearly admirable, but it would be an error to suppose that Faust has finally abandoned the quest for enriching his own experience. It appears that his ambition is more self-directed than other-directed. He wants to see himself as a doer of great deeds; the benefit to others, while undeniable, appears secondary. Faust's vanity and egotism are clearly evident in the episode with Philemon and Baucis.

This old idyllic couple happen to own a cottage in the vicinity of Faust's palace. It does not seem to be in the way of his irrigation project, but its linden trees obstruct his view, and the ringing of the old couple's chapel bell disturbs his peace. Faust is honest enough to admit that what is at work in his annoyance is not due to a particular cause but is an expression of a universal unlovely phenomenon plaguing the human race. 'Thus we are tormented worst by the feeling of what we lack despite our wealth.'

This moment of insight does not, however, diminish his displeasure with this annoying distraction, and he orders Mephistopheles to relocate the couple, having offered them a handsome property on a new land. Mephistopheles, as he is prone to do, adds a devilish little trick. He puts his own interpretation on Faust's ambiguous order, and burns down the cottage with the old couple inside. As in the Gretchen episode long before, Faust is outraged by this act, since he genuinely wanted to improve the couple's lot and not to do them in. He curses the devil and his helpers.

One of these helpers is Care, a personification of a factor so far unknown to Faust. She appears with her three sisters, Dearth, Debt and Trouble, who also announce the approach of their brother, Death. The final trial is at hand for Faust. He has a foreboding of the approach of his final hour, but he does not feel ready for it. And he knows why. He still has not fought his way into the open. He would do so if he renounced magic – and hence also the alliance with the devil. Only then would he stand before nature as nothing but a man, and 'it would be worth the effort to be human'. Once he *was* just a man, but he got himself entangled in an enslaving alliance.

At that moment Care enters silently through a keyhole. Faust senses her presence, and it shakes him. But even in this moment of self-condemnation he recognises that Care is his greatest enemy. All of his life he refused to recognise her power. Understandably so, for Care is the symbol for a paralysis of will. Eternal gloom descends upon those touched by her. She is destructive nihilism personified; where she rules, all values and disvalues become indifferent, the deadened will reduces abundance ·to nothingness, and total darkness descends upon the soul.

Faust's reaction to this threat of Care to take up lodging in his soul is extremely significant. It underscores the essential element that makes him what he is – in his own sight and in the sight of God. He rejects Care vehemently. He knows that demons are hard to keep away, but, even though her power is greater than theirs, because more insidious, he refuses to acknowledge it. The only thing she can do is blind him.

Although blinded, Faust summons all his Care free energies and orders the completion of his great humanitarian task of irrigation, for which he is resolved to be the moving spirit. In the meantime, Mephistopheles, whose alliance with the silent sisters is no secret, knows about Faust's blindness and expects the approach of his death. He orders his grave to be dug. The clanging of spades in this activity Faust takes to be the final assault on the construction of dykes and canals. Conscious of a bright light still shining within him, the blind man delivers his final speech.

> Yes! to this purpose I am wholly devoted, and this is wisdom's final conclusion: he alone deserves freedom as well as life who has to win them by conquest every day. And thus, surrounded by peril, child, man, and graybeard will spend their productive years. Such a throng I should like to see, and stand on free ground with a people free. To that moment I'd have a right to say, 'Do stay with me, you are so good!' Not in aeons can the traces of my earthly days disappear.–In the anticipation of such exalted happiness I now enjoy the supreme moment.

A most unusual blend of mixed modes ensues at this point in the drama: poetry, religious symbolism, humour, a battle of wits between good and evil, melodrama and a happy ending, all rolled into one. Mephistopheles thinks that he has won the wager and has Lemurs carry off Faust's remains. But he is afraid of the angels' trickery, so he calls upon gargoyle-like fellow devils to help him guard his winnings. Sure enough, the Heavenly Host appears strewing roses, which of course burn the poor devil worse than pitch and sulphur. But it is again Mephistopheles himself who botches the job, and the way he does it appears to have deeper significance. Watchful over his booty, he nevertheless lets his guard drop, by being attracted by the angels' beauty! It is as if he remembered his remote ancestral prelapsarian connection with them. 'For I love to see them, those darling boys; what keeps me from being able to curse?' Being a devil, however, he cannot keep his attraction on the Platonic or Christian level, and his fascination turns out to be really lust. 'On the inside I am as amorous as a cat', he says, as he hopes to be looked at by them at least once.

This distraction costs him dearly, for the angels bear away Faust's immortal soul, leaving Mephistopheles once more tricked – but to whom shall he complain? With uncharacteristic honesty, he accepts the blame and attributes his lapse to common lust. He even admits that it was a mistake for him to enter into the wager at all, but worst of all he regrets his final folly.

Faust's soul being carried away by the angels, one may presume that he is saved. But the mechanism of salvation in this case, although presented within the framework of Catholic symbolism, has special requirements. Various saints intercede for Faust, but all of them agree that one more intercession is needed, that of Gretchen, now a Penitent One in heaven. Without her pardon Faust's salvation may be in doubt. In her life, Gretchen proved herself to be Faust's equal in spiritual strength, despite her humble origins and social status. It was his good fortune that on his life path he encountered someone capable of deep love and of moral integrity, and it is to his credit that he recognised the superiority of her firm devotion to his carefree, irresponsible love. It is significant that he could respond to her spiritual strength and even saw himself as her inferior in this respect, in spite of his learning and high ambitions. He was surprised and conquered by that overpowering simplicity of spirituality, embodied in her gentle and innocent soul, that Goethe called the Eternally Feminine. Faust's acceptability by the Eternally Feminine, personified by Gretchen in the final scene, is to be included in what the Lord meant in the Prologue in Heaven when he called him a good man.

Gretchen appears close to Faust and prays to the Lord that he grant her happiness by accepting the beloved of her youth, now no longer afflicted Faust. A host of Blessed Boys, the spirits of those who died young, also add their plea to admit Faust, so he would teach them what they had no opportunity to learn on earth. Significantly, Gretchen adds in her prayer that she be granted permission to instruct Faust of the ways of heaven. In their days of courtship on earth it was he who presumed to expostulate to her about God and religion. The Mystical Chorus concludes the play with these words: 'Everything transitory is but a simile; here, earthly inadequacy is turned into fulfilment; here, the indescribable is fully realised, the Eternally Feminine draws us upward.'

B

Why is Faust saved? Does he deserve salvation? Has he really won the bet with the devil? Mephistopheles certainly does not think so, and accordingly feels himself cheated by his enemies in heaven. But, if we look carefully at the formula which was supposed to decide the outcome, we shall discover that it does not support Mephistopheles's claim. Faust's words just before his death do not say that Faust *is* wholly satisfied. They only say that he *would* be satisfied if he stood as a free man among other free men facing common tasks. The conditional form of his statement is important. It does not satisfy the formula of the pact as Mephistopheles interprets it. But it does bear out Faust's self-conception and God's conception of him. In his pact with the devil he only promised to strive with all his might, and this is what he did, to the very end. He was not wholly satisfied when he died.

And yet, as Gretchen says in her intercession, he is no longer afflicted. He has rejected the devil and his magic by expressing the wish to be just a man, natural man without supernatural powers. That was his final insight into himself before Care struck him blind, and he voiced the desire to be a free man again—free of Mephistopheles and his power – in his final statement before dying. Of course, it was only a desire, not an actuality, but, as the Lord says in the Prologue, man errs as long as he lives. It may seem ironical that Faust, the wise man, learns the truth about human life when his life has run out.

It may *seem* ironical, but it really isn't. The explanation calls for another look at the devil. Somehow he naturally belongs to the scheme of things. In the Prologue the Lord himself indicates that he has sent the devil into the world of a purpose. He is to prod man toward exertion, toward action, for man is prone to inactivity, laziness, resignation. Since all of Goethe's theological – and diabolical – apparatus is used by him to express earthly, human truths, we need to go a step further and to attempt a thorough demythologising of the devil. What does he stand for? He stands for many things, all of them familiar. He personifies a feature of all human experience, a feature which appears in many guises: as antithesis, temptation, novelty, opportunity to venture into the unknown. Because it is unknown, it is potentially dangerous and damaging. This feature of life can be embodied in all kinds of situations, in accidents, in persons. The possibility of making use of this permanent component of life is part of what we mean by freedom. To experience contingency, chance, chaos, defiance is to feel the *force* of freedom.

Goethe's Mephistopheles is a clever creature; his intelligence is a good match at times even to that of Faust. Indeed, Goethe is fair enough to the devil to acknowledge his perceptiveness and insight. Mephistopheles pokes fun, for instance, at the German system of education in a devastating satire when he, disguised as professor, lectures Wagner, Faust's student. Goethe uses this role-sharing between Faust and the devil in order to show that to search, as Socrates was accused of doing, under the earth and heaven, to question the unquestioned but questionable is natural for man, even though it is often dangerous. So there is bound to be an intellectual dimension in the feature of the world personified by the devil. It is not suprising that Mephistopheles, the tempter, is also an intellectual, for an intellectual is often a schemer. He is His Majesty's disloyal opposition, he thrives on being opposed and standing over-against. The spirit of 'over-againstness', of alert resistance, heightens our self-consciousness and sharpens the awareness of novelty, of new possibilities. Transferred into the practical and moral realm, the awareness of alternatives often exposes us to risks and dangers.

These must be included among the components of a vital, experimental, daring activism, which Goethe championed and encouraged. But he was not oblivious to the moral risks which are bound to accompany this attitude to life. Faust's way of acknowledging moral claims on him was to try not to *repeat* moral transgressions, although, as we have seen, he shunned the debilitating effects of remorse. As he accumulated experiences, however, and as his understanding matured, he was also building up a resentment against evils that result from deliberately playing with fire. There is a great moral danger in *cultivating* the element of risk, contrivance, intrigue – in short, in the use of dubious powers – personified in his alliance with Mephistopheles. This accumulated resentment finally breaks through in his renunciation of magic and in his desire to be free of tendencies which increase the danger of evil. This is what Gretchen has in mind when she tells the Lord that Faust is at last free of his afflication.

Goethe's great drama appears to call attention to a feature of human life which already the classical Platonic view took into account. Our world is bound to contain some inherent imperfection because, in Plato's philosophical scheme, it is but a copy of the perfect World of Forms. Socrates inveighs against the disturbing influence of the senses, of bodily needs and desires. The Christian view contains this note as well: the world is often seen as a vale of tears; this view, for one, lies at the centre of the Manichaean version of Christianity. In Goethe's drama the element of imperfection is represented by the negating influence of Mephistopheles, the spirit that denies. When Faust allies himself with the devil, he forms an alliance with something that is not altogether foreign to himself. His better side is confident that it will win in the end, but nevertheless it allows itself to be allied with the devilish side.

Unless one becomes a saint, one will not escape devilish promptings and suggestions as long as one lives. (This may go some way toward explaining the belief of some Christian sects that the devil really inhabits the world.) The desire to be rid of these influences must remain but a desire, a resolve to resist them as much as one can. Faust's insight at the end of the play is the realisation of the importance of the desire to resist the seductiveness of evil, to become immune to its entangling but enticing alliance. That is the moment at which Faust manages wholly to surrender himself, at least for the time being, to the power of goodness in him, or, to put it theologically, when he stands in the light of God's grace, or is subject to divine enlightenment. Because in all his previous undertakings he felt, if only dimly, the pulling power of that goodness, he managed not to surrender to evil without remainder. In this way, he kept his soul from being taken over by the devil. Therefore, in the end there was a soul to save.

Seen in this light, Faust's whole life was as it should have been, and the salvation mechanism is but an allegory. The point of the salvation scene is only to pass judgement on Faust's life as he led it. His introduction by the Heavenly Host into the divine realm is really a poetic affirmation of the goodness of his life, as the Lord in his timeless wisdom described it even before the action began.

Goethe's great drama returns us to the theme of Prometheus, who insisted that man should speak with his own voice and that he must defy natural or supernatural powers that deny him this right. The medieval and Renaissance versions of the Faust legend ring changes on this ancient theme, but they do so against the background of orthodox beliefs that tend to suppress human craving for original self-assertion. That is why Faust's willingness to ally himself with the forbidden, with occult magical powers, strikes a responsive chord in those who chafe under the restrictions of vision, whether these restrictions come from orthodox religious limitations of human creativity or from more neutrally philosophical views that set arbitrary limits to human aspiration.

In portraying his Faust, Goethe combines the ancient Promethean elements with the Renaissance high expectations from man. But he also enlists aspects of Christianity that are not against the Promethean spirit. On the contrary, the Lord in the Prologue expresses approval of Faust's restlessness and finds in it essential goodness. He even takes the responsibility for sending out the devil into the world in order to stir up the human tendency toward complacency and laziness. Goethe in effect is attempting a reconciliation of pagan and Christian virtues. The key to this reconciliation is striving. Goethe's rich drama presents the superabundance of options that human experience offers. The deliberate breaking of boundaries between realistic and fantastic possibilities is a celebration both of activism and of imagination. Faust's hunger for experience is titanic and irrepressible. But it is not mindless. Faust is not indifferent to the way the experiences he undergoes affect him as a person. Without moralising with himself at every stage, he nevertheless grows morally.

Although Faust's motives, as most human motives, are mixed, they do not aim deliberately at producing evil. Evil results are inevitable by products of intense, exuberant pursuits. The crucial question is whether we realise their importance as they unfold. Faust *is* genuinely grieved over Gretchen's tragedy and over the crime committed against Philemon and Baucis. His rage against Mephistopheles in both cases is not just a show. The build-up of Faust's resentment against his voluntarily acquired questionable companion finally breaks through in the renunciation of magic – Faust's final and most important insight of his life.

Man errs as long as he lives, declared the Lord in the Prologue. And yet, the crucial question is what *else* is going on along with the erring. Faust's vital impulse to gain as much experience as possible is not just the exonerating component: it points to the essential purpose of human life. To lack hunger for experience, to be modest in one's aspirations, to keep one's sights low and one's appetites subdued is hardly a prescription for a good life. Without embracing titanism or exuberance, we nevertheless should seek a life characterised by fullness, abundance. This is Goethe's message, even though, to make his point dramatically and powerfully, he chose as his vehicle a titanic character. But Faust's titanism, as the devil's magic, is but a symbol of something universal and natural: namely, the desire of every person to learn and to experience as much as possible of his humanity. Faust's life is saved, affirmed, because he made this his paramount objective.

2 Integrity Preserved: Shakespeare's *Hamlet*

A

Volumes have been written on the meaning of this fascinating work. So many lines of dramatic action and deep thought criss-cross in it that there is no definitive way of interpreting and understanding the play. The interpretation that follows does not presume to compete with the many perceptive and illuminating studies of what Shakespeare has managed to put into his work. Rather, it seeks to call attention to some things which lie at the very surface of the play. Their importance may be overlooked if one seeks immediately to uncover deeper meanings. That such profundities are there cannot be denied. But they arise from features that are simple, direct and inescapable – the most common and familiar factors of human experience. To understand the deeper consequences to which these familiar factors may lead, we must begin with what lies unconcealedly on the surface.

The surface events make up the play's main action. It is the story of a family, a court, a state. The focus of the action is a sudden change in the fortunes of a young prince. Unexpectedly, without warning, his normal prospects are upset by an untoward course of events. Slated to be Denmark's next king, he was preparing for the duties and privileges of that exalted office in the usual royal way. He enjoyed all the advantages of princely life: developing athletic skills such as fencing, no doubt expected of him as the future military leader; acquiring as much academic and literary learning as could be had in the best universities of Europe; enjoying the companionship and friendship of the young people of his choice, male and female. Shakespeare also is anxious to tell us that the young Hamlet was endowed with many admirable personal qualities. He was physically fit, intellectually lively, poetically sensitive, capable of attracting friends, hand-

some enough to win the love of the fairest young woman at court,
and ready to reciprocate her affection with great intensity. Moreover, he deeply loved his parents. His father he admired for his
kingly manliness, courage and wisdom. In his mother he saw a
queenly beauty, and a devoted love for her husband and her son.
It seems, then, that the prospects for Hamlet were marvellous. He
would seriously and properly equip himself to be Denmark's
ruler, worthy of his father's expectations. He would marry the
beautiful, sweet, delicate, and sensitive Ophelia. He would have
the help and loyalty of many friends – companions in youthful
exploits, aides and advisers in his royal tasks.

But something went wrong, and all these things were not to be.
There is a note of foreboding in the very opening lines of the play,
and one may be inclined to search for deep metaphysical reasons
why Hamlet's life suddenly took a tragic turn. Somehow, we may
want to say, the stars conspired against a happy ending. It is just
the way of the world that the brightest and best get tripped up by
mysterious workings of fate. There is even a brand of popular
wisdom according to which the good are too good for this wicked
world, or those whom God loves most he takes into his bosom
early. (So it was said of Mozart and Schubert, Shelley and Keats,
and could be said of many other geniuses who died young.)

We need not take the high path at this point – perhaps later.
For now it is open to us to try out simpler explanations. They may
turn out to be credible and plausible in their own right. True,
what happened to Hamlet's family is neither natural nor normal,
in the moral sense of these words. And yet it was natural and
normal in the sense that such things do happen – unfortunate,
criminal, cruel as they are. For many complicated reasons the
happy and desirable course of events is often thwarted by a strong
ambition, a wicked design, an inability to resist a temptation.
Some such factors, one might surmise, Shakespeare saw at work
when Hamlet's fate was thrown out of joint.

As the dramatist tells us, Claudius, the younger brother of the
old Hamlet, coveted both the queen and the throne. Not a
scrupulous person, Claudius found a way to realise his unbridled
ambitions. Whether he did so with Queen Gertrude's consent and
co-operation, Shakespeare does not make clear, but he has her
son worry about the speed with which she agreed to marry her
brother-in-law. Was it just in order to remain queen? The details
of the murder and the subsequent ascension to the throne by

Claudius need not preoccupy us. Suffice it to say that the disguised killing was ingeniously and successfully contrived and that Claudius had enough leadership ability to command instantaneous obedience and homage from the queen and from the court. The wedding followed shortly upon the funeral, and the new king took the affairs of the state firmly and resourcefully into his hands.

One thing he did not quite expect and found bothersome. Somehow the young Hamlet was slow in accepting the new *status quo*. Claudius meant well by young Hamlet – at least, Shakespeare tells us so without comment. He shows us that Claudius sought Hamlet's friendship and goodwill. The new king hastens to declare openly that the young Hamlet will be the next king of Denmark. In the meantime, it is Claudius's royal advice and desire that Hamlet resume his pursuit of learning and of pleasure at the place where he has made so much progress already, the German university of Wittenberg.

Unhappy as he is with the turn of events – the sudden death of his father and the hasty remarriage of his mother – Hamlet appears resigned to his fate. He does not understand it; he is shaken by its cruel blows; yet what can he do? He is not quite without prospects and friends. For one thing, he loves and has the love of Ophelia. Furthermore, many understanding companions, including the lifelong loyal and learned friend Horatio, stand in the wings to lift spirits. But then comes a disturbing hunch.

I say hunch, and not ghost, for a reason. Here again it is most tempting to go off into the metaphysical blue and to speculate on the role and meaning of old Hamlet's ghost. The temptation is expecially hard to resist because Shakespeare himself makes the ghost episodes prominent parts of the play. The reasons for this are many, and worthy ones. First of all, it is an excellent dramatic device, adding a dimension of mystery to the play. Secondly, neither Shakespeare nor his times were really sceptical about the possibility of ghosts; natural science was still too young to encourage such scepticism and to undermine traditional beliefs, religious and philosophical. Thirdly, even the ghostly presence of the old Hamlet enabled Shakespeare to say more about Denmark's situation preceding the unfortunate turn of events. These reasons alone sufficiently explain why Shakespeare needed a ghost for his play, and he uses him magnificently.

Without questioning either Shakespeare's own beliefs or criticising him as a dramatist, we may, however, discern one essential role the ghost plays. He serves as a device to introduce a disturbing thought in the young Hamlet's mind: is all what I see and hear really aboveboard? Given the magnitude of the happenings, this would not be an idle, easily dismissable thought. Once the hunch had arisen, it was difficult not to follow it up – especially for such an intelligent, discerning and sensitive person as Hamlet. The source of the hunch is really immaterial. Without quarrelling with Shakespeare's choice, we could think up other plausible versions that would lead to the same essential result: Hamlet's resolve to follow up the hunch and to get to the bottom of it. In the play it was the ghost. But it could just as well have been something else–a dream, a subtle material clue, a rumour, someone's perception of a discrepancy or an inconsistency in the accepted accounts of the facts. A multiplicity of possible triggers could be supplied by a perplexed mind – Hamlet's own included. Hence, it is not absolutely essential for the old Hamlet to appear as a ghost to activate his son's disquieted and searching mind. Once more, we need nothing deep and metaphysical to explain the young Hamlet's desire to find out what really happened and how it happened.

Is Hamlet's willingness to doubt the official version and the desire to resolve his misgiving so surprising? Hardly. The events have played havoc with his hopes, expectations, loves and loyalties. His taking seriously the clue to some hidden possibilities, whatever its source, is true to his character as Shakespeare wanted us to see it. He is too thoughtful a person to be satisfied with mere appearances, no matter how ready to accept them are all others around him. Here we may have a clue to something special both about Hamlet and about *Hamlet*. This something special will be the subject of our more intensive inquiry, which may help us to see this play in a new light. But for the time being let us follow the course the young Hamlet takes when he comes to suspect that there *is* something rotten in the state of Denmark, and fears, correctly, that it will not be easy for him to escape the task of setting it right. His forebodings of doom are realistic, and his actions, as we shall see, profoundly admirable.

Since the magnitude of the crime of which Claudius may have been guilty is so great, it is only natural for Hamlet to doubt its real occurrence. It speaks well of him that he does not take the message from the ghost thoughtlessly. In this regard it is well to contrast Hamlet's disposition with that of his friend Laertes. Shakespeare presents this other young man in a favourable light. He is lively, loyal, ambitious, eager to excel, to learn the ways of the world. But, in contrast to Hamlet, he always acts quickly, impulsively. He does not examine or question either the reports or the advice that come his way, even when the reports are based on no more than rumour. Although a lovable young man – and Hamlet loves and respects him – Laertes lacks thoughtfulness. His decisions are too hasty, he does not seem to know the phenomenon of making up one's own mind. His mind seems always made up for him by circumstances. Here the contrast with Hamlet is profound. The latter refuses to be ruled by circumstance, and, even more significantly, he refuses to be ruled by decisions of others, especially when he has reason to quarrel with those decisions.

But first the circumstances. They *are* frustrating. First of all, the source of the clue to Claudius's guilt is not transparently veridical. It needs to be checked. Furthermore, if the clue is correct, then a terrible burden is imposed on Hamlet, in virtue of his special relationship to the wronged man. Here we may assume that Shakespeare endorses the traditional duty of the son to avenge his father, although Hamlet's response to this tradition is very complex and deserves close scrutiny. Among other circumstances of Hamlet's situation was something which, when he perceived it, made his task even more difficult. Shakespeare masterfully presents his hero's gradual discovery that he must carry his burden – both the discovery of the truth and facing its consequences – *alone*.

Here, I believe, we have one of the main psychological themes of the play. From being surrounded by loving parents and loyal friends, Hamlet moves into the opposite circumstance. He comes to realise, with the shocking brutality of a devastating insight, that, heavy as the task appears to be, he must carry it all by himself. This is not a sudden realisation: it is revealed gradually as he is forced more and more deeply into his suspicions and the schemes to clear them up. Of course, he immediately realises that the news received from the ghost must be kept secret from the accused. And so he has his soldiers swear secrecy. They oblige him, and so does Hamlet's closest friend, Horatio. But Horatio's power is limited. He can be trusted to help Hamlet to find out the truth, but he is not close enough to share in Hamlet's spiritual

struggle to decide how to deal with the consequences of the discovery. Somehow Horatio's philosophical detachment disqualifies
him from providing the needed moral support. 'There are more
things on earth and heaven than are dreamt in your philosophy',
Hamlet tells Horatio. Perhaps in virtue of not being in the special
position with regard to the dead king and to the kingdom, Horatio can be only an external, not an intimate, ally.

There is only one person who could provide such inner,
intimate support: Ophelia. Hamlet loves her, and she loves him.
From the way Shakespeare describes their relationship, it is
difficult not to conclude that they are aware of their mutual love
for one another. As Hamlet faces the task of devising some way of
getting at the truth about Claudius's role in his father's death, he
also faces the question of the role Ophelia is to play in this task.
One poignant scene reveals that Hamlet considered confiding in
Ophelia about his heavy burden. But there was a hitch, and the
clear-headed Hamlet, in spite of his inner turmoil, did not fail to
perceive it. The problem was Ophelia's simple-hearted and even
simple-minded devotion and submissiveness to her father. As an
eager servant of the new king, Polonius was bound to be
Claudius's ally in the latter's efforts to learn whether Hamlet is on
the trail of his foul deed. Hamlet is dead right in his conclusion
that, facing the choice between the dictates of her heart and
obedience to her father's will, Ophelia would choose the latter,
and thus agree to act as her father's tool in spying on Hamlet.
This circumstance need not be read as an illustration of a dictum
occurring in the play, 'Frailty, thy name is woman.' It so happens
that the other woman in the play, Queen Gertrude, also suffers
from weakness of character. But, even this coincidence is not
quite enough to convict Shakespeare of male chauvinism in this
play. From his other plays we may conclude that he was not guilty
of such stereotyped thinking.

The fact is that, despite her many virtues, Ophelia is not strong
enough to choose a path independent of her father's will. In its
own way, this too is certainly a virtue, especially when we consider
that she is a very young, inexperienced girl. It would be wrong to
conclude from this that her love for Hamlet is not genuine. She
loves him deeply enough to lose her mind over the loss of him;
nevertheless, in the battle between her lover and her father, the
will of the father would win out. And Hamlet knows this. His
final realisation of this came in that poignant scene, which

Ophelia later reports to her father, when, after looking intently into her face 'as he would draw it', he uttered a deep sigh, shook his head and left her, in utter desolation. From that moment on he knew that he had to go it alone, that he could not count on Ophelia's help, and that therefore even she, whom he loved, had to be treated as part, no matter how unwilling, of the enemy's camp. His mother's role was toó closely tied to Claudius's success to confide in her. There were no other possible sources of confidence and support. Rosenkrantz and Guildestern, his close friends from childhood, soon show their colours and are willing to be used by Claudius as his spies, to play upon Hamlet as upon a flute. Polonius sets his traps, using Ophelia as a decoy. And Laertes is anxious to resume his playboy activities abroad.

Here it seems proper to pause and to reflect on the contrast between young Hamlet's attitude to the situation and that of the rest of the court. Shakespeare appears to be taking into account the general tendency of social organisms to maintain themselves without probing too deeply into factors which keep them going. He who has power shall keep it. Success is its own justification. With this tendency in mind, the hasty marriage is not surprising, nor is the alacrity wich which the members of the court, from the highly placed Polonius to the ridiculously pompous courtier Osric, throw themselves into zealous service to the new king. For all of them Hamlet's doubts and misgivings are just symptoms of quaint behaviour, of 'seeing ghosts' in the metaphorical sense of the expression. It is not for them to question the *de facto* authority of the new king; *they* would not be receptive to ghosts, or hunches, or subtle disruptive clues. This tendency of human nature to avoid subtle truths in favour of obvious facts not only adds to Hamlet's isolation: it also quickly establishes a moral distance between him and the rest of society. All things considered, there is some reason to think that Shakespeare means to present Hamlet as a strange phenomenon: the only moral man in an immoral society.

This conclusion needs to be explained and qualified. It must be qualified because Shakespeare's characters are not drawn in black and white, villains in one camp and heroes in another. He treats them all, or almost all, with compassion and understanding. Even Claudius has moments of self-condemnation, although the sincerity and the motives of his fleeting inner probings may be questioned. When Shakespeare gives us glimpses into the hearts

of his characters, we see some goodness in most of them – and
some badness in the best, Hamlet's included. It would be unfair
to accuse Ophelia of immorality when she does her bit in her
father's scheme to play the cat-and-mouse game with Hamlet.
Ophelia's sweet innocence and loving heart make up for her
ignorance of the world's way. Is Gertrude wicked? Her son does
not think so, and he appeals to her virtue, or whatever is left of it;
it is clear that to the very end she maintains some dignity and
honour. Polonius is a fool, but still a loyal, devoted servant.
Laertes is flighty, but brave and honourable. As persons, of
Guildenstern and Rosenkranz and Osric we know little, and
Shakespeare assigns to them only limited and wholly negative
dramatic functions in the play. Horatio's intelligence and his
sympathy with Hamlet point to an admirable moral character,
but it is significant that Shakespeare distances Horatio from the
action of the play by presenting him as a detached, almost aloof
philosopher. It is Horatio's task to tell the world what took place
at the court, and in order to have credibility he himself cannot be
made into a direct, wholly involved protagonist.

Seen as individuals, all, or almost all, of Shakespeare's characters are complex, multidimensional, credible human beings.
Nevertheless, in this particular play there is a definite alignment
on the crucial front of the action. Somehow the whole court is
hell-bent on *not* knowing the truth underlying its moral status
and legitimacy, while Hamlet is determined to bring the ugly
truth to light. We have already noted that he does have a special
reason for following out his suspicions, part of that reason being
sheer self-interest: he has lost his father, his status; his all-around
prospects look uncertain, in spite of his uncle's protestations to
the contrary. Why cannot Hamlet look at the bright side, as
everybody else around him seems to do? Why does he not indulge
in a bit of positive thinking, accept the new *status quo* and take it
from there – cut his losses, rejoin his friends in Wittenberg, resume
his studies, and return to the courtship of the beautiful Ophelia?
Well, that *would* be a solution – perhaps leading to a happy
ending, with Hamlet and Ophelia living happily ever after.

Why does Hamlet stubbornly insist on defying his uncle and his
mother, his entire society? Why does he sacrifice Ophelia, turn
away from his friends and companions – from mirth, from poetry,
from learning? These are weighty questions, and the answers to
them provide, I believe, the essential artistic, philosophical and

moral motives of the play. But, before we turn to them, we need to trace Hamlet's behaviour and fortunes as he proceeds with his resolve to get at the truth, in the uneasy, agonised knowledge that this truth does not bode well either for him or for those he loves or for his country.

As we follow Hamlet's actions and the events at the court, we witness the unleashing of forces – emotional, psychological and moral – which punish and destroy, but at the same time clarify and purify, making new beginnings and new hopes possible. The tragedy lies in the cost required to make regeneration possible. The tragedy is so great that at times one almost wishes that Hamlet would just surrender to the business-as-usual syndrome and join the acquiescence of the whole court. But do we really want him to succumb to this wish? Do we want the world without Hamlet and what he stands for? The greatness of the play consists in part in the challenge Shakespeare throws out to his readers. He leaves the resolution to us, not just as theatregoers and students of literature, but also as persons who are often confronted by situations similar in kind, if not in magnitude, to that which faced Hamlet.

The play which Hamlet stages in order 'to catch the conscience of the king' resolves the question of Claudius's guilt. According to the tradition within which Hamlet is supposedly acting, his course of action from that point on was clear. It was his duty, of which he was insistently reminded by his father's ghost, to avenge old Hamlet's murder. And that's that, it seems. But the play does not end when the crucial fact of Claudius's guilt comes to light; it does not end quickly. Supposedly we, and Hamlet, know what is the right thing to do: kill Claudius. On the immediately conscious level, Hamlet has no doubts about this. That being the case, what is keeping him from seeking the quickest way of doing his duty?

For one thing, there is his mother. What is to be his attitude to her? Again, Shakespeare has a message from the ghost, who tells Hamlet that Gertrude's transgressions are to be left to Heaven. The son is to *speak* daggers to her, not use them. One can easily imagine why. After all, matricide was not condoned even by the harsh medieval code of revenge. Moreover, Gertrude's guilt was ambiguous. Was it perhaps just the physical attraction to Claudius? Hamlet suggests that much in his early speech. Was she an accomplice in the husband's murder? There is no evidence for that. The most that can confidently be said is that she lacked

moral discretion and decorum in such a quick return to her
queenly role. The contrast between her and her son intrudes also
in another respect: she is not interested in looking for or taking up
clues that might reveal the background of her new marriage. She
has little sympathy with Hamlet's strange behaviour and 'antic
disposition'. Is it that she fears to look too deeply lest she discover
something ugly? In Gertrude Shakespeare gives us a complex
character, ready for a modern psychoanalysis.

Her son practices a bit of basic psychoanalysis in the famous
bedroom scene – and does so with a considerable success. But
Hamlet's motives are not just to find out the truth or to punish
Gertrude. He loves his mother, and he is anguished by the fact
that she has made the transition from one marriage bed to
another so readily and so quickly. He is hurt by it; he feels
rejected as the son of her former husband. So his plea and advice
to her are that she should 'assume virtue' and turn away from
Claudius, even though this means that her life from now on will
not be easy. He is asking much from his mother, but he is asking
it in the name of the moral demand he himself so strongly feels
and cannot shake off. From now on Gertrude's life is poisoned,
even before she *drinks* the poison prepared by her new husband.
After the talk with Hamlet she too is a tragic figure, because she
at least cannot quarrel with her son's anguished nobility, and she
tacitly recognises it.

Having resolved the question of how to relate himself to his
mother under these horrendous circumstances, Hamlet now can
turn to the main task: meting out justice to Claudius. On the
directly conscious and emotional level he is prepared to do that.
Believing Claudius to be hiding behind the curtain during his talk
with Gertrude, Hamlet strikes out with the dagger only to kill the
unfortunate meddling Polonius. In assigning guilt, it would be an
error not to take into account Hamlet's highly emotional state
during his interview with his mother: he was wrought up and
profoundly aggrieved. Under the circumstances the lashing out
against the moving arras was not a premeditated killing: it was an
impulsive act, carried out in the heat of righteous anger. That
Hamlet was capable of such passionate behaviour gives the lie to
the claim, made even by Hamlet himself in self-accusation, that
his actions are characteristically frustrated by the pale cast of
thought. Hamlet is a human being, and a full-blooded one at
that; in spite of what he says against himself, he is not lily-livered.

So what keeps him from killing Claudius resolutely and instantly? He has an opportunity to do so right after leaving his mother's bedroom, when he sees Claudius praying. Shakespeare gives us a straightforward reason, at least as reported by Hamlet. To kill Claudius then, in prayer, would be to do him a favour, for, according to the received belief, a praying soul in death goes automatically to heaven. From Claudius's words we know that his soul is not really praying, that his words lack the authenticity coming from a contrite heart. So Hamlet is mistaken in his appraisal of the situation with regard to divine justice. But could he be even more deeply mistaken – about his own motives, for instance? Could he be self-deceived when he says that he would rather kill Claudius when he is in a drunken stupor or in the clutches of some other vice?

Much of what happens afterwards allows the interpretation that, as in the soul of Faust in Goethe's later drama, there were two souls in Hamlet's breast when he was pricking himself up to the required deed of revenge. For one thing, he becomes deeply philosophical and soliloquous. He is full of introspection and gives himself pep-talks. he discourses on heaven and earth, on life and death, on the glorious spectacle of man in general, on the frailty of womankind. He does allow his thoughtful side to counterbalance his emotional state. But is this a *defect* of character? A sign of irresolution? An inability to act? Or could it be something else?

A case can be made that Shakespeare tells us that there is more in Hamlet than is dreamt in his own philosophy. The presumed melancholy and hesitation, philosophical discussion and psychological soul-searchings may be symptoms of something else: Hamlet is questioning the traditional duty of revenge. It is, of course, not a conscious, active questioning; it is questioning by default. It may be Hamlet's secret desire that this cup may pass from him, although not in the sense in which Christ considers it in the Gospels. The truth of the matter is that Hamlet has no killer instinct, even though he is human enough to kill in anger. But to kill deliberately, premeditately, is another matter. It is not in him. True, he reports that he dispatched Rosenkrantz and Guildenstern to their deaths without any qualms. But in that situation he does not act as a killer himself; he merely allows his uncle's treacherous design to run its full course, merely substituting the victims. To the groundlings in Shakespeare's theatre there may have been here a touch of comic relief, a raw satisfaction of justice done. To do psychological and moral justice to this whole episode in the play would require a study of its own, but even so it would not be conclusive, because Shakespeare contents himself with giving us bare outlines of what happened on the ship. One might even feel that the episode does not live up to the tenor of the play. Whatever the verdict on the meaning of this episode, it is still certain that Hamlet neither planned nor executed the killing of his treacherous friends. It is also an open question what the king of England would do on receiving the message.

All signs point to the conclusion that Hamlet came to regard the act of revenge as secondary. He puts up no resistance when Claudius dreams up the scheme of sending him to England. It does not even seem to enter his head that he had better find some quick way of getting even with the king before he is banished from his presence. If he were really bent on revenge, he would have shown some signs of agitation or of a resolve to frustrate Claudius's design. He does nothing. Consider what happens when he returns from England. His welcoming scene is Ophelia's 'maimed' funeral rites. Shakespeare could not have thought of a more cruel reminder to his hero of what he had lost through Claudius's wickedness. Such a reminder, which unquestionably stirred up the deepest wounds in Hamlet's heart, as the quarrel with Laertes in the grave amply demonstrates, could be naturally expected to inflame the desire to bring down the head of the chief evildoer. Yet this does not happen. Hamlet does not initiate any schemes of action. On the contrary, it is his enemy who once again plans murder – in a most devious, perverse way. He would have Hamlet killed by a lifelong friend, shortfused Laertes, heatedly wrought up by the news of his father's death, which Claudius, true to form, lays at Hamlet's feet, suppressing the mitigating background of this homicide. To secure the outcome, should Laertes be killed in the duel – after all, he is disposable too – there is an alternative scheme to fall back upon, another poisoning.

Hamlet receives the invitation to fence with Laertes in a mood of resignation. At this stage the ways of the world do not please him. He has no plans for the future, for on what could such plans be built? He is sick at heart, but he has no stomach to add more misery to his already miserable world. The court is morally destroyed. Claudius's claim to legitimacy is annihilated; he is unmasked as a murderer. Gertrude's heart is 'cleft in twain'; there is no peace nor joy nor dignity in her present and her future. Ophelia's mind and body are destroyed. Laertes, so dependent on others for inner and outer security, mainly on the moral support from his father and his sister, is hopelessly adrift. There is perhaps Horatio, but that friend seems too unbelievably detached from the affairs of the world to be an effective help in Hamlet's value vacuum. (Indeed, if there is a character in the play whose pale cast of thought makes practical affairs utterly indifferent to him, that character is Horatio.)

How does Hamlet come finally to kill the king? Again, not by premeditation, not out of explicit resolve, but in the cruelly confused situation contrived by the scheming Claudius himself. When Hamlet learns of the king's new treachery from the lips of the fatally poisoned Laertes, of whom he is genuinely fond in spite of the latter's grievance, and when he sees his mother dead as a consequence of Claudius's wicked, criminally bungled scheme, he carries out the deed for which he had no enthusiasm, but which was demanded of him by the traditional code of justice. These complex circumstances under which Hamlet kills Claudius point up the fact that all these many deaths, including Claudius's own, are ultimately to be laid at the chief evildoer's feet. Shakespeare's play demonstrates how evil can be its own downfall, and how the victims of evil can become almost unwilling instruments of the evildoer's self-destruction. From the beginning to the end Hamlet does not become an active agent of violence. He resorts to violence only when it is thrust upon him by those who use violence for their ends.

This circumstance adds another dimension to Hamlet's character. His nobility is not sullied by a willingness to do evil, even when it is an evil done in the name of justice. No champion of non-violence, and yet capable of being hard and merciless when he has no other choice, Hamlet nevertheless never *chooses* the violent path. This trait confirms other traits Shakespeare bestowed on him: sensitivity, gentleness, unwillingness to hurt for the sake of hurting. When he is cruel to his mother it is only in order to be kind. When he excludes Ophelia from his plan, it is only to make her choices easier and his own harder – because he is depriving himself of the tokens of her love. How deeply he needs them is evident from the way he disguises his true feelings in subsequent encounters with her. It is not far-fetched to suspect that the suggestive remarks made to her during the play within the play are ways of coping with the outcries of his own wounded heart. Here again we see at work Shakespeare's deep insight into the self-torturing and tortuous defence mechanisms of the human psyche in distress.

B

The greatness of Hamlet as a human being rests not so much in what he does or fails to do as in what he understands. In turn, his understanding is not just intellectual and theoretical but also practical and moral. He knows, morally knows, that a society based on murder and deceit and hypocrisy is not worth having on any terms. This knowledge, and the willingness to live by it, distinguishes him from the rest of his society. He knows the price he is paying, and he knows what calamities can befall those caught in the workings of an evil design. Those calamities he cannot prevent, although he wishes he could. At the same time, he cannot reconcile himself to the world in which he would stand as a consenting spectator of evil designs and of the satisfactions they seem to produce. Even if one goes along with the argument that some of Hamlet's behaviour betrays irresolution and hesitancy, who can claim that this hesitancy should not be there? After all, the burden which Hamlet had to carry was too large for any person, even one of heroic proportions. It is to Hamlet's moral credit that he refuses to be *merely* heroic. He lives and thinks and feels the moral anguish caused by the criminality, faithlessness, deceitfulness, servility, complacency and shortsightedness of those who should know better and who include those whom he loves and on whose fortunes his own depends. He recognises the intertwining of human destinies and he refuses to participate in a configuration of those destinies that is determined by immoral motives. It is cursed spite that he must set aright the relationships which are out of joint. He does not do this out of a sense of self-righteousness or even righteousness. He suspects that his own fortunes will go down in defeat, but is ready to accept this consequence. The alternative to such readiness is moral decay – that of others and his own as well. This makes him a truly moral person.

Unlike his mother, Hamlet cannot turn 'from this to this' – the way she turned from her first, noble husband to the second, murderous one. When it comes right down to it, Hamlet cannot make the crucial existential choice which would put him back into the swim of things, living contentedly on the surfaces of life, the way the rest of the court is willing to do. The inability to make this choice is the most distinctive thing about Hamlet, his character, the person he is. There is, then, justification for calling him the truly moral man in an immoral society. He does not care to have power, satisfaction, pursuit of happiness on *those* terms. Were he to accept those terms, he would not be true to his own self. Herein, it seems to me, is Hamlet's greatness as a human being, the nobility of his spirit. Hamlet fascinates us because he is *capable* of making that difficult choice, the choice which spells tragedy and suffering.

On a universal plane, it seems that, in many situations, without such a choice on someone's part no moral regeneration for the society is possible. We admire Hamlet because occasionally we feel deep down that such regenerations are indispensable, if the spiritual distinctiveness of the human race is to maintain itself. In that sense, it is not far-fetched to see Hamlet as a Christ-like figure, taking on himself burdens which redeem and justify the rest of us. His suffering is necessary, if we are to see the importance and the weight of his choice. How diminished and impoverished would be Shakespeare's Denmark without his Hamlet. If there is a carry-over from art to life, the quality and the character of human existence are determined, at some juncture of social development, by the sort of choices Shakespeare attributes to his prince. His princeliness is essentially moral. And so is the import of this tragedy.

From where does Hamlet derive his moral wisdom? There is, no doubt, much metaphysical discourse in his soliloquies and asides. But it is important to ask what triggers them and what role they play in his decisions and actions. When he turns to metaphysical and theological thoughts he receives from them little guidance. Although ho looks in that direction, he realises that ultimately *he* has to provide answers to the problem he is facing. That answer is not lodged somewhere in the stars or in the writings of deep philosophers. It must be provided in his own judgement and action. That judgement and understanding, which he makes manifest in his attitude and actions, say something about the metaphysical possibilities of the universe. Without this moral

component that Hamlet *introduces* into the scheme of things the
universe would be metaphysically poorer. His ethical light dispels
the metaphysical darkness.

What precisely does Hamlet introduce into the scheme of
things, and for whose sake? To put the question this way is to be
reminded that Hamlet's character is Shakespeare's creation,
which thought might prompt us to ask about the dramatist's
motives. It must be noted that Shakespeare lived at a time of a
profound cultural transformation. The age of divinely guaranteed certainties (in the play in part represented by the old
Hamlet) is being replaced by the age dominated by science. As
Galileo had noted, the physical universe was written in the
language of mathematics, and the suspicion began to creep in
during the following centuries that the universe could be fully
automatic, not guided by *any* will, including God's. This
conception was bound to threaten eternal verities. Shakespeare's
time is also the time of Cervantes and Montaigne, sceptics and
doubters. The graveyard scene in Hamlet, lamenting the transitoriness of human achievement and suggesting the reducibility of
what is humanly most important to material chemical
composition is worth pondering in that connection.

It is to be noted that the four lyric lines which express Hamlet's
profound love for Ophelia also refer to the uneasiness about the
foundation of the cosmos:

> Doubt that the stars are fire;
> Doubt that the sun doth move;
> Doubt truth to be a liar;
> But never doubt I love.

The two concluding lines, however, may be seen as a symbolic
clue to the position that emerges from Shakespeare's own
uneasiness about the demise of metaphysical certainties. No
matter what the course of the stars is, by what forces they are
moved, and what ultimately they bode for man, Hamlet is certain
about the importance of his love. His love does not depend on the
scientific or metaphysical verdicts about the universe. It is
immovable in its own way, and self-justifying. Similarly, Hamlet's
refusal to surrender his own judgement as to what is right and just
and good is firm and autonomous – it need not shift with the
shifting metaphysical or scientific explanations.

If we are tempted to say that the willingness of the members of Danish society to pursue self-centred personal goals, without probing too deeply under the surface of actions determining the social and political realities, is at least partly conditioned by not clearly understood yet far-reaching changes in the cultural and intellectual climate of opinion, we still have on our hands the question 'Why is Hamlet's stand so different?' The answer to this may be that Shakespeare himself was looking for a way in which human beings could face up to the creeping scepticism and metaphysical uncertainties of the time. Hamlet's way of facing up to them, as they expressed themselves in the behaviour of people around him, was one possible answer to the question 'What is possible for man under such trying circumstances?' In preserving his integrity as a person, in refusing to accept a way of life that is indifferent to such human values as trust, loyalty and honesty, Hamlet calls attention to their crucial importance as providing the foundations of meaningful life *regardless* of whether one believes the sun to be fire or does not believe the earth to move.

Human beings *can* defy augury and need not be deflected from the vision of humanly desirable social and interpersonal relationships, no matter what is happening on the horizon of scientific and metaphysical explanation about the origin and ultimate destiny of our planet. The fact that the dust which once was Alexander the Great's body is now covering a bunghole in a peasant's cottage does not diminish the stature of Alexander as a human being. That stature – the moral qualities it comprised and the acts that flowed from it – is by no means affected by what happened to Alexander's body after he died. Analogously, the course of the stars, and the fate of the universe, do not take away an iota from the meaning that human persons achieve in their lives. *Hamlet* is a great play because it portrays such a glorious achievement. By conceiving, if only in imagination, of the possibility of reacting the way Hamlet does to his circumstances, Shakespeare paid a high compliment to the human race, of which he himself was such an extraordinary manifestation.

3 Evil Conquered: Dostoyevsky's *The Brothers Karamazov*

A

In this great novel Dostoyevsky forcefully presents his conviction that human life revolves around 'eternal questions'. The reader cannot escape the conclusion that the human condition matters centrally in the scheme of things. The author's philosophy is at the opposite pole of all forms of reductionism which would deny man a special status in the universe. Dostoyevsky's irrepressible exploration of the meaning of life is summarised in Ivan Karamazov's words spoken to his younger brother Alyosha, 'We in our green youth have to settle the eternal questions first of all.' His words, preceding the telling of the legend of the Grand Inquisitor, do not express a mere interest in ideas, a disembodied intellectual reflection. Throughout the novel we are given to understand that ideas are desperately needed to inform the human situation, to disclose its essential and profound features.

The concern with ideas, with the question of the meaning of life, is passionate because life itself is a passion. This is the most immediate and powerful message of the book. Dostoyevsky speaks of the Karamazov passion as if it were to be applicable to the human race as such. When the two brothers agree that life 'is not a matter of intellect or logic, it's loving with one's inside, with one's stomach', they characterise themselves, their family, their nation, the human race. The startling feature of Dostoyevsky's novel is that he makes this point so unabashedly, so brashly. The 'objective consciousness' of a cautious, sober, restrained reader is likely to object that the intensity of the Karamazovs is not typical of all human beings and that it at most characterises this bunch of wildly vital Russian characters.

40

This objection does not account for the amazing popularity of the novel. Millions all over the world respond to it. They do so for many reasons, among which must be included its serious struggle with such perplexing and fascinating questions as the problem of evil, the nature of justice, the essence of Christianity. But among the attractions of the novel must also be counted something which communicates itself directly and with great force: the invitation to love life more than the meaning of it. The author is serious when he has Ivan say that only when one loves life regardless of logic will one understand the meaning of it. The novel as a whole is an eloquent statement of this conclusion.

The resounding affirmation of life is the alpha and the omega of the book. That life is good was for Dostoyevsky the main message of Christianity. He championed an unquestioning acceptance and a resolute living of it. For a being endowed with a mind, the acceptance of life also involves a passionate desire to understand it, to make sense of it. All its manifestations, including one's own, must be subjected to attentive scrutiny. The reader of *The Brothers Karamazov* is bound to be struck by the intense self-consciousness of its characters. Almost without exception they are deeply introspective, really concerned about their essential identities. This applies even to minor characters and to those whose self-analysis results in grief, in terrible disasters for themselves and for others. Much of the time, Dostoyevsky show us how one can give *wrong* answers to the question of the meaning of life. But even that wrongness proceeds from impulses which we can understand and even share. We can see how and why the characters in the novel are prompted to believe and to act as they do. Repeatedly we are led to recognise that their impulses, tendencies and conclusions could be ours as well. Even the best cannot deny the attraction of evil. When Alyosha discovers in himself the dangerous thoughts and impulses that agitate his brothers, he is only being honest. The force and cogency with which Ivan or Dimitri present their arguments leave no doubt that the author himself found them attractive; there is much autobiographical reflection in the novel. Dostoyevsky's sympathy for all his characters is undeniable, and his success is due to this fact; the reader can sympathise with them, and through them with him. He shows that nothing human is foreign to a human being, even when that being is in danger of lapsing into inhumanity. Dostoyevsky's deep respect for man includes his conviction that between inhumanity and pure beastliness there is an unbridgeable gap.

There are many reasons for regarding Ivan as the central character in the novel. He is deeply reflective and articulate. He formulates Dostoyevsky's main problem, both abstractly (in part through the legend of the Grand Inquisitor) and concretely, through his own behaviour and, most crucially, through his response to the consequences of his own action. Ivan's agony over these consequences powerfully expresses some of Dostoyevsky's chief philosophical concerns. In an important sense, Ivan clearly is the initiator of the main action of the novel. One of its fascinating features is Dostoyevsky's gradual but relentless disclosure of the workings of Ivan's obscure, subtly hidden desire for his father's death. In the course of the book's development, Dostoyevsky makes clear that, if it were not for Ivan's very special state of mind, there would have been no murder. His abstract agonised grappling with fundamental questions had a concrete, practical side and determined the course of events. This is *one* reason for calling this novel philosophical.

Let us recall the novel's main action. Fyodor Karamazov, a selfish, exploitative landowner, is at odds with two of his four sons. (Although Dostoyevsky leaves some uncertainty whether Fyodor was Smerdyakov's father, he pretty much intends the reader to draw this conclusion.) Quite justifiably, Dimitri and Ivan believe themselves to be cheated of their inheritance. In addition, Dimitri falls in love with Grushenka, a young woman whom the old man is trying to seduce. The conflict is exacerbated by Fyodor's character traits. He is a lascivious sensualist, lacking any sense of honour. He exploits his own bad reputation to gain his ends, and he plays the fool to his own shameless advantage. He has no one's interest at heart but his own.

The impulsive, reckless Dimitri, frustrated in his aims and desires, physically abuses his father and publicly threatens to kill him. Ivan's grievance is less direct. Although he also hates his father, his attitude toward him is generalised, diffuse. He condemns his whole way of life, seeing in it a perfect example of pervasive social injustice and malaise. A possibility of influencing the course of events suggests itself only by the circumstances, in a rather complicated way. Smerdyakov, the illegitimate son, smarting under the abusive status and from insulting treatment, obliquely indicates to Ivan that, while feigning an epileptic fit, he may kill Fyodor. The tacit assumption is, of course, that the removal of the old Karamazov would not be a bad thing. Ivan would get his inheritance unfairly denied him, and Smerdyakov would also come into some money (the 3000 roubles the old man keeps in this bedroom as a bribe for Grushenka, should she visit him). Under the circumstances, the whole business can be done in such a way as to attribute the murder to Dimitri, who, as Smerdyakov knows, in Ivan's eyes is also a 'reptile', not much different from his father in life-style. It is quite natural that 'one reptile should devour another'. In addition, Dimitri is an obstacle in Ivan's desire to win Katerina Ivanovna's love.

The way in which Ivan actually influences the execution of the murder is far from straightforward, and the unravelling of the psychological and physical chain of events is one of the most important developments in the novel. The essential drama of that unravelling takes place in Ivan's mind. That he actually was a key contributing factor in the murder becomes clear to him only later, as the whole evidence is gradually but devastatingly presented to him by Smerdyakov. The psychological relationship between Ivan and Smerdyakov is subtle but far-reaching. Eventually Smerdyakov accuses Ivan of using him as a tool, or at least of having tacitly provided a moral and practical sanction for Fyodor's murder. But we are also shown by the author that Ivan can be seen as Smerdyakov's tool; he has allowed himself to be manipulated into acquiescence with, even tacit approval of, the murder plan. When the truth finally dawns on Ivan he is morally devastated. In Dostoyevsky's detailed account of this dramatic inner struggle within Ivan's soul we have a gripping revelation of what a human being is capable of.

Ivan's overwhelming problem is not only how to come to terms with his guilt. Since his part in the murder appears to follow logically from his consciously articulated philosophical position, he is now facing the question whether he can really *live* with his convictions. It is to his moral credit that he doubts whether he can. There is enough goodness and honesty in him to see that his philosophical position is morally bankrupt, no matter how logically correct it may seem. Abstractly conceived, the slogan 'if God does not exist, everything is permitted' may strike a Euclidean mind as perfectly acceptable, but what happens to Ivan when he faces the consequences of *acting* on this slogan shows that he is not *just* a Euclidean mind. He is appalled by the terrible wrongs that result from acting on this slogan, and he is shaken to the very depths of his being. He is honest and decent enough to recognise his own guilt, and he resolves to correct as much damage as he can. He can do so only at a terrible price for himself, his reputation and his self-esteem; his body and his mind are almost destroyed in the attempt. He might have succeeded in realising his resolve, but his efforts are undermined by Smerdyakov's suicide. By this final act Smerdyakov revenges himself on the man he envied and emulated but who was willing to use him as murderous tool.

The details of Ivan's mental anguish as his role in the events relentlessly reveals itself belong to the most absorbing developments in the novel and certainly lie at the centre of Dostoyevsky's interest in the nature of the human soul. Ivan's debate with the devil, his *alter ego* who shows him his secret thoughts and desires, is no less of a psychological masterpiece than is Goethe's analogous account of Faust's dealings with Mephistophles. Indeed, the subtleties of self-deception, as unmasked by Dostoyevsky, out-Freud Freud. Moreover, it is impossible not to feel deep sympathy with Ivan's passionate desire to be honest with himself, even at the cost of losing his grip on life. In that sense, Dostoyevsky presents Ivan as a tragic hero.

Compared with him, Dimitri has less depth. The lack of depth, however, is compensated by exuberance. Passion for life in Dimitri is almost wholly translated into pursuit of full-blood sensuous enjoyment. Like his father, he is a sensualist. He lives to the hilt; as he himself confesses, when he leaps into the pit, he leaps headlong, heels up. But there is one profound difference between father and son. The latter has an acute sense of personal honour. He cannot stop his recklessness, admits to being often a scoundrel, and yet he cannot conceive of himself as a thief. Although his nature and his circumstances almost force on him the need to steal, he rejects, sometimes a bit disingenuously, the possibility of being one. Even more importantly, he is capable of self-reform. Although he lacks Ivan's dialectical acumen, he is taking his philosophical–moral impulses seriously. Conscious of having done much harm to others, even though that harm was not really intentionally inflicted but followed from his impulsive intensity-seeking nature, he is willing to repay with his own suffering. Although not guilty of his father's murder, he acknowledges his other wrongdoings and is prepared to pay a price for them. Like Ivan, he is powerfully struck by the problem of evil. It is not a bare coincidence that both Ivan and Dimitri point to the suffering of innocent children as a serious challenge to the belief in the goodness of God's world. Ivan's reasons for not accepting God's world include a vivid account of a child ripped apart by dogs upon the command of a cruel landowner. Dimitri's dream about the babe crying of cold and hunger is similarly a potent jolt to his moral consciousness. Their reactions, however, differ significantly.

Ivan uses the account to justify taking things firmly into one's own hands and by Euclidean thinking ruthelessly to eliminate injustice in the world. Dimitri's dream plants in his mind the need to repent, to curb one's egoistic desires, and to accept punishment for one's wrongdoings. Dimitri's impulse to expiate the suffering he has inflicted on others is one form of passionate response to a challenge; Ivan's response is another. The latter is no less passionate for taking place in his intellect, his understanding. His initial conclusion is that one must fight evil with evil, but he is intelligent and sensitive enough eventually to learn better. Although understanding of Ivan's motives and respectful of his inner struggle, Dostoyevsky enlists the reader's sympathy with Dimitri's instinctive responses, not with Ivan's Grand Inquisitorial scheming. There is much about Dimitri that is genuinely positive and lovable: his honour, his directness, his generosity, his search for close human contact – with his brother, with his beloved. His entire unfortunate entanglement with Katerina is doomed because from the very first encounter he senses her dishonesty with herself, her masochistic impulse toward 'self-laceration'. Similarly, he doesn't quite know what to make of Ivan, because Ivan to him is a tomb, or, as Alyosha more perceptively describes him, a riddle.

Dimitri's instinctive reactions, while betraying an essentially good, generous heart, are nevertheless unstable because not rooted in deep understanding. For this reason, his resolve to change, to turn over a new leaf, to control himself in the future, does not quite produce conviction. Innocence, observed Kant, is a glorious thing, and yet it is prone to error, because it lacks principle, a steady direction. In that sense Ivan, for all his shortcomings, is a more representative human being than his older brother. He is a deeper person, and therefore his agony over evil, including the evil in himself, is more acute.

What about Alyosha? What is his role in the novel? How does he live through the family drama? One contrast becomes quickly apparent. Unlike his brothers – and his father – Alyosha seems to lack a goal, ambition, direction for himself. Fyodor's philosophy of life is extreme sensualistic hedonism. Dimitri also has a great appetite for life, for intoxication, but he is capable of falling in love, of deep personal loyalty, and his self-image is controlled by his sense of honour. Ivan's ambition transcends the bounds of his own well-being. Although his need for love and for fulfilling human contact is strong, as his relationship to Alyosha and to Katerina indicate, he is obsessed by the presence of evil in the world, and is willing to take it on, in terms of his philosophical, social and political schemes. In contrast. Alyosha lacks anything analogous to such personal aims and ambitions. Instead, he gravitates to the monastery and to people such as Father Zossima – to renouncers. What prompts him in that direction?

Not an anaemic sense of life. There is nothing world-denying about Alyosha. Dostoyevsky presents him as a healthy, robust, cheerful and happy young man. One character trait becomes quickly and clearly evident: the capacity to become absorbed in the goals of others. Dostoyevsky points to this trait in a brief account of Alyosha's childhood experiences and attitudes. He describes him as 'an early lover of humanity'. The suggestion is that this unobtrusive but genuine interest in the well-being of others is completely natural, unself-conscious, inborn. In religious terms it is captured in the phrase 'a man of God'. Of Alyosha, as of Faust, God would have said to the scoffing devil 'He is a *good* man. Go and tempt him, and you will see what I mean.'

As natural and instinctive as Alyosha's goodness is, it certainly is not mindless. He is far from being a saint and even farther from thinking himself one. In fact, he confesses to Ivan and to Dimitri the presence of low impulses that agitate him; he too is a Karamazov. What keeps him from indulging them, in the same way as they do? For one thing, Dostoyevsky is saying and showing, the circumstances. Alyosha does not *resolve* to follow the course he takes. The opportunity to be what we can often comes from outside, from the situation into which we are born or thrown. We do not choose that situation; it presents itself. A mark of a naturally unselfish person may be to allow himself to be distracted from his own pursuits by the consequences of others'. This is very characteristic of Alyosha. Perhaps he entered the monastery as a novice partly out of inertia, partly from a desire to escape the unpleasant family situation, and partly from a diffuse sense of admiration for the good works emanating from the monastery and, more conclusively, from the influence of Father Zossima. But soon he is drawn back into the world by the actions of the members of his family. When his brothers appear on the scene there is no way for Alyosha to stick to his chosen life of meditating and praying in the monastery. But he does not leave the monastery out of the impulse of *wanting* to be helpful. It is simply natural for him to become selflessly absorbed in what is going on in the lives of his brothers.

Here one may come to think of Jesus's saying that he who loses his life shall find it. But in applying it to Alyosha we must add that in becoming absorbed in the drama taking place in the souls of others he is not looking for the salvation of his own soul. There is a total absence of self-consciousness in him on this point. He does what he does because it simply does not occur to him that there might be something more important to do. Herein may lie the essence of his goodness, not to be further explained as a manifestation of some mysterious psychological or religious phenomena but simply to be accepted as a marvellous human possibility. Even if Dostoyevsky wishes to give a religious explanation of Alyosha's goodness, this wish is of secondary importance; his very account of the possibility of the occurrence of such goodness is an inspiring human act. What would *The Brothers Karamazov* be without Alyosha?

His special gift is the ability to become a sympathetic reflector and sounding-board for the inmost agitations in the souls of others. Because of this gift, the anguished souls seek him out. They do so because they are sure that their concerns can become genuinely his as well. Not obtrusively and ostentatiously, but quietly, tacitly, covertly. His concern and interest lighten the burden of their anguish and break down their isolation. Sharing their inmost feelings, worries and fears with Alyosha makes these emotions less oppressive, less burdensome. His brothers' most intimate stirrings are released to the scrutiny of one who truly listens and understands. This capacity to understand, however, cannot be abstract and condescending. It must be rooted in the consciousness that the listener himself is capable of feeling the attraction of what the confessor confesses. That is why

Dostoyevsky presents Alyosha as a self-conscious Karamazov, as at least a potential Ivan or Dimitri. He may be on a lower rung of the ladder of degradation, but he is not innocent of where it leads to. That is why he can be sympathetic and supportive without self-righteousness or sentimentality.

Alyosha is neither self-righteous nor sentimental. Dostoyevsky calls him a realist. Part of his realism is due to the knowledge, obvious when one spells it out, that people need other people, that no one likes to stand alone. Responding to this need is for him a matter of course. But he does not conceive of this response as a matter of moral obligation, of duty, of something required. Somehow he feels that this is the way for him to be, to find himself, to make sense of his own life. This is the way in which, by losing his life, he finds it.

One thing is certain about the world, Dostoyevsky seems to be saying through his novel. There is always plenty of action. The world is full of Ivans and Dimitris. To be human is to act, to choose, to pursue objectives, to seek happiness, to manifest ambition, greed, lust for power or women, need for revenge or retaliation, desire to improve or reform, to erase infamy or injustice. Pick up your newspaper and you see countless examples. But, if such a world, full of enterprise and drama, were to be devoid of Alyosha-like presences, it would be much bleaker than it is. That evil is real cannot be denied. But if we are to come to terms with it, if it can be at all redeemed or perhaps diminished, we need people who can think and feel and act like Alyosha.

Alyosha is a realist because his kind of response enables truth to come to light. Consider his reaction to Ivan's Grand Inquisitor legend. The telling of it is directly relevant to the action of the novel, although the story is sufficiently self-contained to be of interest outside the context of the novel. For Ivan the legend is not an idle mental exercise. He made it up to formulate, first of all for himself, his answer to the most serious 'eternal question' – the problem of evil. The Grand Inquisitor speaks Ivan's own disillusionment with man, with his apparent inability to use his freedom constructively and effectively. Man is not glad of his freedom: it is a burden to him. When he tries to use it, he makes himself miserable. He is therefore pleased to surrender that freedom to some strong-willed leader who is prepared to take his welfare into his hands. He knows what his subjects really need:

miracle, mystery, authority. If the weakness, viciousness and rebelliousness of man can be subdued, he may attain a degree of happiness. The question that Ivan is exploring in the story is whether the Grand Inquisitor was right in taking the course he did, and he is careful to emphasise that the Grand Inquisitor took the fate of millions into his hands out of his love for them. He thought that he loved them more than Jesus did, because he would like to relieve their self-inflicted suffering through the use and abuse of freedom. Jesus's work needed to be corrected because he did not love men enough in demanding from them the impossible: a loving, constructive use of freedom.

It is obvious that Ivan himself is uneasy about his own supposed championing of authoritarianism. That is why he places the story in the context of the inquisitorial practices of the Catholic Church. And yet he seems to agree with the Grand Inquisitor's logic: sometimes a person is justified in taking the fate of others into his own hands – namely, when they make a mess of it. Ivan is looking for a justification of power, both in the general political realm and in interpersonal relations. In his political thinking he is inclined to advocate the merging of socialist authoritarianism with church authority. On the personal level he is wondering whether a person with his father's qualities and behaviour deserves to be alive. He expresses his thoughts, even to himself, indirectly and obliquely, presenting them in a legendary and hypothetical form. Clearly he senses that his logic entails morally dangerous consequences. That is why Dostoyevsky says that Jesus's kiss was burning on the Grand Inquisitor's lips, even though he went about his grim inquisitorial business. The Grand Inquisitor was not unaware of the force of Jesus's silent gesture. It contained the truth he fought hard to suppress.

This train of thought explains Ivan's discomfiture when Alyosha plagiarises his story and kisses Ivan when invited to respond to it. Alyosha is reminding his brother of the truth which Ivan was uneasily aware of but tried to dismiss because it ran counter to his logic. At the same time he is secretly pleased with Alyosha's response, because that response takes account of Ivan's capacity to see through his own self-deception. In this way Alyosha goes straight to the heart of the matter and sees through Ivan's ingenious but disingenuous manoeuvres to appease his moral conscience. Deep down Ivan loves Alyosha's response, because it tells him the truth about his conflicting motives and brings out his latent receptiveness to Christ's message.

Alyosha's realism consists in his sensitiveness to the stirrings of self-doubt and self-condemnation in our criminal promptings. Somehow he is reluctant to accept the view that any human action can be *wholly* evil. 'Between the lines' he is able to read the despair which haunts an evil impulse or act. Repeatedly he makes people realise that in fact they are better than at the moment they thought they were. Consider the startling move Alyosha makes at the end of Ivan's moral odyssey, when Ivan finally becomes convinced of his own guilt in Fyodor's murder. Reading Ivan's anguished mind on this topic, he tells him suddenly without being asked, 'Ivan, you did not kill father.' Ivan is taken aback by this blunt declaration and appears offended by it. Alyosha has hit the centre of Ivan's self-questioning: am I a murderer, a parricide? From Dostoyevsky's account the reader knows the facts. Ivan's *mens rea* is not that of a murderer, although in tracing back in his mind his influence on Smerdyakov he thinks himself into believing that he must take direct responsibility for his father's death. This verdict is too harsh, it is not quite true, and Alyosha's remark is intended to communicate just that. Alyosha is in a position to arrive at a true estimate of the situation because he has known all along, at least from the time of hearing the Grand Inquisitor legend, about his brother's inner moral struggle. He does not deny that Ivan *wished* his father dead (that thought might have crossed even his own saintly mind), nor would he disagree with Ivan's own estimate about the drift of his behaviour with regard to Smerdyakov's intimations of his designs, including such episodes as Ivan's listening in the hallway of his father's house prior to the murder, which behaviour he later found despicable. But the fact is that Ivan himself did not commit the murder and most probably would never have been able to bring it off, should an opportunity have arisen, precisely because of that nagging suspicion that his 'logic' was wrong and that he had no right to arrogate to himself the power over life or death of others. That is why Alyosha hits the nail on the head when he tells his brother, 'You did not kill father.'

Dostoyevsky gives may other examples of the way in which Alyosha's perceptiveness enables the truth about people's real motives to come to light. This almost uncanny ability to read off the secret stirrings in other people's souls explains why those who become aware of this ability gravitate toward him. They seek him out, are anxious to know his opinion. Besides Ivan, Dimitri, Grushenka, Katerina, Ilyusha and Kolya learn something important about themselves from their encounter with Alyosha.

B

The truth which Dostoyevsky succeeds in communicating through his novel is that there is a residue of goodness in every human being. No person is *essentially* evil. Human life is a positive force in the universe bacause of the presence of this ineradicable deep convicion in every person that something good can be realised in the very fact of his existence. There is in us a power that affirms sense-making, value, fulfilment, happiness, joy. Dostoyevsky expands the judgement made by God about Faust in Goethe's drama. As Goethe has God pronounce in the Prologue in Heaven, Faust is a *good* man. That *every* person is good is Dostoyevsky's amplification. The desire to point to this truth explains why the novel so passionately celebrates human life across its entire sweep and in every moment of living. When the novel ends, with Kolya's exclamation 'Hurrah for Karamazov!', the exclamation is meant to apply not just to this one family, because what is found in the Karamazovs can be found throughout the family of man. This explains why millions respond to the message of this novel.

Human goodness is, of course, not unalloyed: usually it is mixed with its opposite, and the mixture of good and evil is different in each case. The way in which man's essential goodness can come to the surface also varies from person to person. If we were to put all five Karamazovs on the evil–good scale, we should have the following line-up: Smerdyakov, Fyodor, Ivan, Dimitri, Alyosha. Smerdyakov is the most evil, Alyosha almost incredibly good. But even for Smerdyakov Dostoyevsky elicits sympathy. First of all, he is a victim of inhumane treatment. Although economically much better off than most inhabitants of the town, he smarts from psychological oppression. Probably aware of being at least biologically a Karamazov, he is a servant, pushed around and ridiculed, contemptuously dismissed as a 'soup-maker'. It is no wonder that Smerdyakov's suppressed and enraged ego revolts against such treatment and seeks revenge. In all of us there is an ineradicable need to count as persons, Dostoyevsky is saying through his portrayal of Smerdyakov's plight. This craving to be recognised as a person is good: it testifies to our respect for the human life in each of us. The sense of honour is honouring the individuated humanity in ourselves. Smerdyakov's wounded sense of honour leads him to assert himself in round-about and perverse ways. Even his suicide is a form of one-upmanship: his dying thought must be a deep satisfaction at having paid back Ivan for his contemptuous way of using his illegitimate half-brother for his selfish ends. Even Smerdyakov refuses to be treated as a means only. To that extent he deserves if not our respect then at least our pity. His embracing of evil ways is at least understandable if not condonable.

Fyodor's lust for life is so excessive that, subconsciously, even he is ashamed of it. So he deliberately plays a buffoon. He is a victim of his own vitality, which, unfortunately, is rather narrowly channelled. Although incorrigible and unrepentant, he senses the distance between himself and others. Especially in the presence of Alyosha he is aware of the fact that his ways *deserve* condemnation. That is why he is struck by Alyosha's refusal to condemn him. You are the only one, he tells his youngest son, that does not condemn me. Such inklings of honest self-awareness, such occasional truthful self-perceptions, creep up in old Karamazov's speech and behaviour, even though a genuine regeneration seems impossible for him. It is almost as if he had decided to talk himself into being and remaining bad.

As we have seen, Ivan's evil is even more dangerous and insidious because it has an intellectual, philosophical basis, and, hence, may have social and political applications. He too talks or rather thinks, himself into being evil. That that evil does not reach the core of his humanity is borne out by his behaviour when he realises the consequences of *acting* on his beliefs. As he faces their consequences, he cannot face *himself*. The ensuing conflict within his soul is bitter and prolonged, but his good impulses are very much astir: in his desire to save his brother from unfair accusation and in his willingness to humiliate himself – not to speak of other, less central matters, such as his love for Katerina or his solicitousness over the drunken peasant whom he previously, in a daze, had knocked down in the snow. Even more importantly, his constant admiration of Alyosha, the almost inexplicable eagerness to confide in his younger brother and to be well thought of by him, betray a tender, generous, receptive, good-loving side in Ivan.

A similar responsiveness to goodness is even more evident in Dimitri. That responsivenss is in part a consequence of his general impulsiveness and impressionability. But Dimitri is no fool, and, more than any other Karamazov, he is intent on preserving his honour. He sins bravely, but he does not want to escape punishment; indeed, he welcomes it, because it assuages his guilt for inflicting so much harm on others. Quick and impulsive, he often regrets his actions afterwards and is willing to compensate for them. He is not a sheer sensualist as is his father, and he is capable of falling in love, not just of desiring women.

Alyosha's evil, if it can be discerned, is at most potential, although we have no reason to question his self-ascription of evil impulses. What is most puzzling about him, however, is his goodness. Perhaps it will become less puzzling when we consider in what it consists. In almost every case Alyosha refuses to accept the conclusion that fellow human beings are wholly incapable of goodness. In each one of them he sees some good and addresses itself to it. That is why Grushenka, induced by Rakitin to seduce the young monk, finds to her surprise that he sees in her not a seducer but a person, a sister, in contrast to the way other males have been treating her so far.

In short, Alyosha's secret is rather simple. He conquers evil by turning his attention to potential goodness. He knows that people are not indifferent to the question of whether they are good or not. Here his insight merges with Dostoyevsky's conviction expressed throughout the novel: life itself is a positive passion. It seeks joy, happiness, fulfilment. But such experiences are poisoned by the presence of pain and frustration. As Ivan comes to learn, those who inflict pain and suffering on others are not immune to reverberations which this pain and suffering have on their souls. They themselves are bound to feel miserable, if they have not become completely hardened and have not lost all their capacity for compassion and fellow feeling. That is the reason why we regard hardened criminality and sadism as akin to illness: they are humanly unnatural states.

Alyosha is a realist because he acknowledges the craving for mental health in all of us. Mental health includes the capacity to affirm life, in oneself and in others. To affirm it in oneself without affirming it in others is, besides being a moral failing, a logical mistake. A person's understanding of what, for instance, pleasure *means* includes the understanding and appreciation of the fact that it is welcomed by all living creatures, which realisation includes the knowledge that pain is experienced as unwelcome. Knowledge of good and evil, then, is not something that is confinable to oneself alone. If something is good, its goodness cannot be limited to one person. So, if I affirm life in myself, I cannot be indifferent to the affirmation of life in others. If it is true that life is a positive passion, that all living creatures can and want to experience it positively, then the very knowledge of this fact commits us to affirming the lives of others. One crucial corollary of this conclusion is that, if one is indifferent to the suffering of others, one undermines, logically and morally, one's own love of life.

This is the philosophical wisdom that Alyosha has somehow acquired. More correctly, it is the wisdom which he demonstrates in his actions. He acts in the light of the conviction that potentially all human beings are mentally and morally healthy, that they have a natural desire to allow the seeds of goodness to sprout in their souls. This is the explanation, or rather the analysis, of *his* goodness. It consists in his willingness to stand by his brothers and neighbours, waiting for such seeds to sprout. What is so unusual about him is the amount of patience he expends on this positively expectant waiting. He waits by the side of his brothers and of his father. He is not equally successful in all cases, because one person's goodness cannot *make* those seeds sprout in other persons. It functions, rather, as the sun and air, which facilitate their germination. And, since, in Dostoyevsky's book, all people have such seeds, even if dormant and submerged under the debris of confused and self-concerned motives, all persons are strangely stirred by Alyosha's presence. He becomes Grushenka's 'conscience', as she puts it, and he is the sounding-board for confessional self-revelations in his brothers. Even persons who seem to be consciously or blindly oriented toward evil, such as Rakitin, are uneasy in Alyosha's presence. Rakitin's failed scheme to engineer a seduction of the young novice by Grushenka stems from his desire to deny the disconcerting powers of Alyosha's character. It is also significant, I believe, that the only person to whom Alyosha does not seem to get through at all is Smerdyakov, the person farthest removed from good on the good–evil scale. This may be seen as Dostoyevsky's admission that in some cases even an angel's intervention would do no good. Here again we do not have a comment on the inefficacy of goodness but rather a realistic acknowledgment of the posibility that evil can *kill* all seeds of goodness in a human self. It is also significant that the person in whom this happens does not see any reason for further existence and commits suicide.

The affirmation of the goodness of human life in Dostoyevsky's novel is total and absolute. That affirmation is presented not in terms of an idea but through life itself, most tellingly in the character and actions of Alyosha but also in the lives of the whole Karamazov family, which may be seen as standing for the whole human family. Dostoyevsky does not *argue* the truth of his position; he presents it to us in character and plot. He seems to be saying, 'This is what life has to offer.' To the extent that the reader can find in his own soul an echo of motives which move the characters in the novel he confirms Dostoyevsky's verdict about the human situation.

Whether this view of human possibilities is to be labelled as characteristically Christian is not crucial. Dostoyevsky believed it to be centrally connected with the message of Christianity, and there is no denying that Father Zossima and Alyosha are Christ-like characters. But whether to *call* this position Christian or not is secondary. The important question is whether one is impressed by the portrayal of humanity as Dostoyevsky's novel presents it. He based it not just on studying the Scriptures but also on acquaintance with the book of life.

PART II
TWILIGHT

Faust, Hamlet and the Karamazov brothers say an absolute yes to life. They conquer their circumstances in ways that reveal something grand about themselves. In perpetually living up to the unconquerable urge to seek experience and to learn from it, Faust confirms the Lord's judgement of him as a good man. In refusing to succumb to the rottenness of Denmark, Hamlet, at a terrible price to himself, preserves the nobility of his soul. Ivan Karamazov, who philosophises himself into fighting evil with evil, shrinks in confusion, agony and horror when he finally realises the full extent of his guilt and presumption. He struggles with the devil inside his own soul, and achieves a victory over the spirit that denies when, at the risk of suffering a breakdown and worse, he tells the truth to the court.

Dostoyevsky's sympathy with Ivan is undeniable. He watches his character drift into criminal thought and behaviour without realising that and how this is happening. Ivan's catching himself and heroically setting himself aright when the truth finally dawns on him is spectacular and impressive. And so is Dimitri's acceptance of the punishment for the crime he did not commit. He is honest enough to see the cosmic justice of his punishment; but he does not allow it to break his spirit, and accepts the verdict, resolved to celebrate life as a better human being under difficult conditions. He is fortunate to have the solace of being loved by a vital woman who admires his love, his bravery, his undaunted spirit. Finally, there is Alyosha Karamazov's uncanny understanding that those too serve life who stand in the wings but are patiently and actively attentive to the uneasy stirrings of conscience and goodness in their brothers and fellow men. Like Socrates, who busied himself as a midwife to truth, Alyosha devotes his attention to helping tender, generous desires to assert themselves.

In short, the authors of these works present human beings who affirm the worth of their lives fully and without reservations. They succeed in making sense of their destinies, in showing how impressive human life can be – in ceaseless striving, in noble self-sacrifice, in resolute self-regeneration, in steadfast altruistic devotion. The three works that follow do not exhibit such an unambiguous affirmation of life's possibilities. Melville, Conrad and Mann explore characters and situations in which the verdicts are not clear-out. A note of inconclusiveness found in these works is not only persistent but also disquieting. We are shown that life is often such that no amount of goodwill can guarantee a good outcome. Or the social conditions may be such that even the most promising, most talented individuals can succumb to corruption. Or, finally, the entire culture may find itself at the crossroads of movements and tendencies that war against one another and leave to the next generation nothing but uncertainty and ambiguity. In other words, the atmosphere in which the questions of the meaning and the sufficiency of human values are explored is not that of high noon and clear air but that of dusk and twilight. The human experiment on earth strikes our writers as inconclusive.

4 Innocence Sacrificed: Melville's *Billy Budd*

Much metaphysical content is packed into Melville's and Conrad's sea stories. That content is not superadded as extraneous intellectual baggage, but forms an integral part of the events described by the authors. If this philosophical interest seems surprising in men so closely identified with the profession of sailor, that surprise may be counterbalanced by the thought that a profession that has for its home the treacherous watery medium connecting continents and races can naturally generate uneasy reflection. Coincidentally perhaps, our authors muse about the ocean of time; both Melville and Conrad reflect on the historical past of present-day England. When Melville speaks of Billy Budd as a barbarian (in a special sense, as we shall see), he thinks that an inhabitant of England of those days, if captured by the Romans, might have struck the dark Italians as an odd sight indeed: his 'clear ruddy complexion and curled flaxen locks' might have led them to think that there was indeed a connection between Angles and angels. On the other hand, Conrad observes that England too, once upon a time, was a dark place.

Melville and Conrad have something else in common. Both are concerned with the way men's lives fit into the larger destiny of the world. It may be more correct to say, however, that both are struck by the fact that the cosmic ways often *fail* to fit human objectives. This appears to bother both writers in a profound sort of way. Conrad does not hide his amused astonishment about the pretentiousness of the human race in presuming to handle that vast dumb thing we call nature. In the long run it is bound to handle us, reducing all human habitations to dark places again. The flame of the candle only flickers, until it dies down altogether. The meaning of the human story may lie only in the telling of it.

Melville is also struck by the ways in which that which to us

humans seems beautiful and grand is so vulnerable, so open to
destruction, the way Billy's life in its lovely youthful bloom is
struck down by seemingly inexorable forces. Both authors are
poignantly reacting to the dark side of human existence; they
ponder the enigmatic evil against which we ultimately have no
defence. But in *Billy Budd* there is also a further dimension
which complicates matters. What destroys Billy is not only Claggart's evil nature but also Captain Vere's goodness. To compound
the irony, Billy believes to the end in the goodness of the man who
condemned him to die. If evil results from good, what sense can
we make of human life?

Billy's story, though not its meaning, can be told briefly. A
foundling, he does not even know who his parents were. His physical features and his bearing are strikingly beautiful, emanating
strength, grace, easy charm, cheerful disposition. Indeed, the
naturally aristocratic characteristics make Melville speculate that
he is the abandoned offspring of a nobleman. As he grows up,
Billy becomes a sailor, a handsome sailor, popular with his mates
and with his superiors for his skills, his willingness to work, his
helpfuless, his ability to inject goodwill and good cheer into any
situation. His illiteracy does not prevent him from showing good
sense. Although lacking sophistication and proper unbringing, he
wins the hearts of others by straightforward honesty and
constructive innocence. He seems an almost angelic, simple-
hearted barbarian, a representative of the state of nature in its
guileless, blessed form.

In 1797, when Melville places the action, Britain and France
were at war and it was a common practice for British war vessels
to impress into the King's service sailors from merchant ships. In
such a manner Billy was transferred from *The Rights of Man* to
the *Indomitable,* to the chagrin of the captain and crew of the
raided merchantman. This change of circumstances Billy accepts
with his usual equanimity and soon becomes popular with his new
companions at sea – with one important exception. Lieutenant
Claggart, master-at-arms of the *Indomitable,* shows a secret but
inordinate interest in Billy. That interest is hard to explain, as is
all of Claggart's character and motivation. His background is
unknown, although Melville speculates that he sought refuge in
the navy after committing some crimes. Claggart's personality,
although unfathomable, is unquestionably sinister. It seems as if
he inexplicably envied Billy all his natural attractive qualities,

which so eloquently contrasted with his. Perhaps mixed with this envy was also a subconscious attraction, resented by the conscious part of his evil mind.

Out of this murky mixture of malevolent motives Claggart decides to do Billy in. After some unsuccessful covert attempts to implicate Billy in an imaginary plot, he attacks the matter head on and reports to Captain Vere that Billy is fomenting mutiny. Aware of Billy's faultless reputation and pleased by his performance as the foretopman, Vere is incredulous and demands that Claggart repeat the accusation in Billy's presence. When Claggart does so, Budd's reaction is unexpected and fatal. Unbeknownst to the captain, Billy has a speech impediment which manifests itself when he is upset. Stunned by the accusation and unable to express it in words, he impulsively strikes out at Claggart, who is instantly killed in the fall. The captain convokes a court-martial, and Billy is sentenced to be hanged. The execution is performed at dawn the next morning.

In this brief summary I have compressed to the bare minimum the events surrounding Vere's actions and Billy's response to them. The circumstances surrounding Vere's decision and motives are complex and crucially important. Their fuller exploration is needed not only to explain the course of events but also to develop the philosophical concerns Melville brings to bear on Billy's tragic end. Captain Vere's personality, values and reasoning need to be discussed in some detail in order to bring out the salient features of the situation.

One important preliminary fact must be mentioned. The action of the story takes place at a very special juncture of British history. Shortly before the incident Melville describes, the British navy was racked by a series of mutinies on its warships. These mutinies had been in part conditioned by the political events across the Channel – the French Revolution – and in part by the appalling conditions under which sailors were expected to live, work and fight. The mutiny at the Nore was particularly dangerous. It was ruthlessly put down, but the Admiralty remained nervous. Commanding officers of all ships were apprehensive that a mutiny could unexpectedly recur and that therefore the utmost vigilance was required. The situation was especially perilous because Britain was at war with France, and mutinies on warships could spell disastrous defeat.

Vere's handling of Budd's case must be seen against this background. But we also need to consider the personal qualities of the man in charge of the *Indomitable*. Although Billy Budd is undoubtedly the focus and the hero of the story, Melville's portrait of Captain Vere is drawn in more perspicuous detail. Part of the reason for this is that the handsome sailor was hardly explicable in ordinary terms; not unlike Alyosha Karamazov, Billy was almost too good do be true. We can understand Vere better because we can follow his thoughts and reasoning; we can weigh, with him, the pros and cons of the case and see the force of the dilemma he is facing. Being more accessible to our understanding, Vere may strike us as a more interesting character than Billy Budd. He also strikes us as the more tragic of the two, precisely because of the clarity with which he understands his and Billy's problem.

Let us try to see the situation from Vere's point of view. On the level of character appraisal the captain does not have much difficulty in determining the facts of the case. An experienced judge of men, he clearly sees the difference between Budd and Claggart. The first is transparently good, the second unaccountably evil. Like the rest of the ship's company, Vere takes a strong liking to the impressed sailor, and, watching his fine performance, seriously considers promoting him to a more responsible position. Claggart's background and behaviour have looked dubious to him from the time he came on board, which was only recently, at the start of this voyage. Claggart's manner of accusing the young sailor of fomenting mutiny strikes him as suspicious, and he is sure that the falsehood of the charge will be exposed if repeated to Billy's face. What he does not and cannot foresee is that the outrageous attack will provoke Billy to the fateful emotional and physical outburst. He does not know of his speech impediment, but, as he watches his futile effort to express his anger in words, he understands why the swift motion of his powerful arm follows instead: it is the only way in which Billy at that moment *can* speak. He has to give vent to his outraged emotion, and in doing so he does not think that his reaction will kill or even hurt. Hurting others is not in his nature. Only an extreme provocation can force from him such a physical response. Claggart's provocation is too much even for his patient, nonviolent, almost angelic disposition.

His clear perception of the two personalities involved, however, did not solve the captain's problem. He is in charge of the ship in wartime, with special weighty responsibilities for the whole Mediterranean fleet. The mutiny at the Nore is fresh on everyone's mind, and its recurrence a constant possibility; anything could set the smouldering embers on fire. In his own mind Vere is convinced that Billy is innocent and that the blow that killed Claggart was an uncontrolled outburst, almost an accident of fate. He also thinks Claggart to have been an evil man, responsible for initiating a chain of causes that had his own death as one of its results. But one thing is unaffected by the considerations of guilt or desert: namely, his responsibility for preventing an outbreak of mutiny on his ship.

Is there a chance that a mutiny will break out? The reader may feel that the captain's fears are exaggerated. Even one of the officers in the court martial feels no imminent danger, and suggests a less drastic course of action: confine Billy to the brig and later turn him over to the Admiralty for decision. But Vere does not see it that way. It is of importance to follow not only his reasoning but also Melville's account of the facts that bear on that reasoning. One lesson for moral philosophy is clearly implicit in the way Melville handles this case. To arrive at a justifiable moral decision it is not enough to appeal to moral principles alone: a correct perception of all relevant facts cannot be dispensed with. And, if we heed carefully the author's clues, we shall have to conclude that Vere's perception of relevant and important facts is accurate.

Vere tells the other two judges in the court-martial that not Billy's deed alone but also its consequences must be examined. It might be tempting to interpret this remark as indicating Vere's adherence to the consequentialist theory of morality: an act is morally wrong if its consequences are bad. This view is rightly criticised for sanctioning the punishment of the innocent. If Billy was innocent, then he does not deserve the punishment prescribed by the naval code. But Vere seems to be of the opinion that in this case the consequences of the act should be regarded as part of the act. Claggart's death is still Billy's doing, or, at least, it would be perceived as such by others. And that perception, in these circumstances, cannot be morally ignored. This is made clear in Vere's response to the junior lieutenant's question of whether it might not be possible to convict Billy and yet mitigate the penalty, which under the code then in force was death by hanging.

The people (meaning the ship's company) have native sense; most of them are familiar with our naval usage and tradition; and how would they take it? Even could you explain to them – which our official position forbids – they, long moulded by arbitrary discipline, have not that kind of intelligent responsiveness that might qualify them, to comprehend and discriminate. No, to the people the foretopman's deed however it be worded in the announcement will be plain homicide committed in a flagrant act of mutiny. What penalty for that should follow, they know. But it does not follow. *Why?* they will ruminate. You know what sailors are. Will they not revert to the recent outbreak at the Nore? Ay. They know the well-founded alarm – the panic is struck throughout England. Your clement sentence they would account pusillanimous. They would think that we flinch, that we are afraid of them – afraid of practising a lawful rigour singularly demanded at this juncture lest it should provoke new troubles.

Vere's perception of the facts is such that they make it 'imperative promptly to act'. 'The greater the fog the more it imperils the steamer, and speed is put on though at the hazard of running somebody down.' What shows that the fog is hazardous? Several things. First of all, even though the striking of the officer was itself already an act of mutiny, in informing the crew about what transpired in his cabin and what is to be Billy's punishment the captain carefully and deliberately avoids using the word 'mutiny'. He also refrains from talking about the necessity of maintaining discipline, 'thinking perhaps that under existing circumstances in the navy the consequence of violating discipline should be made to speak for itself'. That the situation is explosive is evident also from the occurrences reported by Melville. Although the news of Billy's court-martial is at first heard by the sailors in dumb silence, at its conclusion a confused murmur goes up and begins to wax. But then, at in instant sign, presumably from the captain, a shrill whistle of the boatswain and his mates pipes down the watch and sets the sailors in motion to their assigned posts. The same sort of psychological nipping in the bud of an incipient revolt is enacted, once more by the discipline-demanding whistle of the officers, right after the execution, when a similar indistinct but waxing murmur arises from the assembled crew. Still another instance of prompt control of the sailors' collective mind occurs when Billy's body is about to enter the billows. 'An uncertain movement began among them, in which some encroachment was made. It was tolerated but for a moment. For suddenly the drum beat to quarters, which familiar sound happening at least twice a day, had upon the present occasion a signal peremptoriness in it.'

Only willfully can we ignore these details to which Melville wants to draw the reader's attention. They are meant to serve as evidence that Vere's fears are not imaginary, and that they bear out his analysis of the situation at the court-martial, as quoted above. At least, they seem to count as such evidence in the author's mind. Throughout the story, and long before the tragic incident takes place, Melville has emphasised the precarious conditions in the British navy at that time. The mutiny at the Nore

was indeed a demonstration more menacing to England than the contemporary manifestoes and conquering and proselytizing armies of the French Directory. To the British Empire the Nore Mutiny was what a strike in the fire-brigade would be to London threatened by general arson.

Discontent foreran the Two Mutinies, and more or less it lurkingly survived them. Hence it was not unreasonable to apprehend some return of trouble sporadic or general. . . . So it was that for a time on more than one quarter-deck anxiety did exist. At sea precautionary vigilance was strained against relapse. At short notice an engagement might come on. When it did, the lieutenants assigned to batteries felt it incumbent on them, in some instances to stand with drawn swords behind their men working the guns.

If the reader disagrees with the author's view of the circumstances, he must rewrite the story.

But, even if one agrees with Vere's perception of the facts of the situation, one may still be inclined to say that it was morally preferable for him to face mutiny rather than allow Billy's execution. In response to this, one must once more consider what Vere saw included in the consequences of Billy's killing of Claggart. Melville's repeated warnings in the story about the disastrous consequences of naval mutinies for England are intended to be taken at their face value. Captain Vere clearly

identifies himself with the cause he is serving, and he perceives his
formal duties as morally tied up with that cause. Included in that
cause is the responsibility for lives, immediately those that would
be lost in a mutiny, and mediately those that would result from
defeat at the enemy's hands, should the British navy be crippled.
Vere considers that such would be the consequences of Billy's
action should he fail, as captain, to stay in control of the ship.
Again, this is not consequentialist morality, but only an analysis
of the implications of acts the direction of which is to a crucial
extent in Captain Vere's hands. He cannot abdicate this responsibility: it is objectively his, whatever his 'private conscience' may
whisper to the contrary.

It must be also recognised that Vere does not think of himself
as the only person who can read the situation correctly. First of
all, he does not act alone. In the courtmartial proceedings he does
not *tell* his fellow officers what the right decision should be. He
presents arguments, for them to accept or reject. They accept
them because they cannot refute them. Even more significantly – startlingly, perhaps – Melville takes pains to indicate to
the reader that Billy himself understood and accepted the
arguments on which his condemnation was based. Vere's perception of Billy Budd's character made him confident that he would
understand what was at stake. As he says to the other two judges,
'I feel as you do about this unfortunate boy. But did he know our
hearts, I take him to be of that generous nature that he would feel
even for us on whom in this military necessity so heavy a
complusion is laid.'

Vere's prediction, as Melville shows, is borne out. After the
court-martial the captain talks to the condemned and discloses
the motives which led him, and the other officers, to the decision.

It would have been in consonance with the spirit of Captain
Vere should he on this occasion have concealed nothing from
the condemned one – should he indeed have frankly disclosed to
him the part himself had played in bringing about the
decision, at the same time revealing his actuating motives. On
Billy's side it is not improbable that such a confession would
have been received in much the same spirit that prompted it.
Not without a sort of joy indeed he might have appreciated the
brave opinion of him implied in his Captain making such a
confidant of him. Nor, as to the sentence itself could he have

been insensible that it was imparted to him as to one not afraid
to die. Even more may have been. Captain Vere in the end may
have developed the passion sometimes latent under an interior
stoical or indifferent. He was old enough to have been Billy's
father. The austere devotee of military duty letting himself
melt back into what remains primeval in our formalized
humanity may in the end have caught Billy to his heart even as
Abraham may have caught young Isaak on the brink of
resolutely offering him up in obedience to exacting behest.

We are left with a feeling that father and son share a decision
difficult for both of them. That Billy actually does feel the way
Vere predicted he would is borne our by Billy's final utterance,
seconded by the entire crew, before his execution: 'God bless
Captain Vere! Melville's description of the way Billy looks and
acts up to the very end also indicates that he accepts his martyrdom as morally inevitable. The author even goes as far as to sur-
round Billy's death with poetic imagery traditionally associated
with the sacrifice of the Lamb of God. There is also a suggstion,
in a sort of popular-metaphysical digression in section 27, that
Billy's way of expiring violated physiological laws and in that
sense, was almost miraculous.

The thoughts and feelings with which the handsome sailor
accepts his fate are rendered by Melville with deeply religious
piety and with heavy metaphysical pathos. The poem which ends
the telling of the story equals and even surpasses the heart-
rending poignancy of Queen Gertrude's account of how Ophelia
found her final peace ('There is a willow grows aslant the brook
. . .') Billy's natural goodness and innocence, and his unquestioning acceptance of the necessity of his sacrifice, are to be counted
among incomprehensible human phenomena toward which no
other attitude seems appropriate except wonderment and reverence.

What about Captain Vere? We have said that he is no less, and
perhaps more, tragic than the young sailor. Melville leaves no
doubt that Vere loved Billy for what he was, loved him like a son.
And yet he believed that he had to demand his death. This belief
was morally wrong and irrational if Billy's innocent death was
pointless. But was it? Once again, let us look at the situation as
Vere saw it. He believed that he, Billy, and the rest of the crew
were charged with a vitally important task, the defence of the

country at a time of peril. As he saw the circumstances, the failure to execute Billy would amount to an abdication of that responsibility. Melville portrays the captain as a rational, judicious, fair person whose life and profession are commited to the service of the country. He is a patriot in the best sense of the term. His kind of patriotism has nothing in common with the puffed-up officious patriotism displayed in the distorted account of the events on the *Indomitable* which appeared in a naval chronicle of the time. Ironically, that chronicle celebrates Claggart as hero and presents his actions as refuting 'that peevish saying attributed to the late Dr. Johnson that patriotism is the last refuge of a scoundrel'.

Melville did not think that Vere's motives and actions would be correctly understood and appreciated by the world around him. The captain continued to do his duty in the usual quiet, efficient, unostentatious way. While moving to rejoin the rest of the British fleet, shortly after the Budd incident, the *Indomitable* was engaged by the French ship the *Athéiste*. In the course of directing from the deck the attack on the enemy, Captain Vere was wounded and was carried below, where he died a few days later. Led by the second officer in command, the English ship was victorious and the *Athéiste* had to flee. The fighting spirit of the English crew may serve as a clue that the crisis just lived through enhanced the unity of the crew and its determination to fight the enemy. (The manner in which Captain Vere met his death bears a strong resemblance to that of Admiral Nelson, described and commented upon by Melville at the beginning of the story. Are we to draw some conclusions from the symbolic similarities?)

Vere's last words were, 'Billy Budd, Billy Budd.' According to the witness, the senior officer who as a member of the drumhead court was the most reluctant to condemn Billy. 'these words were not the accents of remorse'. What accents, then? They were accents of sorrow and suffering. Vere mourned the loss of such a wonderful human life, knowing that the evil that befell Billy had to come about through his, Vere's, decision and action, as the person charged with the security of the ship in the militarily and morally important mission. To be the bearer of evil in virtue of one's inescapable position of responsibility is no easy task. What Melville intends and succeeds in doing is to present an upright, noble person's inner anguish. Vere's consciousness of his heavy burden is concealed in the author's masterful understatments.

B

At the beginning of this interpretative narrative we noted that there are occasions when human concerns are frustrated by the larger course of events. Sometimes we cannot, and, as the story shows, morally cannot, change the facts that destroy our most cherished values. Vere was condemned to preside over such a destruction. He could not avoid it because what forced his hand were weighty moral considerations. Of course, all of us often wish that things were different from what they are. We are reluctant to accept Vere's reading of the facts because we *hope* that he was wrong, that some other, perhaps more imaginative handling of the course of events, or possibly some external intervention, would make Billy's execution unnecessary. We may say, for instance, that the captain could have taken the crew into his confidence and told them all the facts as he knew and understood them (an action that, as he says in the longer passage quoted above, 'our official position forbids'), thus possibly both saving Billy and preventing the mutiny. Instead, as Melville shows, he was engaged in manipulating the crew in such a quick, subtle and eficient way as to prevent them even from getting their thoughts together.

Such an objection, however, ignores another set of facts. The situation was not one of collectively choosing the right decision, with all persons concerned allowed full away of reasoning and deliberation. To have succeeded in bringing around the simple sailors under his command to his personal view of the matter, the captain would have had to undertake a laborious process of moral education, of exploring all the complexities of the case, and even of instantly heightening their sympathies and sensitivities. But under the circumstances there was no chance for success in such a course and great jeopardy in attempting it. To have risked such a chance would have been, again, to abandon control of the ship under these perilous circumstances. The speed had to be put on. One may be inclined to say that in this regard the sailors under Vere's command were treated, to use Kantian terminology, not as ends in themselves but as means. Even more correctly, Vere's proximate objective was by a series of quick commands merely to control their bodies and their behaviour, bypassing their judgement. But this was not just an option for him: it was part of his responsibility as commander of the vessel. In that sense, Vere

did not fall foul of the Kantian formula, because, having agreed
to serve on the ship, the sailors had accepted the captain's control
of their behaviour as it concerned the well being of the ship, and
thus they were not treated as means only. On the other hand, if
they had resorted to *mutiny,* then, as the word itself sufficiently
indicates, they would have broken the agreement which kept
their relation to the captain morally intact. It may seem
paradoxical that in this case Captain Vere's efficient way of
nipping a possible mutiny in the bud was precisely the sort of
action that helped the sailors to keep *their* part of the moral
bargain. But the paradox here, in this case, seems to be a truth
which stands on its head in order to attract attention.

In this story Melville deals with a crisis situation in which it
seems fitting to invoke the wise old saying 'God, have pity on us
who have to make decisions.' Captain Vere significantly modifies
this insight when he exalaims, after it has become clear that
Claggart is dead from Billy's blow, 'Struck dead by an angel
of God! Yet the angel must hang!' This exclamation has
philosophical depth not immediately discernible from its surface.
It is spoken by a pious, religious person who appreciates the
divine spark in man, in this case manifested by the angelic
qualities of Billy. Yet at the same time Vere quickly perceives that
the other God-given quality – the ability to take on and faithfully
to discharge one's responsibilities – is in conflict with that first
God-given blessing. Captain Vere's moral maturity is evident in
his accepting the challenge to take sides in the dilemma. His
behaviour shows that it is possible to respond to such a dilemma
without losing one's religious piety. Perhaps he remembered the
story of Job.

Melville's story shows how the exigency of a social situation may
sometimes require a decision which destroys beautiful innocent
lives. The author refuses to draw any metaphysical or theological
conclusions from this fact, even though he underscores the
poignancy of Billy's death by invoking images from the account of
Christ's death. There is a Christ-like element in Billy's willingness
to be sacrificed for a good cause. The moral impact of this event
is tremendous. The fact that Vere feels it so acutely says
something about his moral character. The uncomprehending awe
with which Billy's execution is met by the crew, both officers and
simple sailors, also testifies to their vague awareness of the
unfolding tragedy. And yet, Melville is also soberly aware of the

fact that simultaneously with the moral feelings there may also be forces at work which would lead to further, greater tragedies, if the sacrifice of the innocent were not there to keep these destructive forces from erupting. The question should of course be raised of whether it would be better for them to erupt rather than allow the sacrifice and self-sacrifice to take place. The answer to this question depends on how seriously one is committed to moral values which are attained by preventing the impending eruption. Captain Vere is convinced that it is his moral responsibility not to allow the possibility of mutiny to arise. The way he reads the facts, he cannot avoid it without sacrificing Billy, and Melville's depiction of the facts suggests that the captain's estimate is correct.

We may hope that such terrible moral conflicts as the one depicted in Melville's story do not occur frequently. This consoling thought, however, does not diminish the pain of the tragic impasse produced in our moral conscience. The question raised by the story falls clearly within the domain of the theological problem of evil. Under some circumstances evil is unavoidable. But its occurrence is more disturbing to us than that of the evil resulting from floods and earthquakes. For in our story Billy's innocent death is the result of a deliberate human decision, brought on not by blind natural forces but by an act, or acts, of free will. This moral feature in the circumstances of Billy's death weighs heavily on Captain Vere's mind even at the moment of his own death. The only way in which Vere's decision to sacrifice Billy and Billy's acceptance of the need for this sacrifice can be made sense of morally is by making a plausible case for the importance of values which are being secured by that course of events. Those values are briefly summarised in the phrase 'prevention of mutiny'. But we also need to refer to the positive implications of this negative objective. They involve the preservation of the fighting capability of Vere's ship, and, given its important role in the task of the British Mediterranean fleet, also the success of the entire military enterprise and England's future. The success or failure of that enterprise spells out either death or life for many persons, and is therefore directly connected with the requirement of patriotic duties. One cannot close one's eyes to the weight of that factor in Vere's decision and Billy's support of it.

There is a further dark element in Melville's treatment of the ending of the story. The world is not likely to understand and appreciate its heroes' motives. The truth about the events on the *Indomitable* was hopelessly distorted when it reached England. Claggart was presented as a hero, Billy as a villain, and the captain's difficult and agonising role was not even noted in the official world. Nevertheless, Billy's sacrifice was recognised, instinctively and almost mystically, in a ballad inspired by the innocence and beauty of his moral personality. The last lines of 'Billy in the Darbies' are devastatingly powerful in rendering human sorrow.

5 Truth Retrieved: Conrad's *Heart of Darkness*

Conrad tells his story through a narrator, Marlow. It is difficult to avoid the impression that in this story the author is revealing his own thoughts about the human condition. The details of the narration, though sparingly delineated, draw the reader immediately into the deeper undercurrents of emotion and reflection on many weighty topics. The persistent imagery of darkness and light, playing against each other, effectively blends the physical and metaphysical dimensions of this metaphor. One aspect of this metaphor soon obtrudes itself: the immense darkness of the overwhelming cosmos is illumined – briefly – in human consciousness. That illumination is flickering unsteadily, ultimately doomed to oblivion in the immensity of time. Yet, while it lasts, the author seems to suggest, it can become a target of fascination – the way Kurtz becomes the all-consuming object of Marlow's imagination.

It is doubtful that Conrad intended to draw any parallels between Kurtz and Goethe's Faust, yet the parallels are there. Kurtz, like Faust, is not a common man: his abilities are extraordinary. Marlow thought that he was a 'universal genius'. Although Kurtz never committed himself wholly to any profession, he could have utilised many of his impressive talents to become a successful musician, journalist, poet or politician. In Kurtz we seem to have a representative of concentrated human energy seeking expression. The story traces this energy as it actually manifested itself in Kurtz's life and death. In contrast to Geothe's play, Conrad's story does not give us a didactic, edifying picture of man's role in the world. With some important qualifications, to which we shall come later, his estimate of the human lot seems darkly pessimistic, sombre. If he does intend to convey wisdom, that wisdom is wintry.

Conrad's method is indirect. Slowly, gradually, he comes to the kernel of the enigma. The object of his quest is to unravel the real

75

being of Kurtz, and thereby to comment on the being of man. An impressive array of psychological observations on the varieties of human charcter is condensed into deceptively brief comments and descriptions. If one but pays attention to them, a portrait of humanity may come into view. All of life is teeming underneath the spare account of a small band of persons. While telling their story Conrad seems to be reflecting on the history – and prospects – of the human race.

The story is told on the deck of a ship sitting at dusk in the estuary of the Thames, a symbol of the movement of mankind through the open gateways of the world. The Thames is one such watery gateway; the Congo is another. As the European seekers of conquest and profit used the latter to penetrate the African continent, so the Roman conquerors used the former for entering Britain. The parallel allows Marlow to comment that England like Africa was one of the dark places of the earth, enduring the savagery inflicted on man by man – in the name of civilisation. Almost in a Schopehauerian vein, Conrad looks at human history as a melancholy spectacle of either strong or weak but rapacious devils spreading their lust for power and wealth all over the one inhabited planet we know.

Conrad is a competent witness. He lived at the height of the European imperialist period and observed at first hand the behaviour of colonising nations. Perhaps the example of the Congo is not altogether typical of what took place on all continents during the centuries of expanding international and interracial conquests. There is no doubt that what is now known pejoratively as 'colonisation' often can be credited with positive, constructive accomplishments. For example, it was not uncommon during the still recent time when France was trying to hold on to Algeria to hear the argument that French culture wuld not have come into being had not France been colonised by the Romans. But it can be safely assumed that the attitudes and practices described in subdued yet shocking detail in Conrad's story were rather prevalent in all corners of the world. A belated indigenous comment on them can be found in such works as Frantz Fanon's *The Wretched of the Earth*.

The cosmic–historical frame of the story is not irrelevant. Indeed, it seems central to it. Conrad, in effect, is weighing in his mind the course of human civilisation and makes a judgement on it through his account of Kurtz's career. The salient features of this career are given to the reader only toward the end of the story. For our purposes it is more important to begin with them, although, obviously, this reversal undoes the gripping suspense element in the narrative. But it is not our purpose here to consider the aesthetic virtues of this gem-like work of art.

Who is Kurtz? Conrad means to make him a representative of the talented, productive, efficient, aggressive, enterprising European civilisation. Kurtz's ethnic background is mixed: part English, part French, part something else. We are told that 'all Europe contributed to the making of Kurtz'. The word 'making' is to be taken not just in a genealogical sense but also as indicating his cultural heritage and legacy. Conrad pokes fun, not too well disguised, at the pretentious claims of Europe's leading circles that by entering the territories of what are now somewhat sanctimoniously called 'underdeveloped nations', the European settlers and traders were bringing light into the dark corners of the globe. Kurtz the journalist is commissioned, and gladly undertakes, to write a pamphlet for the 'International Society for the Suppression of Savage Customs'.

This aspect of Kurtz's career launches us well into the inner workings of his mind. Here lies the centre of Conrad's interest, both as a psychologist and as a philosophical interpreter of human consciousness. His problem is to explain how such a talented, sensitive, sentimental idealist as Kurtz could be so easily transformed into a vicious savage. The brief answer is that the jungle 'patted him on the head' and the veneer of civilisation disappeared. What lends poignancy to this transformation is that Kurtz was justifiably believed by all who knew him at home to be a brilliant, promising protagonist of the European spirit. Although temporarily, as a stepping-stone, he chose business as his career and became a trading agent for an ivory-collecting enterprise in Congo, he was expected, and was himself sufficiently motivated, to become a resounding success in whatever area he chose: trade, politics, art.

But here we have it. The writer of inspiring pamphlets for the colonist cause himself winds up performing unspeakable rites, atrocities and human sacrifices. His intelligence and adaptability allow him to succeed in establishing himself as a god amidst an African tribe in the heart of the jungle. That status Kurtz obtains through his audacity and his skill in convicing the natives that he is a supernatural being. The use of thundering deadly guns is not a minor ally in this undertaking. Having gained power over the tribe, and having become for the natives an object of worship, Kurtz uses his power to his own ends. For one thing, he can now fulfil his ambition to become the most effective supplier of ivory. What is more, his extraordinary feats will not only lead to the acquisition of personal wealth, but also prove that he is qualified for greater things in the higher arena of European politics. Conrad shows us how, in seeking to satisfy his ambitions, this spectacular specimen of European culture loses all restraints of civilisation. He chooses to preside over murders, decapitations and other incredible degradations.

What may seem unusual is that the tension within the telling of the story by Marlow oscillates between abomination and admiration. Marlow is an acute observer and a sharp, yet detached, critic of the exploitative spectacle he observes in the Congo. He is repelled by the rapaciousness of his fellow-Europeans, unredeemed by any trace of constructive, compassionate, idealistic thought. His devastatingly satirical accounts of the goings on in the trading expeditions manage to blend the ridiculous with the macabre. The characters and practices he describes show us the underside of human designs and ambitions. Referring to the Congo conquest Marlow comments, 'It was an unreal as everything else – as the philanthropic pretence of the whole concern, as their talk, their government, as their show of work.' 'To tear treasure out of the bowels of the land was their desire, with no more purpose at the back of it than there is in burglars breaking into a safe.' The horror of cruelties is hidden behind the facade of ignorance and stupidity, assisted by a blind but obstinate need to preserve appearance. Often the reader does not know whether the author wants him to laugh or to condemn, or, even more insidiously, whether the object of comment is the fictional characters of the story or ourselves.

Within this context of colonial exploitation, and as contrast to the mindless, stupefied and stupefying pursuit of profit, Kurtz stands out as a positive relief. In fact, for Marlow the very phenomenon of Kurtz is a magnetic attraction and, later on, an electrifying experience. The narrator's mind appears to be suffused by a pessimism born of a repeated disappointment with human nature. His life has been saturated with the spectacle of men scrambling for dominion over nature and other men, driven by nothing but greed and petty self-interest. That is why the ears of his spirit perk up when he first hears of Kurtz. It is not so much Kurtz's success that impresses him, spectacular as it is both in extent and in method. What most impresses Marlow is that here is someone who goes about his business with a coherent understanding of what he is doing, someone with a deliberate plan, someone with ideas that seem to go beyond his own petty existence. And that is why Marlow is eager to learn more about this anomaly, this unusual manifestation of humanity. This provides his chief motivation for pushing the steamer deep into the jungle against incredible odds.

Kurtz's exploits, as they gradually become revealed, show a man of extraordinary powers: daring, intelligence, toughness, endurance, and the ability to impress and to dominate others. He shows these traits both in his own civilised world and in the jungle. Conrad at times appears to be giving us, prophetically, a picture of a mover of men and nations, as we have come to know such men in the recent ideological, political and military events of this century. Here is a man with a magnetic personality, who can evoke deep love from a pure-hearted woman; respect, awe, even fear from co-workers; the attachment and affection of such an existentialist free spirit as the Russian sailor; and the profound admiration of such a wise, reflective sceptic as Marlow.

The question is how, underneath such admirable, even inspiring, personal qualities, there can reside an impulse to kill, exterminate, abuse and degrade other human beings. Conrad convincingly shows us that such a possibility is real. His message, however, appears to be more than just an account of an unusual phenomenon; even mankind's brightest and best, he seems to tell us, can move 'from this to this', to recall Hamlet's words in an analogous context. Kurtz the civilised man hardly knew what he carried inside him:

> But the wilderness had found him out early, and had taken on him a terrible vengeance for the fantastic invasion. I think [Marlow says] it had whispered to him things about himself which he did not know, things of which he had no conception till he took counsel with this great solitude – and the whisper had proved irresistibly fascinating. It echoed loudly within him because he was hollow at the core. . . .

The distance between the so-called savages and civilised men did

not appear to Conrad very great, and not necessarily to the credit
or discredit of either. Unusual as the idea may have been in his
time, when racist thought was pretty well entrenched, Conrad
expressed in more than one instance of the story the sense of
kinship that all human beings, from whatever time or culture,
can feel toward one another. In one telling understatement, while
describing the spectacle of the dancing natives, he says 'No, they
were not inhuman. Well, you know, that was the worst of it – this
suspicion of their not being inhuman.' He felt a 'remote kinship
with this wild and passionate uproar'. He even allowed himself a
rare direct speculative metaphysical comment in this context:
'The mind of man is capable of anything – because everything is
in it, all the past as well as all the future.

Conrad's sense of the unity of all mankind comes out also in
Marlow's feeling of kinship with the simple black helmsman. The
description of his death and of the way Marlow reacts to it is one
of the most touching episodes in the story. There is, however,
another element in this context, an element that seems to betray
something of Conrad's own attitude to the enigma of human
existence. The key word is 'work' – not necessarily work of some
special significance. 'I don't like work – no man does – but I like
what is in the work, – the chance to find yourself. Your own
reality, for yourself, not for others – what no other man can
know.' Any real work transforms the directionless flow of life into
a concentrated purposeful beam – like a beam of light. One is
tempted to use here Conrad's key metaphor, the contrast between
a beam of light and the diffused scattered motion of entropy.

For Marlow work *is* a way of finding himself. Even if everything
around us is meaningless and deserves to perish, as Mephistopheles claims, a job done purposefully and conscientiously
makes a difference. Even if Marlow has no stomach for the larger
enterprise in which he participates, he at least finds his
opportunity and obligation clear: to make the steamer run. (The
indifference to the effectiveness of human effort is the most
frustrating experience for Marlow at the trading station. Consider
the matter of bungled rivets alone. However, there may be
another reason for the constant delays: the manager is not in a
hurry to rescue Kurtz, since he is afraid that Kurtz may get his
job.) What Marlow finds so dispiriting about both the 'pilgrims'
in the jungle and the upright citizens of a safe city is precisely this
aimless mechanical 'everydayness', to use Martin Heidegger's

term. Perhaps Conrad was on the track of something which Heidegger regarded as the characteristic feature of our time: namely, thoughtlessness, the fact that we still have not learned to think.

To bring together work and thought is to come back to Conrad's central character, Kurtz. Early in the story we are given clue as to why Marlow will find Kurtz fascinating. The pitiless desolation of the ivory-trading post and of other ventures in Africa is mainly due to their mindlessness. When you look into the conquest of the earth, 'it is not a pretty thing. . . . What redeems it is the idea only.' Kurtz's activity seems to Marlow to be redeemed by the idea. Marlow's greatest purpose, after his arrival in the Congo, is to learn what that idea, what Kurtz's thinking, is, and he runs considerable risks to discover it. 'I was curious to see whether this man, who had come equipped with moral ideas of some sort, would climb to the top after all and how he would set about his work when there.' Marlow admires Kurtz for having imbued his work with a definite purpose and wants to know what that purpose is. In the end he is disillusioned, even shocked. Judging by this story, we must conclude that Conrad's estimate of the role of the spirit of man on earth is much more pessimistic than Goethe's. But, oddly enough, there is a kind of affirmation in Conrad's pessimism. Perhaps it is pessimism transcended. One may think ahead to Camus's *Myth of Sisyphus* to see a similar idea at work. But Conrad is an optimist compared with Camus. Since this is a rather strong statement, it calls for an explanation.

So far we have considered only part of the reason why Marlow finds Kurtz fascinating and admirable. Kurtz's pursuits are not mindless: they are imbued with an idea, however we might want to qualify it. Still, all of his activities come to grief. Somehow they prove to be vitiated by his decision to embrace immoral methods and practices. The manager is not altogether wrong in saying that Kurtz's method is unsound, although the irony lies in the fact that such a judgement is not for *this* manager of make. In the end, even in terms of his personal designs and ambitions, Kurtz fails. Here we come to the heart of the matter.

What Marlow cannot get over for the rest of his life is the *way* Kurtz reacts to his own failure. It is not just the matter of his uttering the final words, 'The horror! the horror!' Marlow observed carefully what was going on in Kurtz's soul. He also learned much about him from the Russian sailor. 'This man suffered too much. He hated all this and somehow couldn't get away', says the sailor of Kurtz, and he was close enough to Kurtz to count as a reliable witness. Marlow regards Kurtz's final cry as 'an affirmation, a moral victory paid for by innumerable defeats, by abominable terrors, by abominable satisfactions'. Marlow gives great emphasis to Kurtz's last words, because what is behind them elevates Kurtz above the common man, the narrator included. (Contrast Marlow's account of Kurtz's death with the account of himself facing the prospect of death.) Not only these words but also Kurtz's whole moral development indicate that Kurtz was *judging* his own transformation. He was doing so not just at the moment of dying: he was at it all along, thus imbuing his actions with thought. He was tormented by the consciousness of having made the transition 'from this to this', from a nobly motivated idealistic son of Western civilisation to a perpetrator of unspeakable deeds.

The torment was there when, upon embarking on his enterprise in the Congo, Kurtz postscripted his peroration, described by Marlow as dominated by 'the notion of an exotic Immensity ruled by august Benevolence', with the exploding exclamation, 'Exterminate the brutes!' Torment was there when that sensitive would-be musician, poet, writer, statesman, a person admired by those who fell under his spell and loved by an equally idealistic but innocent woman, was gathering ivory by means which later so shocked another sensitive soul: namely, Marlow's. Torment was there when Kurtz could not make up his mind whether to allow the natives to kill the members of the small expedition when it arrived on the steamer (to save Kurtz, in the self-deceived words of the manager), or whether to leave the post and to salvage the gains made up to that point. Torment, intensified to the highest pitch, was in that incredibly dramatic scene when Marlow persuaded the escaping Kurtz, thirty yards away from the camp-fires of his tribe, to return to the steamer. Marlow saw then a soul struggling with itself, a soul which, as he told Kurtz, would be utterly lost if he failed to go back to civilisation. Torment was in that pilot-house when, deathly ill, Kurtz reviewed his whole career and sought an honest way to describe it. Because Marlow was impressed by the honesty and power of Kurtz's final words, he remained forever loyal to him and tried to preserve his memory in the best possible way.

It was not an easy thing to do, because the world to which Marlow was to disclose the spiritual struggle – and victory – of his unique friend, could not and would not understand the justification. Perhaps the only way to tell it to the world was through a story, told by an almost anonymous narrator to a band of anonymous listeners on the deck of a ship moored at dusk at the mouth of the Thames.

In his accounts about Kurtz Marlow repeatedly refers to Kurtz's voice and remarks on its surprising strength and vibrancy, in spite of the fact that it came from a weak, ill body. Kurtz's voice voiced his ideas, which at least up to a point redeemed what he was up to in life. At times Marlow wondered whether there was anything more to Kurtz than a voice; the whole episode, and the telling of it, have a dream-like character. But the voice dispelled the silence of the darkness, the mute uncomprehendingness both of man and of nature. It must be noted that, when he comes to look at the relation between man and nature, Marlow does not find that man cuts much of a figure. Indeed, much of the power of the story comes from Conrad's being able to show the powerlessness of man against the ageless durability of mute unconquerable nature. A ship firing into a continent, into 'the empty immensity of earth, sky, and water', was incomprehensible insanity. 'Pop, would go one of the six-inch guns; a small flame would dart and vanish, a little white smoke would disappear, a tiny projectile would give a feeble screech – and nothing happened. Nothing could happen.' Although these illustrations came from *a* period of human history, Conrad probably has all of human history in mind when he makes this point.

Talking about the Congo, Conrad contemplates the flicker of mankind's history in the immensity of time. But it is not abstract time. It is time teeming with life, of which the jungle is such a fitting symbol. That life, contrasted with man's, is dumb, speechless. Will we handle that dumb thing, or will it handle us? asks Marlow. The sense of being overwhelmed, overpowered, silenced by the elemental forms of life irradiates darkly from Conrad's descriptions – of the dark continent, of the impenetrable darkness of densely packed vegetation on the banks of the river. Besides the appeal to the sense of sight – light or darkness – there is also a strong use of contrast between sound and silence. For the most part, when it is not made alive by the voices, penetrating voices of the natives, the jungle is silent: 'an implacable force brooding over an inscrutable intention'. Nature, in the image of a dark forest, seems to be *waiting* – it knows neither work nor speech. It is imbued with neither voice nor idea. And we are surrounded by it.

That is why man's role is to be a messenger of light. He should at least relieve – if he cannot redeem – the darkness by which he is surrounded. At the very least he should not allow himself to do things which would be 'too dark', as would be telling the truth to Kurtz's intended when she wants to know his last words. Although Marlow has previously told us his conviction that lying has a taint of death in it, he does not hesitate to go against his own conviction, this time in the service of life. Kurtz said that he wanted nothing but justice, but for Marlow, to do justice in this case would be to show no restraint. He cannot bring himself to destroy the underpinnings of meaning and hope in the young woman's future.

There is another symbolic feature in the story, although its deeper significance is not immediately apparent. The picture of the Russian sailor is marvellously cheerful. One can hardly think of a better specimen of an existentialist hero. Here it is, that fantastic phenomenon of a young man sustaining himself in the jungle, supported by nothing more than his audacity, the seaman's handbook, a pinch of good English tobacco, and a few cartridges for his Winchester rifle. The very appearance of the man is a motley of colour on his improvised clothing. It is difficult not to sense Conrad's fondness for this secondary character. He needs nothing, or hardly anything, to exist. Moreover, he exists cheerfully. Like Marlow, he is impressed by Kurtz, by his voice, his articulate ideas ('He enlarged my mind!'), his boldness and effectiveness, even though, like Marlow, he is uncomprehendingly nonplussed by Kurtz's audacity to lose all moral scruples in dealing with the natives, of his kicking himself loose from the earth. Unlike Marlow and the sailor, Kurtz had no restraint – and that was his downfall.

Neither the sailor nor Marlow wants to emulate Kurtz. To them he was a spectacular human being, wondrous to behold, because so far removed from the ordinary and common. But both sense in him (Marlow naming it) the inevitable cause of every downfall: a lack of restraint. In Kurtz's case it was absolute lack of restraint. He went mad, and, as Shakespeare knew, madness in the great should not go unwatched. The idea of restraint goes with the idea of setting one's limits. The poor black helmsman perished because, in his eagerness to join the battle with the invaders of the steamer, he had no restraint. The idea of restraint goes also with the idea of work, because, as Marlow says, work, if it is something you choose for its own sake, gives your life a direction, a set of parameters within which you can find yourself. In that sense, your chosen task helps to define your destiny, your *own* destiny. 'We live, as we dream, alone', and that is why it is important to give some substance to one's solitude.

The motif of restraint can also be found in less admirable characters of the story. Even preserving appearances is restraint. It is manifested by the accountant who insists on wearing regularly impeccable clothes, white starched collar and all, in the midst of the steaming jungle. The pilgrim wishing Kurtz to be spared shows restraint, although, knowing that he in fact is jealous of Kurtz and considers him to be his rival for the position of station manager, we may consider Marlow's remark to be meant ironically in this context. Even more incredibly, the hungry cannibals employed on the steamer show restraint. Even though they are starving and could easily overpower the few pilgrims, they refrain from eating them. Out of what: restraint, primitive honour? Marlow puzzles over the question; the whole phenomenon of restraint is to him a great mystery.

Although the Russian sailor imposes on himself his own kind of restraint, the symbolic significance of his mode of life is that he gladly, bravely, with full abandon and no fear of risk, entered the jungle and made it his preferred habitat. 'His need was to exist, and to move onwards at the greatest possible risk, and with a maximum of privation.' This too is a victory of light over darkness, of voice over silence, of human life over dumb vegetation. It is not a gesture of defiance, nor is it presented as a grandiose ambition to make the jungle – life, history – secure for the human spirit. All of human existence is still 'inconclusive experience'. There cannot be security in the human venture, but who needs it? Not the sailor: he is happy enough without it. He expresses his superiority by ignoring security, by *not* needing it. Is it incorrect to interpret the sailor's character as Conrad's restrained gesture toward the question of the meaning of life, his form of affirmation? If one thinks it wrong, how would one explain the Russian sailor? He certainly is not a drunken sailor; he seems sober enough. If he can be said to be drunk, then he is intoxicated by his own appetite for adventure, for a challenge of his natural human skills, for a meaningful, thoughtful, though unpredictable human contact he found in Kurtz.

Listening to Kurtz's vibrant voice, almost instinctively comprehending the power and the scope of his ideas, the simple sailor was responding to the mysterious powers of human life. Conrad, through the voice of his narrator, tells the story. After the story is told, the voice remains. In its own special way it redeems, or at least lightens, the darkness surrounding the ship. Perhaps this is the way of art. Somewhere in the middle of the story, Conrad gives a hint that this was his view: 'but I have a voice, too, and for good or evil mine is a speech that cannot be silenced'. At least, Conrad's speech may enable us to see life 'in the august light of abiding memories'.

B

The setting of Conrad's story – shadowy figures on the deserted deck of an idle steamer, brooding at dusk about inconclusive experiences – provides a fitting atmosphere for his theme. Conrad was sensitive to a hidden and disturbing feature of the colonising enterprise. He questioned the self-righteous mood in which the industrialised nations of Europe were pushing themselves into lands inhabited by peoples still untouched by Western civilisation. Ugly things were happening alongside the energetic drive to 'civilise' the primitive world. The most obvious among them was the brutal, unconcerned extermination, for the sake of economic gain, of the people who, in their own culture, lived in peace with themselves and with nature. Conrad's almost clinically detached descriptions of the cruel, inhumane treatment of the Africans by the colonisers gave the lie to the hypocritical claim that the colonisers were motivated by august benevolence or by any motive resembling the Christian respect for fellow human beings. This factor alone makes the story into a profound indictment of the behaviour of whites on the dark continent of Africa, or, by a natural extension, in every other corner of the globe touched by the colonising enterprise.

The questioning of the dubious motivation of the allegedly civilised, proud human heart takes place not only at the level of abominable collective practices of the 'emissaries of light'. Conrad is deeply interested in what is going on in the soul of the more gifted representatives of the 'advanced' nations. The reason why Kurtz becomes a focus for Conrad, via Marlow's reactions, is that he appears to be equipped with qualities of which Western civilisation is proud: intelligence, eloquence, ambition, initiative. In addition, Conrad endows his hero with two other characteristics highly prized by the proponents of occidental humanism: artistic sensitivity and talents, and receptivity to tender romantic emotions. Kurtz's fellow men in the sepulchral city, including the person who was very close to him – namely, his fiancée – were deeply impressed by his fine character traits and had from him great expectations in many areas of high endeavour: learning, politics, business, journalism and art.

Kurtz's moral distinction, admired by Marlow, is that he still musters enough honesty and courage to look into his soul – only to shrink in horror. That capacity to judge oneself strikes Marlow as a kind of victory – a victory over one's own blindness and wickedness. But the implications of that victory are not sanguine. On the contrary, Kurtz is an exception even in that respect. His insight into himself is not shared by the people around him: they understand neither him nor themselves. At least, they appear oblivious to their own blindness and rapaciousness, perpetrated in the name of enlightenment, achievement and progress. The official world had a distorted idea both of Kurtz's activities and of his motives. It was hopelessly caught up in practices the dubious character of which became apparent to him at least in the fleeting glimpse as he lay dying. Others were far from comprehending and appreciating his insight, and, in Conrad's view, not realising their self-deceiving immorality. Conrad, in the person of his narrator, penetrates to the heart of human motivation and finds it dark, even if redeemed by a flicker of truthful self-insight on the part of such gifted individuals as Kurtz. Perhaps this flicker creates a momentary twilight in which the truth about human nature may be glimpsed. It is not a cheery discovery. In fact, it profoundly questions man's claim to essential goodness and healthiness.

It is difficult to imagine the Lord in the Prologue to Goethe's *Faust* proclaiming Kurtz to be a good man. There was enough fairness in him to render a true judgement on his activities, but, alas, it had to take the form of self-condemnation. There is, of course, an approving echo of this insight in Marlow's soul, who admires Kurtz's capacity for self-condemnation. Man, as repre-

sented by Kurtz, has not sunk below the
appraisal, and that is perhaps a beginning
reform. The shadowy figures to whom Mar
on the deck of the steamer are at least *list*
they learn from Marlow's narration will hav
future behaviour is an open question, and C
about their reaction or attitude.

Perhaps Conrad thought of his position
commentator on human affairs as analogou
with regard to his listeners. The story i
significance will be taken up, if at all, is u
about human nature and human affairs
intermittent flickers, it is not likely to provi
to the dark scene. But at least the artist, th
observer, can tell the truth, and at least wi
world may not be moved by the telling, and
not risk revealing the whole truth, becaus
stances that truth may be 'too dark'. Ne
the artist's, the sympathetic narrator's, s
state of affairs, and to his willingness and abi
who listen may become more sensitive to
them – in what ways, and in what directio
cannot affirm man to be good, he cannot co
bad, because man is at least capable of self- c
self-condemnation is genuine and sincer
reform, of turning away from evil, is not pr

more gifted representatives of the 'advanced' nations. The reason why Kurtz becomes a focus for Conrad, via Marlow's reactions, is that he appears to be equipped with qualities of which Western civilisation is proud: intelligence, eloquence, ambition, initiative. In addition, Conrad endows his hero with two other characteristics highly prized by the proponents of occidental humanism: artistic sensitivity and talents, and receptivity to tender romantic emotions. Kurtz's fellow men in the sepulchral city, including the person who was very close to him – namely, his fiancée – were deeply impressed by his fine character traits and had from him great expectations in many areas of high endeavour: learning, politics, business, journalism and art.

Kurtz's moral distinction, admired by Marlow, is that he still musters enough honesty and courage to look into his soul – only to shrink in horror. That capacity to judge oneself strikes Marlow as a kind of victory – a victory over one's own blindness and wickedness. But the implications of that victory are not sanguine. On the contrary, Kurtz is an exception even in that respect. His insight into himself is not shared by the people around him: they understand neither him nor themselves. At least, they appear oblivious to their own blindness and rapaciousness, perpetrated in the name of enlightenment, achievement and progress. The official world had a distorted idea both of Kurtz's activities and of his motives. It was hopelessly caught up in practices the dubious character of which became apparent to him at least in the fleeting glimpse as he lay dying. Others were far from comprehending and appreciating his insight, and, in Conrad's view, not realising their self-deceiving immorality. Conrad, in the person of his narrator, penetrates to the heart of human motivation and finds it dark, even if redeemed by a flicker of truthful self-insight on the part of such gifted individuals as Kurtz. Perhaps this flicker creates a momentary twilight in which the truth about human nature may be glimpsed. It is not a cheery discovery. In fact, it profoundly questions man's claim to essential goodness and healthiness.

It is difficult to imagine the Lord in the Prologue to Goethe's *Faust* proclaiming Kurtz to be a good man. There was enough fairness in him to render a true judgement on his activities, but, alas, it had to take the form of self-condemnation. There is, of course, an approving echo of this insight in Marlow's soul, who admires Kurtz's capacity for self-condemnation. Man, as represented by Kurtz, has not sunk below the level of honest self-appraisal, and that is perhaps a beginning of wisdom and self-reform. The shadowy figures to whom Marlow's voice is directed on the deck of the steamer are at least *listening*. Whether what they learn from Marlow's narration will have any efficacy in their future behaviour is an open question, and Conrad tells us nothing about their reaction or attitude.

Perhaps Conrad thought of his position as an artist and a commentator on human affairs as analogous to Marlow's position with regard to his listeners. The story is told, but how its significance will be taken up, if at all, is uncertain. If the truth about human nature and human affairs comes only in such intermittent flickers, it is not likely to provide much illumination to the dark scene. But at least the artist, the occasional attentive observer, can tell the truth, and at least will get a hearing. The world may not be moved by the telling, and often the teller must not risk revealing the whole truth, because under the circumstances that truth may be 'too dark'. Nevertheless, thanks to the artist's, the sympathetic narrator's, sensitivity to the real state of affairs, and to his willingness and ability to reveal it, those who listen may become more sensitive to what really moves *them* – in what ways, and in what directions. Even if the Lord cannot affirm man to be good, he cannot condemn him as wholly bad, because man is at least capable of self-condemnation. If that self-condemnation is genuine and sincere, the possibility of reform, of turning away from evil, is not precluded.

6 Vision Blurred: Mann's *The Magic Mountain*

Thomas Mann wrote this novel at a time when Europe was in the throes of a deep crisis. The crisis was multiple: political, cultural, spiritual. The novel was conceived two years before the First World War began and was completed a dozen years later, appearing in 1924. The original idea was to write a light-hearted counterpart of *Death in Venice*, but what eventually resulted was a weighty tome dealing with the profound changes which not only Europe but the whole of Western civilisation was undergoing during these fateful years. The novel is a record of what was coming to an end, and projects a glance, an anxiously prophetic glance, into the future. One might describe that record by borrowing a term Mann used to describe the favoured activity of his hero, Hans Castorp: 'stock-taking'. The author, along with his hero, takes stock of what was going on around Hans, as German, a European, a son of the West. The occasion for such an activity was not only propitious: to a person who saw signs of a convulsive, earth-shaking transformation, it was unavoidable.

Not only a long-lasting, seemingly unvulnerable political arrangement came to an end: all of a sudden the very foundations on which Europe's political, social, moral, and spirital order was built appeared to be crumbling. Stock-taking on all levels was clearly in order, and Mann uses the novelistic genre to undertake it in all seriousness.

The narrative vehicle is the story of a young engineer who is initiated into the complexities of life, both his own and that of his epoch. The initiation takes place in very special surroundings. Literary commentators have labelled the book a *Bildungsroman*, an educational novel, so grouping it with such famous works as

Goethe's *Wilhelm Meister's Apprenticeship**. In such a novel a young person is initiated into the mysteries of the surrounding world by some specially selected circumstances and by uniquely placed individuals. The simple, inexperienced, guileless youth grows in experience and knowledge, achieving in the end mature understanding of what the world around him and his life in it are all about. The novelist's task is to create circumstances that will lead to an enhancement, a heightening of the process by means of which this transformation is brought about. By undergoing that process, the person's life is also enhanced, heightened, thus illustrating possibilities open to others.

Not everyone is equally capable of being a good pupil in the school of life; a special talent may be required. This talent is receptivity, plasticity, a willingness to open oneself to a range of influences and experiences which in turn help to clean the windows of one's soul. Mann's novel abounds in examples of bad pupils. Indeed, in this respect there appears to be a great contrast between Hans Castorp and most of the people around him. This might be seen as a pessimistic verdict on the receptivity, the potential for growth, of most people. But we should not read into the author's motives any intent to pronounce such a verdict. His objective may have been just to emphasise the special features of his hero's talents. In addition, the circumstances of the people with whom Castorp is fated to share the seven formative years of his life are most unusual.

The action begins in the summer of 1907 and takes place at Davos, in an Alpine sanatorium for tubercular patients. Hans Castorp, who has just completed his engineering training and is about to enter employment with a shipbuilding firm in Hamburg, comes to visit has cousin Joachim Ziemssen, who is undergoing treatment in the Berghof sanatorium. The visit is to last three weeks. Before that time elapses it is discovered that Hans himself is suffering from a lung infection, and he is advised to prolong his visit. Eventually his stay is extended to seven years and is interrupted only by the outbreak of the Great War. The influences exerted on Hans during these years are profound and far-reaching enough to deserve being labelled magical, in the special sense with which Mann endows the word. The magic

* The translation is by H. T. Lowe-Porter (New York: Alfred A. Knopf, 1955).

wrought upon our guileless yet talented hero comes first of all in the form of illness, which 'heightens' his temperature and accelerates certain not necessarily desirable but stimulating bodily processes. Secondly, the mode of life prescribed every patient at this hospital introduces much time for leisure, contemplation, stock-taking, and for exploration of things for which the busy, energetic but phlegmatic flatlanders simply do not have time. Thirdly, Hans Castorp is thrown into the company of persons who, each in his or her way, teach him things that are never dreamt of in a shipbuilding firm in Hamburg or in any other straight, healthy, unproblematic enterprise.

Among the persons who play the central role in Castorp's magic transformation four stand out: Ludovico Settembrini, Clavdia Chauchat, Leo Naphta, and Mynheer Pieter Peeperkorn. Besides these four eminently memorable and superbly drawn characters, other persons play an important role in Castorp's life on the mountain. The two physicians, Hofrat Behrens and Dr Krokowski, have much to do with what he does and what he learns. Not to be left out are, of course, all the other patients, whose attitudes and mode of life furnish telling counterexamples to our hero's special talents.

The reader might want to distinguish between influences exerted on Castorp as a private person and on him as a representative of his time. Thomas Mann, however, through his mode of telling the story, quickly makes clear that the two aspects cannot be easily separated. Of course, we learn much about Hans's character, his assets and liabilities. But we also learn much, perhaps more, about things that every reflective, culturally sensitive European must have been thinking during the crucial transition Europe was undergoing. Within this global concern there is also the question of what it meant to be a German of that time, of what was to be the role of Germany, *das Land der Mitte,* in European and possibly global politics. Beyond politics, again, there are larger questions: namely, those of fundamental values on which Western civilisation was relying up to that point. For those values themselves have become deeply questionable. That questioning will be the central focus of *our* interpretation.

Hans Castorp, an indifferent engineer, comes from a wealthy Hamburg family with traditional connections with business and commerce. His aristocratic family background, placing him in the social and cultural mainstream of Europe, makes it possible

and accurate to refer to him as a son of the West. Herr Settembrini treats him as a representative of the spirit which animated
European life and politics for centuries. According to the Italian
humanist, Germany, where the printing press was invented and
where the idea of a progressive national state was realised, must
be in the vanguard of social, moral and political progress for
centuries to come. She must be so, of course, in collaboration
with all other Western countries dedicated to humanistic values
of freedom, economic prosperity, and cultural growth of all
peoples. The concern for human values must be translated into
resolute efforts to remove all vestiges of political oppression and of
the material barriers toward wellbeing and happiness of all
people. Settembrini's family heritage includes a dedicated service
to classical humanistic values and to the ideal of political liberty,
as expressed in the aspiration of the Italian people to free themselves of external domination. Ludovico Settembrini, *homo
humanus,* pedagogue, a member of organisations aiming to
transform Europe through the rational process of international
conferences and by means of a sustained effort to educate the
masses in the classical spirit of humanism and utilitarianism,
offers himself as a spiritual tutor to the newly arrived representative of the industrious flatland.

Unfortunately, soon after his arrival at Davos the object of
Settembrini's pedagogical attention begins to exhibit tendencies
which do not look healthy to his self-appointed moral guide.
Mann treats the causes of his young hero's deviationist behaviour
in a calculatedly ambiguous way. Castorp is ill, subject to the
disruptive influences of tubercular fever under physical and
climatic conditions which, as Dr Behrens says, are good *for* the
disease. But that susceptibility to bodily abnormalities which the
disease facilitates at the same time produces a susceptibility and
receptivity to influences to which the normal, healthy, busy
flatlander would be oblivious or indifferent. The first disrupting
influence on Castorp, the son of the West, is Clavdia Chauchat, a
Russian fellow-patient at the sanatorium – a daughter of the East.
Castorp's reaction to her person and her behaviour is complex,
not easily attributable to any one kind of motivation. From the
very start he is strongly attracted to her physical appearance. But
there is something disturbing about her behaviour: it is not
proper in terms of the etiquette of polite Hamburg, or any West
European, society. For example, she habitually slams the door

upon entering the restaurant – usually late, too (Castorp's first angry reaction to her noisy entry may be symbolic of the loud, disruptive intrusion of new, unsuspected elements into his life). Her bearing is informal, even lax: she sits in a relaxed slouching manner – another minus in the book of proper etiquette. And yet somehow Hans finds her ways attractive, magically charming, once he gets used to them. To his surprise he finds for instance, that a relaxed, unrigid posture at table is indeed pleasant, satisfying.

Castorp's sympathetic interest in the Russian table in the hospital's restaurant alarms Settembrini. He regards the very presence of the representatives of Eastern culture as an incipient danger. Beneath the surface of lax social manners of Russian patients he sees other Eastern, Asiatic values which he finds inimical to the West. He suspects that bad table manners are but a symptom of deeper attitudes toward life. The Russians, inhabitants of vast uncultivated spaces, have a different sense of time. They do not feel the urgency to husband it, to use every minute in advancing humanly important projects – agriculture, industry, business, transformation of natural resources for human uses. Much space, much time, they say. That lack of the sense of urgency to use time constructively diminishes, in Settembrini's eyes, a proper respect for human life. Hence the history of serfdom, of political repression, cruelty, prisons and Siberian exiles. The Italian humanist warns Castorp not to fall under the spell of the spirit emanating from the East.

The warning, however, has no effect, at least as far as Hans's relation to Clavdia is concerned. He watches her from a distance, across the room or during walks, and he falls in love, without even getting to know her. When they finally meet, several months later, during a carnival celebration in the hospital, he confesses his love for her in the course of their dream-like conversation, conducted in French. (To speak French, he remarks, seems to absolve him of some responsibility; it is speaking, so to speak, without really speaking.) How much Clavdia reciprocates Hans's feelings at that time Mann does not really tell us, at least right away, but she is sufficiently attracted to him to allow him to spend the night with her. Their conversation prior to his going to her room, to return the borrowed pencil, carries further Mann's interest in exploring the relation between East and West. Although neither of the conversationalists is an intellectual by inclination, they nevertheless manage to say weighty things to each other, perhaps stimulated by the carnival's 'heightening mood.

Clavdia, for her part, offers some remarks which the author probably presents as criticisms of the Western spirit, especially with regard to its political implications. If Germany is to be taken as typifying Western values, then her neighbours may find some of these values threatening. Referring to Joachim, Castorp's cousin, who is impatient to get well as soon as possible so that he can return to military service in his regiment, Clavdia remarks that Germans love order more than they love liberty. Moreoever, she finds in them a disconcerting combination of contradictory qualities. When Hans indulges in a bit of metaphysical–lyrical exploration, she dubs him as follows: 'Bourgeois, humanist, a poet – here is a complete German, as he should be!' She also produces for his benefit an account of morality that brings out the contrast between her and him, between East and West. Morality, she explains in French, should be sought not in virtue – that is, reason, discipline, good manners, honesty – but rather in opposite qualities: sin, abandonment to danger, to that which is useless, that which consumes us. It seems to her (she continues to speak on behalf of the Eastern point of view) that it is more moral to lose oneself and to allow oneself to be destroyed than to preserve oneself. The great moralists were not the virtuous but the adventurers in evil, in vice, the great sinners who bade us to take a Christian attitude toward misery.

Her attitude towards Hans, and what he represents, is not hostile, but there is a note of condescension toward his cultural milieu and the role he is likely to play in it when he returns to the plains. The suggestion seems to be that the cultural tradition to which he belongs has spent itself and no longer speaks to the world in brave, challenging tones. She regards Castorp as a good conventional fellow, from a respectable family, of pleasant appearance, a docile disciple of his teachers. When he returns to the plains he will, she claims, completely forget that he even indulged in this carnival dream with her and will use all his energies and honest labour to make his country strong and powerful. That is what she thinks of him and, most likely, of his countrymen. This abstract philosophical exchange between them does not prevent Hans from wooing her in metaphysico-poetical terms, and, as the sequel shows, not unsuccessfully. She is impressed by the profound, German manner of his wooing.

Although Clavdia Chauchat leaves the sanatorium shortly afterwards, Hans Castorp's relation to her remains the main thread in the narrative, and, as we learn later, the main reason for his remaining at Berghof. He is deeply in love with her, or, at least, magically fascinated (one way in which West may meet East, according to Mann?), and when she returns many months later we witness a profoundly human contact of the two souls under unexpectedly strange and difficult circumstances. But of that later. It is time to turn our attention to other factors that contribute to Castorp's initiatory, heightening experiences.

There are many of them. The most important pedagogical influence comes from Settembrini – *homo humanus*, as Castorp dubs him. He is very concerned about the young man's soul and tries to steer it in the right direction. He is upset by Castorp's interest in Clavdia, but, by the time the two get together, Settembrini has called his pupil's attention to many things and ideas. Hans, we should also note from the start, is not an uncritical person. His receptivity to the type of morality championed by Clavdia is partly conditioned by what he himself disapprovingly observed in the straight, honest, bourgeois flatland. When Settembrini praises the energetic quality of Castorp's phlegmatic people, he remarks that this quality may also have a highly unattractive side: it may lead to hardness and coldness. 'And what do hard and cold mean? They mean cruel. It is a cruel atmosphere down there, cruel and ruthless.' Hans is surprised to hear Settembrini link technology to moral progress. Down below he never thought of progress in these terms, never connected the subjugation of nature by means of science and technology with the furthering of distinctly human values such as fellow-feeling and enlightenment, goodness and joyousness. But Settembrini suggests to him that Europe's genius lies in the ability to give cultural and aesthetic form to the lives of her peoples, since to cherish form is to enhance human dignity. The written word, literature, is one exemplary mode of cherishing form: there is a direct connection between writing well, thinking well and acting well. In that sense, the word is the moving spirit both of humanity and politics. Settembrini's own contribution in this domain was to prepare a series of volumes on the sociology of suffering for the League for the Organisation of Progress, of which he is a member. In that work he wanted to show how important it is to understand all forms of suffering in order to work toward its rational abolition.

There is no doubt that Settembrini's eloquent, rhapsodic accounts of the glory of human reason and of its promise to make life more glorious, more beautiful for all mankind strikes a responsive chord in his pupil. It has never before occurred to him to think in that way of activites that are so much taken for granted down below, in the world of practical affairs, of which the shipbuilder's lift and tackle are such solid, fitting symbols. At the same time, Hans is somewhat taken aback by the rhetorical flow of the humanist's speeches. Something about him does not square with the great ideas he is propagating. For one thing, Hans is not sure about the motives behind them. Preaching international brotherhood and co-operation, Settembrini is nevertheless hotly nationalistic, ready to take up arms over the Brenner frontier. Hans finds too much personal or national animus in his sonorous words. The nationalistic spirit does not seem quite consistent with international brotherhood.

Furthermore, there is a discrepanacy between the way Settembrini sounds and the way he looks. His external appearance, although neat and well kept, betrays poverty. Somehow the wealth of his mind, his lofty ideas, does not translate into economic affluence. To Hans this seems to signify, perhaps subconsciously, that ideas are not as powerful as his mentor makes them out to be. The eloquent humanist is a threadbare humanist: he wear the same check trousers day in and day out. A bit maliciously, Hans likens him to an organ-grinder, the simile referring not only to his teacher's poverty but also to a monotonous repetitiveness of themes on which he tirelessly expostulates.

Thus, in spite of his willingness to be an attentive, responsive pupil, Hans does not accept everything he hears without reservations. The humanistic philosophy expounded to him sounds too bombastic to be sure of itself. There are also the simple facts of life to consider. In spite of his impassioned defence of wellbeing and health, Settemrini is an ill man: he has to grapple with a deadly disease. To be sure, he does so nobly and with a certain air of condescension toward illness, and yet his optimistic philosophy is being undermined by the work of the bacilli in his lungs. At times it seems that Settembrini is ashamed of his illness and, unrealistically, closes his eyes to its effects – not a confidence-inspiring trait in a writer who undertakes to help us understand the meaning of suffering.

Hans, on the other hand, becomes fascinated by the fact of disease. By recognising its reality, its power, perhaps even its positive possibilities, he shows a talent his mentor seems to lack. Once he has discovered his illness he begins to show an almost scientific, objective interest in its organic causes. The initial explanations given to him by Dr Behrens during his first physical examination grow for Hans into a veritable research project. He borrows medical books from the hospital library and spends countless horizontal hours devouring their contents. The conclusions he draws have a distinctly philosophical flavour. He is struck by the mystery of organic processes and by their intimate relation to the lifeless, inorganic. Indeed, he seems to be moving toward a sort of monistic evolutionism in which life is continuous with its physical and chemical underpinnings. He is startled to discover, in a conversation with Behrens, that the same chemical process, oxidation, underlies both the growth and the death of organic cells. There appears something distinctly magical in the way life emerges from non-life and then joins its inorganic substratum at the moment of death. This objective, calmly exploratory attitude toward death is not common among the patients at the Berghof, nor, for that matter, in any part of the flatland. The author suggests that Hans has been conditioned for such an open, unanxious and interested exploration of the phenomenon of death by his familiarity with it since childhood. Both his parents died when he was still a child, and he has vivid memories of the way his grandfather looked in his coffin, when Hans was still a young boy.

Without indulging in a long-winded justification of his actions, Castorp institutes, for himself and his cousin, a practice which is frowned upon by the hospital authorities and shunned by the patients. The cousins begin to pay visits to the *moribundi*, patients on the verge of dying. They bring them flowers, and within feasible limits establish personal contacts, sometimes spending a good deal of time with people who are still in a position to be diverted or entertained. One outcome of this activity for Castorp is the discovery that dying people are not necessarily closer to wisdom and deeper insight about themselves or the life around them. The terminally ill patients they visit exhibit all the foibles and weaknesses of healthy people, even though sometimes their eyes seem to betray an unspoken

understanding of their fate. Hans discovers that it is good for
them to become aware in such moments of the presence and
kindliness of others. Thereby a link is established between the
dying and the living, because the latter through such contacts are
bound to to be called back to their mortality. Both parties gain in
dignity as the result of such encounters.

Castorp's philosophical interest in disease and death is not
shared by other inmates of the sanatorium. Mann's account of
their behaviour does not support the thesis that illness as such
tends to make people more thoughtful, more moral, more
spiritual. In many cases the opposite is the case. Most patients are
hell bent on having as much good time as possible. Bored by their
routine, even though affluent, existence, they seek all kinds of
diversions and pleasures: parties, celebrations, gambling, contests
and sexual conquests–using the balconies to effect nightly
visitations to each other's rooms. The feverish search for
enjoyment and thrills need not be interpreted as an escape from
the seriousness of one's condition; disease and stupidity are quite
compatible, Mann appears to be telling us – whether in the
mountains or on the plains. The magic quality that Hans Castorp
finds in Davos is the result of the 'alchemic' combination of his
own sensitivities with some of the factors, natural and human,
that react on them. His is an exceptional case. The coming
together of some special influences produces transformations in
our hero, and the author uses the changes that take place in him
to tell us something about the cultural epoch in which he lived.

Mann appears to suggest that the deeper insight into the reality
of the human situation is always individual. Personal insight can
be seen as a sort of alchemic emergence from the confluence of
factors impinging on a person's life. A human personality is,
then, a unique heightening of the life process. Hans is an example
of such a heightening. That he grows spiritually and grows so
rapidly in the abnormal hothouse of his fever and his special
surroundings is something that can and sometimes does happen.
It is not guaranteed either by the life process or by any sort of
abstract humanistic programme, although intellectual stimula-
tion may be one of the necessary components of such a growth.
When Mann calls Hans Castorp 'life's delicate child' he is calling
attention to the fragility, tentativeness and vulnerability of man
as individual, personalised phenomenon. Life does not guarantee
either wisdom or power to its bearers, and yet the emergence and

creation of personality bespeak the magic potency of life.

Hans's special talent lies in his willing openness to experience. His guilelessness makes him unitentionally oblivious to its dangers. When he exposes himself to various influences he is taking a chance, for he may be harmed or even destroyed as a person. Often he skates on thin ice, as in his encounters with the seductive charms of Clavdia, or in giving himself to Settembrini's silver-tongued eloquence. And yet, as we shall see, he manages to transform the relationship with Clavdia into something beautiful, and he does not allow himself to be brainwashed by the *homo humanus*. In fact, he is sometimes clever enough to borrow weapons from his mentors' arsenals and uses them to assert himself against them. For instance, during the eventful carnival night he makes clear to Settembrini that he appreciates all he has done for him, but will nevertheless be guided by his own will in matters that matter to him in more than an abstract way. He decides to establish contact with Clavdia's 'Kirghiz eyes', supposedly so dangerous to his Western soul, in spite of the well-meaning mentor's warnings. Like Faust, Castorp is not afraid to use for his own development special advantages put in his path by people or by circumstances that may often be dangerous. But he remains his own man; he does not lose sight of his goal to grow as a person, to keep on striving. In that sense, like Faust, he could be called *homo Dei*.

Some time after the carnival night, which on the verge of her departure from Davos brought Hans close to Clavdia, a new protagonist appears on the scene. He also shows interest in the state of Castorp's mind and soul. Leo Naphta's influence, as Settembrini comes to think, constitutes an even more sinister danger to Castorp's spiritual wellbeing than the perils hidden behind Clavdia's Eastern charm. Interestingly enough, Naphta also has a connection with the East. An East European Jew, he came to Germany as a young boy after his father had been killed in a pogrom. Highly intelligent and knowledgeable, Leo was taken in by Jesuits and put through rigorous schooling, with priesthood as the goal. Tuberculosis intervened, and Naphta, a Jesuit novice, found himself an inhabitant of Davos, but not an inmate at the Berghof. He had private lodgings in a modest house in which Herr Settembrini by then also had a room, having been forced by financial circumstances to forgo the amenities of the hospital.

There may have been a symbolic intent in Mann's choice of the name Naphta for the newcomer. Naphta is a name for crude oil, usually a black, murky substance. Remembering that Settembrini is an exuberant spokesman for the Enlightenment (in the novel he literally turns on the light on some occasions, an appropriate symbolic action for him), we are alerted by Naphta's very name to something dark and sinister about him. This is at any rate the way Settembrini perceives him when the two get acquainted and come to know each other's philosophical and political views. Naphta is not an attractive person; Mann portrays his physical appearance as rather ugly, in spite of the elegant clothing he is wearing. His physical unattractivness, however, is compensated for by his erudition and eloquence. Settembrini and Naphta are bitter intellectual antagonists. Sharp and clever, often witty in a malicious sort of way, they provide sparkling, sometimes electrifying dialogues. Hans Castorp, always the willing listener, learns much from the two lively conversationalists. The exchanges between the two pedagogical antagonists attract other listeners besides Castorp, although he is singled out by them for special attention, each of them vying for his assent.

What are Naphta's views? They offer a direct and radical challenge to everything Settembrini stands for. That challenge is quite different in kind and in form from the instinctive, diffuse, somnolent, obstinate opposition of Eastern inertia which Settembrini divines in the behaviour of Russian guests and governments. It meets Settembrini head on at the level at which he is master: the discursive, philosophical. Naphta is an enemy of humanism because, in his opinion, it undercuts the essential, transcendental dualism of faith. The attempt to construct the City of Man is an affront to the promise of the City of God. Naphta perceives the entire history of European humanism as a destruction of the only real value of the human soul: the supernatural. In his learned discourses he shows how science and the cult of reason have gradually destroyed the essential connection man has with the transcendent God. To restore that relation is the ultimate imperative which it is the duty of a truly religious person to follow. This duty entails the destruction of man's pretentions to construct his wellbeing by his own hands through humanistic endeavours. History has proved, claims Naphta, that all such endeavours are bound to end in failure, and deservedly so, because they turn man's back on God's ultimate power unfathomable to human reason. He believes that man is *essentially* ailing, and that religion aims *beyond* human life and its earthly values.

What is startling about Naphta is his willingness to resort to terror in order to force man to see the error of his ways. Surprisingly perhaps, the vehicle of this terror is communism. Communism, says Naphta, rightly perceives the viciousness of the bourgeois attachment to private property and to all indulgence in the pleasures of the flesh. The whole capitalist economic system must be destroyed root and branch, in order to force man away from worship of the Golden Calf. With that radical purification accomplished, man will be ready to perceive his ultimate goal and to turn himself over to God and his will. Thus, in the name of the future Kingdom of God, Naphta is ready to support political revolutions which would reduce to rubble the edifice which the benighted humanistic libertarians were futilely trying to erect.

Naphta's position closely resembles that embraced by Ivan Karamazov. Ivan also advocates a marriage of socialism with the Church, because only through such a unification of power can man be forced to give up his misguided evil ways. Correspondingly, Naphta may be regarded as the model of an updated Grand Inquisitor, willing and eager to take away man's freedom 'for his own good'.

It is difficult not to perceive in Mann's portrait of Naphta a very important cultural phenomenon of our epoch: disillusionment with the efficacy of human reason, in both its theoretical and its political employments. Mann is calling attention to the likelihood that our times will see the emergence of *enfants terribles* who will proclaim the demise of humanistic-rationalistic aspirations and declare allegiance to trans-rational divinities. Naphta's divinity is not altogether new: it wears the garb of old-fashioned, medieval Christian religion, even though a Dostoyevsky would point up its radical divergence from Christ's message. It is not the particular form of the irrational or anti-rational faith that is at stake here: what provokes concern is the very fact of invoking forces lying beyond the ken of ordinary human intelligence. For anyone who still finds attractive the basic humanistic thrust of Settembrini's position, which sees the ultimate meaning as lying in human freedom and creativity, Naphta's views will look threatening indeed. No wonder that the *homo humanus* is anxious to protect Hans Castorp from their influence.

There is a prophetic note in Mann's characterisation of the
kind of ideology Naphta is prepared to propagate. The disillusionment with the course of Western civilisation before and in the
wake of the Great War sowed similar seeds. Provoked by the circumstances of history, leaders could arise who would dream of
establishing political systems on the basis of quasimystical visions,
such as that of the 'thousand-year *Reich*'. It is no accident that
the ideological basis of Hitler's programme was shrouded in the
mists of quasi-religious pagan mythology. But fascism in its
various forms is not the only example of the loss of faith in the
possibility of arranging human affairs – social, economic and political – with an eye toward preserving and strengthening individual
human freedoms. There is much anti-humanist mysticism in the
idea of the perfect communist state, even though its proponents
are willing to make use of the technological fruits of natural
science. Not without justification has communism been likened to
a new fanatical religion.

How does our young hero, Hans Castorp, take to Naphta's
views? As usual, he keeps his eyes and ears open. It does not
escape him that the the earthly-pleasure-condemning 'little Jesuit
with a moist spot' (in his lungs) is himself living in utter luxury.
His sumptuously appointed room (in an otherwise humble house
of a tailor) does not square with the philosophies expounded by its
inhabitant. What a contrast with the almost bare walls of the
Spartan attic occupied by the threadbare humanist! Even more
seriously, Hans perceives outright contradictions in Naphta's
cleverly and eruditely argued views, and concurs with Settembrini's verdict that 'His form is logic, but his essence is confusion.'
The Italian also points out, echoing Nietzsche, that Naphta's
attraction to terror, to inquisition, is a perverted assertion of the
sickened (both in the physical and moral sense) will to power.
Naphta, declares Settembrini, is a voluptuary, in a broader,
intellectual sense of the word; in other words, a champion of
extreme irrationalistic voluntarism.

In time, Castorp gradually works his way toward a position of
his own. Stimulated and stirred up by what each of the two
warring pedagogues put before him, he cunningly concludes that
neither of them is wholly right or wholly wrong. They push
everything to extremes, he tells his cousin on one occasion. But
his judgement and his insight reach fullness of comprehension
and formulation under rather unusual circumstances, which

Mann describes in the central section of the novel, entitled 'Snow'.

The circumstances are in part of Castorp's own making. True to his resolve to expose himself to as much expereince as possible, he learns how to ski, and one fine snowy day he ventures far beyond the safe limits for a beginner. He wants to be alone with the limitless expanse of wintry mountain scenery. His calculations are under normal circumstances rational and safe enough, but he is surprised by a snowstorm as he winds his way through empty, unfamiliar mountain slopes on his skis. The blinding storm keeps him going in circles. Almost wholly exhausted, he reaches a hut and leans against it, seeking protection from the icy wind. The temptation to lie down is irresistible, even though his brain signals the deadly danger of succumbling to sleep. Nevertheless, he dozes off for a time and has a dream. He sees an idyllic scene: beautiful country, meadows, trees, a brook, with people, young and old, in various poses and gestures of love, contentment, serene and joyful peace. But hard by he sees horrible witches tearing apart the body of a small child. Significantly, one of the youths in the idyllic scene seems to be aware of the human sacrifice being performed just a short distance away. The horror scene of the dream rouses Hans to consciousness, thus saving him from certain death. Before resuming his return to the valley, he ponders the meaning of the dream.

He takes the dream to have its origin, almost in Jungian fashion, in the memories of the whole human race. 'We dream anonymously and collectively, if each after his own fashion' (an echo of the phrase 'anonymous and communal' which he had used to characterise some of Naphta's ideas). He sees now that the interest in disease and death is just the other side of the interest in life. Both of his mentors fail to see the true position of man.

> Their aristocratic question! Disease, health! Spirit, nature! Are those contradictions? I ask, are they problems? No, they are no problems, neither is the problem of their aristocracy. The recklessness of death is in life, it would not be life without it – and in the center is the position of the *Homo Dei,* between recklessness and reason, as his state is between mystic community and windy individualism. . . . Man is the lord of counterpositions, they can be only through him, and thus he is more aristocratic than they.

As a result of such deep pondering Hans arrives at a conclusion italicised by the author: *For the sake of goodness and love, man shall let death have no sovereignty over his thoughts.* This statement may be taken as a summing up, as Hans's, or Mann's, synthesis of ideas and positions explored in the novel so far. But the novel does not end there, and the young man's initiation into life's mysteries is not over. As it progresses, the reader may ask himself just what is the status of that preliminary 'summing up' in the 'Snow' section. Does Hans live up to his vision? Is this vision for his benefit alone, or is it to be taken symbolically as the author's intent to call European civilisation back to itself, to warn it against the optimistic delusions of humanistic liberalism and the horrible consequences of allowing mystical ideologies to institute a reign of terror?

One thing is sure. Hans is neither a pedagogue nor an ideologue. What he has learned from his dream on the snowy slopes concerns *him*, his wisdom, his understanding, his verdict on the meaning of human life. His talent does not include a tendency toward leadership, philosophical or political. He does not draw up any programmes for action from his vision. Indeed, Settembrini later reminds him that he ought to bestir himself as a citizen of a great European power and help decide what political role it is to play. '*Caro amico!*' says the Italian.

> There will be decisions to be made, decisions of unspeakable importance for the happiness and the future of Europe; it will fall to your country to decide, in her soul the decision will be consummated. Placed as she is between East and West, she will have to choose, she will have to decide finally and consciously between the two spheres. You are young, you will have a share in this decision, it is your duty to influence it.

It is sobering to ponder Settembrini's, and Mann's challenge, in the light of what was happening in Germany ten years after the publication of the novel.

Hans does not take up his mentor's challenge. He remains silent, thus provoking another almost epigrammatic warning from Settembrini (is there a symbolic meaning in his name as well?), directed not only at his young friend but also at the nation he represents. 'The articulate word does not know where it is with you. My friend, that is perilous. Speech is civilisation itself. The word, even the most contradictious word, preserves contact – it is silence which isolates.'

In the remainder of the novel there is a conspicuous absence of references by Hans to the message of his vision in the 'Snow' section. Indeed, one may gain the impression that it is lost and has no real effect on what he later does, thinks or says. That such an interpretation would not be wholly correct subsequent events demonstrate. Nevertheless, Mann's philosophical conclusions as conveyed through his hero are not transparent, and we shall need to grapple with their possible meaning. In the meatime, we must meet another fascinating character, Mynheer Peeperkorn.

Castorp's parting with Clavdia is sudden, unannounced. During the following months he does not know where she is or what she is doing. She may have returned to her husband in the Asiatic part of Russia or she may have gone elsewhere. She never writes to him. Although Hans is eager for news from her or at least about her, he has none. And then, just as suddenly and unannounced, she reappears; not alone, however. She is accompanied by Mynheer Pieter Peeperkorn, an elderly Dutchman, whose conspicuous wealth was acquired in Indonesia in coffee business.

From the moment of his arrival Peeperkorn dominates the Berghof scene. Everyone's attention is fastened on his magnetic personality. Mann takes pains to make clear that in using the term 'personality' with reference to the newcomer he wants to emphasise one of its special connotations. That connotation is connected with his physical appearance. Although no longer young, his body manifests muscular strength. His bearing and gestures are on the grand scale. That scale, however, has nothing to do with intellectuality. Peeperkorn has none of the gifts which distinguish our pedagogical orators, who have so far dominated Castorp's education. On the contrary, his speech is incoherent, disconnected, punctuated by an emphatic repetition of some stock words, such as 'positively', 'by all means,' 'absolutely' and 'settled'. It definitely is not the power of his mind that commands attention. Castorp has only one word for it: 'personality', in the elemental, almost mysterious sense of the word, having nothing to do with cleverness or stupidity.

From the time of his arrival, Peeperkorn presides over social life at the sanatorium. He enhances it considerably by arranging special parties, games and excursions – paying, of course, personally for sumptuous provisions on every occasion. These provisions include generous quantities of his favoured brand of gin, to which he refers, euphemistically, as bread. As Castorp learns from Dr Behrens, Peeperkorn is an alcoholic who also suffers from rheumatic fever contracted in Asia. Hence his visit to the sanatorium. He is treated for his illness, but not with much success. His fever returns every fourth day, and on those days he has to stay in bed. When relatively free of his illness he rouses his fellow patients to renewed revelry.

As Castorp quickly observes, Settembrini and Naphta, the two masters of cerebral gymnastics, who often join the lively social occasions, suffer in comparison with the inarticulate Dutchman. Although he treats them with distinguished attention, his occasional mocking interjections play havoc with their discussions. His 'participation' in their conversations is inane, but somehow his stupidity seems to come off better than their cleverness. As Castorp remarks about this effect, 'he puts us all in his pocket'. Such is the power and magic of Peekperkorn's personality. By a series of seemingly relevant yet disjointed and uncompleted remarks, accompanied by a few elegant and pointed gestures, he reduces the learned interlocutors to powerless despair.

Mann's new character succeeds in exposing another weakness in those whose assets are merely cerebral. If we are inclined to call Peeperkorn 'life without mind', we nevertheless must reckon with the electrifying force of that elemental life itself. Hans is genuinely impressed by this new discovery. He enjoys the presence and the performance of Peeperkorn's magnetic personality and soon becomes his friend. This development surprises all those who know of Castorp's attachment to Clavdia, including Clavdia herself. By all of them he was expected to show jealousy and hostility toward the man who had conquered the heart of his beloved. We know that he had prolonged his stay in the sanatorium for her sake, hoping that she would return, although it is also true that she had made no commitment to him. Nevertheless, he is at first deeply hurt when he learns that she is the Dutchman's mistress. But soon his hostility evaporates and the incipient jealousy disappears. Why?

In part, this must be counted as another facet of Hans's special talent: to learn from life and to turn his attention to the new things it has to offer. Again he finds something new and special to wonder at, and it is more complicated than it at first appears. It does not take Hans long to discover that there is a certain sadness about the inarticulate life-loving giant. Paradoxically, that weakness lies precisely in his strongest point: the intense need to live on the level of feeling. That is Peeperkorn's sore spot, a *point d'honneur* analogous to the insistent sense of duty which leads poor Joachim to 'desert to the colours', thus precipitating his death. Hans observes that being such an extraordinary, life-celebrating personality has something military about it, like guarding an outpost. The question which the 'civilian' Castorp asks is what happens when one is no longer an effective soldier at this post.

Hans's perception proves accurate. As it turns out, in the triangular relationship Hans–Clavdia–Pieter some intriguing undercurrents come to the surface. As their mutual friendship grow (and Hans genuinely cultivates it), Peeperkorn discloses to him his philosophy of life. Like his personality, it is elemental. Resting in his bed from an attack of rheumatic fever and consuming great quantities of red wine to fight his thirst, he confesses that he sees no point in life if he cannot respond to physical desire. 'Man is intoxicated by his desire, woman demands and expects to be intoxicated by it. Hence our holy duty of feeling, hence the shame of unfeelingness, in powerlessness to awaken the woman to desire.' Peeperkorn reinforces his point by propounding what sounds like a religion of eroticism.

> For feeling, young man, is godlike. Man is godlike, in that he feels. He is the feeling of God. God created him in order to feel through him. Man is nothing but the organ through which God consummates his marriage with roused and intoxicated life. If man fails in feeling, it is blasphemy; it is the surrender of his masculinity, a cosmic catastrophe, an irreconcilable horror–.

We also learn that Clavdia, the willing object of Peeperkorn's feelings, is aware of this sore spot in her lover. She is worried about his grip on life, should his health deteriorate to the point where he can no longer respond to physical feeling. A new disclosure comes to light. In a touching scene Clavdia confesses to Hans that she came with Peeperkorn to Berghof in order to be with Hans while facing this difficulty. The scene in which this disclosure is made is one of the most moving in the whole novel. It takes place when Clavdia decides to talk the matter over with her former lover. She is a bit hurt that Hans shows no jealousy towards the new lover. But then she is moved by his confession that he spent all those months in the sanatorium waiting for her return. When asked whether she loves Peeperkorn she answers that she could not help responding to his strong feeling for her (thus bearing out his philosophy). More importantly, she reveals that the person with whom she felt like sharing her deep worries was Hans. That is why she came back to the Berghof.

What can we make of this confession? Hans, of course, is profoundly touched by it. It signifies that what they felt for each other during the carnival night was not insignificant and did not evaporate into nothingness. The encounter established a bond between them, a bond which did not remain merely on the sensual level but was transformed into mutual need and trust. The first act of their new and deeper friendship is to enter into a pact to be helpful to Peeperkorn in his difficulty. That Clavdia needs Hans in this way pleases him immensely. 'Oh, Clavdia! That is beautiful beyond words! You came back to me with him? And yet will you say that my waiting was silly and wrong and fruitless?'

The following paragraph is a classic example of Mann's subtle irony, in which he indulges throughout much of the novel. At the same time, it is one of its deeply moving moments. Hans and Clavdia exchange a kiss – a Russian kiss on the mouth. Its meaning, however, as Mann tells the reader, is far too multi-faceted to fit any one description. That kiss appears to be bringing together into a single unity seemingly disparate, even opposed elements: friendship, sexuality, morality, loyalty, spirituality. The opposites sometimes meet. 'In the most raging as in the most reverent passion, there must be *caritas*. The meaning of the word varies? In God's name, let it vary. That it does so makes it living, makes it human; it would be a regrettable lack of "depth" to trouble over the fact.'

The triangle is strengthened in still another way, disclosing for Hans, an inveterate learner, a further valuable dimension in interpersonal relationships. A man of feeling, Peeperkorn is not indifferent to pangs of jealousy. He suspects that Hans and Clavdia had been lovers in the past, and the thought worries him. When he finally manages to ask the question directly, Hans is torn between the desire to be honest and the wish not to hurt his sensitive friend. Fearful of Peeperkorn's reaction, he nevertheless manages to tell the whole truth, disclosing in the process his inmost feelings.

> For love of her, in defiance of Herr Settembrini, I declared myself for the principle of unreason, the *spirituel* principal of disease, under whose aegis I had already, in reality, stood for a long time back; and I remained here, I no longer know precisely how long. I have forgotten, broken with, everything, my relatives, my calling, all my ideas of life. When Clavdia went away, I waited for her return, so that I am wholly lost to life down below, and dead in the eyes of my friends.

Hans's confession means much to Peeperkorn. They both feel that their love for the same person, instead of dividing them, is bringing them closer together. The bond merges into a brotherly feeling. 'Young man, we are brothers', says Peeperkorn, as they join in the ritual of drinking their *Bruderschaft*. Mann's rendition of this scene is tender without being maudlin. Perhaps to our surprise, he manages to produce a convincing example of a counterpart to the daemon of jealousy.

The new friendship, however, does not deter Peeperkorn from acting on a previously made resolve. Having become convinced that the rheumatic fever is rendering him irreversibly impotent, he commits suicide. In the light of his philosophy, his life has no point any longer, although, as we have seen, Castorp diagnosed this to be precisely the sore spot in his point of view. But that was Hans, not Pieter. Even his departure from the world Peeperkorn manages on a grand scale. He administers himself a deadly poison by means of an ingeniously contrived mechanical device, imitating the fangs of a snake. After his death, Clavdia again leaves and disappears from Castorp's life.

The remainder of chapter 7, the last in the novel (the number seven recurs repeatedly through the book), is difficult to interpret. It begins with the author's own, highly philosophical disquisition on the nature of time. The weight of Mann's musing on this topic falls on the radical relativity of time. It is reminiscent of Bergson's view that to measure time objectively, by means of clocks and other mechanical devices, is to distort its actual experiental content. The mathematical matrix of time is but a formal grid and can accommodate varying amounts and kinds of content. Depending on how we fill that grid, the sense of time, its subjective duration, will feel very differently. When a boy tells his girl, 'I've been waiting here for hours' though she is only twenty minutes late, what he says is true in its own way. Filled with impatient and eager longing, every second extends for him far beyond its objective limits. In the same way, the first three weeks of Castorp's stay in the Berghof take up the first four of the seven chapters of the book. As he becomes a regular resident, he is able to confirm Settembrini's observation that the smallest unit of time on the mountain is three weeks, and, indeed, the passage of time speeds up as its contents become regularised and uniform. After Clavdia leaves for the second time, Hans remains at Davos for another four years, but it takes Mann less than 100 pages, of the total 700, to describe their content.

   Their content is puzzling, even problematic. Apart from the duel between Settembrini and Naphta, nothing of real import happens. On the contrary, boredom, ennui, seem to set in. There are no enriching personal encounters, no heightening discoveries. To be sure, our hero is initiated into some new experiences, but they are disturbing rather than enlightening. Some of them are in fact, as Mann's one section-heading indicates, 'highly question-able'. The upward curve of Castorp's education seems to have reached its zenith with his memorable brotherhood pact with Peeperkorn. The novel could have ended there, perhaps even on a happy note, with Clavdia and Hans joined in happiness. Or, it could have ended even sooner, with the 'Snow' section, where Hans apparently reached a firm philosophical position of his own. In the latter case, of course, we should not have met the kingly Dutchman and should have been deprived of the most humanly touching 'pacts' made by the members of our romantic triangle.

   We must, however, defer to the author's choice to make the novel as long as it is. As Mann observed in 1933 in reference to his book, 'It is possible for a work to have its own will and purpose, perhaps a far more ambitious one than the author's – and it is *good* that this should be so'. It is, therefore, only proper to consider the possible objectives which the work was carrying to completion after the dramatic highlights have been left behind. Shocking as the duel between Naphta and Settembrini is, it merely rounds out the characterisation of their two philosophical and moral positions already essentially accomplished in the earlier sections of the book. The windy individualist, in spite of

his bellicose nationalism, has no stomach for bloodshed and fires
into the air, openly exposing himself to Naphta's bullet (a manly
behaviour, according to Castorp, the civilian), and the little Jesuit
terrorist turns the terror against himself, firing into his own
temple. (Is this Mann's not-too-subtle symbolisation that all
terror is bound to be self-defeating?) It is also to be noted that,
although he earnestly tries to prevent the duel, Castorp's efforts
are rather inefficacious and utterly unsuccessful. His lack of
vigour and resourcefulness in this episode may appear morally
questionable.

What words can we use to describe the content of Castorp's
time during the years between Clavdia's second departure and the
thunderbolt of the war? He languishes. Some such word needs to
be invoked to characterise his mood. Surprising? Well, the urge
for an explanation is strong; the reader's mind is teased by what is
happening. There may be even a temptation to speak here, *à la*
Joseph Conrad, of inconclusive experiences. There is something
puzzling, inexplicable, even questionable about our hero's
behaviour. One possible explanation must be considered, even if
it is to be rejected outright. We know from Castorp's confessions
and Mann's narrations that the young man was deeply in love
with Clavdia. He stayed for years on the mountain for her sake.
He was hurt when she returned as the mistress of another. It
speaks well of him that he transformed his jealousy into a
beautiful act of fellow-feeling. And yet, despite her professions
that Hans means a lot to her, Clavdia does not stay with him: she
takes off immediately after Peeperkorn's suicide. Is Mann trying
to say something about her in terms of her actions rather than
words? During their *tête-à-tête* Castorp and Peeperkorn accept
the possibility that there were other men in her life, and she is, of
course, in some sense married to the absent Russian, about
whose strange relation to her Castorp sometimes wondered.
Could it be that by presenting her as she is and acts, her
conception of morality and freedom included, Mann wanted to
indicate a certain unreliability, symbolised by feminine fickle-
ness, in the wind blowing westward from the East? Or is Mann
calling attention to the impermanence of all human relationships? While on this topic, one may speculate about the possible
symbolic significance of the fact that our free-spending, life-loving
Dutchman acquired his style *and* rheumatic fever in exotic
Indonesia, even farther east than Clavdia's Daghestan. (The

plague in *Death in Venice,* the work written just before *Magic Mountain* was begun, also comes through a gateway to the East, and the object of perilous fascination for Aschenbach is a Polish boy.)

Whatever inconclusive conclusions we draw about Clavdia, it still remains a possibility that Hans's gloomy state of mind is in part induced by having lost his beloved. Is he waiting for her second return? He does not refer to her, she does not seem to be consciously present to his mind, and yet some 'alchemic' changes may occur because of the absence of some 'magic' ingredients. If the ironic German (as Mann has been dubbed by Erich Heller) meant to tease us with this possibility, he certainly has done a good job in disclaiming, or covering up, any responsibility for it. We are on our own and in turn may, just as ironically, disclaim any responsibility for our speculations.

If the speculation about the negative effect of Clavdia's absence is correct, then the fact that Castorp succumbs to 'the great God Dumps' is easier to understand. But Mann directs our, and our hero's, attention to things that also contribute to making this glorious promontory seem stale and unprofitable. Life may dump us into gloom, despair and nameless anxiety without warning, without rhyme or reason (Mann the existentialist?). There is no guarantee that the greatest insight, once had (snow scene), and the greatest heights once scaled (Hans's *hu-man* experiences with Clavdia, Peeperkorn and, on a different level, with his brave, amiable *homo humanus,* Ludovico Settembrini) will equip us with wisdom and strength to fill the remainder of our formally available time with positive content.

We seem to be told by Mann in these last sections of the novel that there is such a phenomenon as the spirit of the times, or even the spirit of the place. Some of the follies, irritabilities and irrationalities described in this part of the book the author often attributes to the 'prevailing temper'. He seems to hint that sometimes that temper renders individual intervention helpless. With Clavdia gone, and Settembrini enfeebled by rapidly failing health and the *hysterica passio* of the duel, there are no positive magic influences to keep Hans Castorp stimulated and interested. As he told Clavdia, it was for her sake that he cut off all of his connections with those below. No duty calls him to return, as it did, fatefully, his cousin. The bulk of the patients carry on as usual their inane games and diversions, flitting from one craze to another and outwitting the hospital managers in finding new ways to indulge in sexual escapades.

Even Hans seems to be caught up in the indolent way of living. He forgets his mentor's warning not to abandon his divinely given reason and takes part in spiritual seances supervised by Dr Krokowski, relentless researcher into the unconscious and occult powers of the mind. A new young patient, Elly Brand, is discovered to be a very talented medium and is used as transmitter of messages from another world. During one seance Castorp agrees to summon Joachim Ziemssen from beyond the grave. Mann renders the scene as if Joachim's apparition actually did turn up before the gathering. But he also shows us Hans's moral revulsion against disturbing the spirit of his departed cousin; in a truly Settembrinian manner, with one quick movement, Hans turns on the white light, putting an end to this 'highly questionable' activity. (There is a question on this episode for the reader. So far in the book, Mann, when dealing with facts has never presented anything that is not objectively credible. The appearance of Joachim as a ghost is treated on a par with other objective events. Unless we try to explain the events as a collective hallucination, for which interpretation Mann seems to give no encouragement, we must assume that the author himself was allowing for the possibility of such happenings. But here too we are left with nothing but inconclusive speculation.)

One section of the final part introduces a more positive diversion into Castorp's life. Indeed, it is more than a diversion and can be seen as a manifestation of our hero's talent to stay responsive to further significant dimensions of experience. When the management installs for the benefit of the patients a high quality gramophone with a library of records, Hans becomes its custodian and the most assiduous user. Long after the novelty of the new gadget has worn off for other patients, he takes time to explore in depth the riches of the musical world, especially the opera. This section gives Mann, a serious student of music, an opportunity to comment on its moral and spiritual possibilities. Hans certainly sees such possibilites and immerses himself, with understanding and discernment, in the magic messages of music. The themes in *The Barber of Seville, La Traviata, The Tales of Hoffman, Aida* and *Carmen,* operas to which Castorp for a time gives all his attention, show a connection between them and some of the themes that so far have contributed to the initiation, the heightening of our hero.

This connection is especially evident in the final part of the section on music, when Hans Castorp falls in love with Schubert's *Lied 'Am Brunnen vor dem Tore'*, with Goethe's poem for the text. That text, and Schubert's music, captures something simple and yet profoundly dear to those who appreciate peace, nature, love, and home. The *Lied* is a most suitable medium to transmit such feelings, and Hans is susceptible to them. 'To him the song meant a whole world, a world which he must have loved, else he could not have so desperately loved that which it represented and symbolised to him.' What Hans discovers, however, when he broods over the song's meaning, is that the world behind it is death. He recognises that the spiritual sympathy with that world 'was none the less sympathy with death'. This insight brings back the message of the 'stock-taking' after the dream in the snow-storm: what makes life so poignant, so tender, so delicate, is the imminent presence of destruction by death. The conclusion Mann wishes to draw from it, however, is not wholly pessimistic. Without being death-denying, it nevertheless affirms life. 'Ah, it was worth dying for, that enchanted *Lied*! But he who died for it, died indeed no longer for it; was a hero only because he died for the new, the new world of love and the future that whispered in his heart.' The vision at the ski hut is not forgotten.

What tears Hans away from the ambiguous enchantment of the mountain? Not his own resolve, not the prompting of a friend or lover. It is the thunderbolt of the war. 'He saw himself released, freed from the enchantment – not of his own motion, he was fain to confess, but by the operation of exterior powers, of whose activities his own liberation was a minor incident indeed!', although Mann suggests, tentatively, that this effect on one tiny individual destiny may be taken for a manifestation of divine goodness and justice. He even has his hero sink to his knees, grateful for being liberated from the 'gloomy grotto of his state of sin'. But we must be wary of our ironic German. His messages are often not easy to disambiguate.

The last glimpse we have of Hans Castorp is as he dodges the rain of shrapnel explosions, running across the field of battle. His chances for survival are slim. Life in general has no special protection for its 'delicate child', in spite of the insinuation of God's justice and mercy. And yet the reader, aware of the horrible slaughter in the trenches of the Great War, of the merciless destruction met in them by millions of indifferent engineers and talented human beings, cannot help but feel that the loss of Hans is our loss as well. His exposure to death and destruction are also ours. Why? Because what he has learned in the hermetic atmosphere of his mountain concerns us as well. Hans was talented in learning *for us* what possibilities, opportunities and dangers life has to offer. If we have followed him in his explorations, his informal classroom with his mentors, his experiences with love and friendship, his seclusion with books and records, his walks across the mountain meadows and ski-trips across snowy slopes, we have learned something about ourselves, *our* options, talents and limitations. For all of us are 'life's delicate children', threatened by secret workings of disease, caught in the crosscurrents of changing beliefs and values, subjected to the whims of 'prevailing opinion', vulnerable to the dispensations of 'thet great God Dumps', and expendable in the whirlwinds of historical forces beyond our control.

B

Mann's novel brings home to us Nietzsche's claim that man is an experiment in the cosmos and that all his endeavours are always on trial. Nietzsche's message was that we should boldly welcome our experimental status and join in the cosmic laughter when our personal part in the experiment fails; as long as we have done our best to serve life, our conscience is clear, proclaimed the fiery philosopher. But Mann's book does not invite cosmic laughter. Its ending encourages a different kind of response. For one thing, Mann's hero lacks the puffed-up grandeur of a 'higher individual'. In his Hans he shows us that the sensibility to the mysteries of life may be present not only in 'higher individuals' but also in 'indifferent engineers'. With the author, we wish Hans Castorp well as he works his way through the battlefield. He did not fail in the task of trying to make sense of life, even though, when we take leave of him, he did not succeed in working out his private destiny. In wishing him well we show some of the talent with which his author endowed him.

But Hans's, and our, situation is not enviable. Mann's diagnosis of the state of health of Western civilisation is inconclusive. A sense of uncertainty seems to pervade the scene.

The optimistic humanism of the Age of Reason, which pinned its hopes on scientific, social and political progress, appears now shabby, threadbare. Blind and contradictory ancestral instincts, to which the human race has been always ready to respond, seem to submerge the civilising impulse. On the one hand, sloth, lasciviousness and abandonment to sheer pleasure raise their ugly heads; on the other, the appeal of force, authority, martial discipline and terror threaten to sweep aside rational humanitarian protests. On the one hand, Hans experiences the seductiveness of the attitudes represented by Clavdia and Peeperkorn; on the other, he resists the appeal of martial adventure, which has such a strong hold on his cousin Joachim and to which Naphta is ready to resort in the name of his totalitarian transcendental, transhuman ideals.

Mann's perception of the vulnerability of the rationalistic –humanistic ideal is indeed prophetic. Our rationalistic self-conception is always in danger of being undermined by more instinctive – voluntaristic and libidinal – forces. If we regard reason as the typical, essential feature of man, then we shall be inclined to call such a reversion to instinctive forces a lapse. But such a reversion may also be seen as a defensive reaction of the complex human entity against the overeagerness of reason to subordinate to itself everything else in human nature. Settembrini's self-conscious rationalism has a prudish and conservative side. In spite of his proud adoption of the libertarian slogan *Placet experiri*, he is anxious to set arbitrary limits to experimentation. Hans senses this overcautiousness and is more open to experience than is Settembrini. He is more realistic about the life–death relationship and does not look upon ailment and suffering as merely providing a target for social action. Hans is fascinated by the entire dialectical health–disease spectrum, and in that sense he is more of a philosopher bent on understanding things as they really are in their full scope. He does not close his eyes to deeper phenomena just because they appear inimical to his moral preconceptions. Hans discovers that disease and death are much closer to life than Settembrini is consciously or unconsciously willing to admit.

Had Castorp found himself among the Berkeley students of the 'flower-children' generation, he would be quite sympathetic to their causes. They too found their world too disciplined, too square, often repressive of spontaneous feelings and closed-minded about new, unheard-of experience. To the extent that their objections to the unfeelingness of the technocratic political system was rooted in their general attack on 'objective consciousness' as such, the flower-children's behaviour was analogous to Castorp's gravitation toward Clavdia's undisciplined, lax charms and Peeperkorn's exuberant life-style. Conversely, the outraged Establishment's reaction and concern were analogous to those expressed by Herr Settembrini with regard to his pupil's wayward, suspect behaviour.

Just as shallow rationalism tends to close its eyes to, or sweep under the rug, some important aspects of the human situation, so it tends to overestimate the degree to which it can be effective in organising mankind socially and politically. Mann is pointing out how even in Settembrini's own case we perceive an inability to escape the instinctive appeal of tribal bellicosities. Settembrini preaches internationalism but gets all worked up over the Brenner frontier. His case is not an exception: moving forward in time we find this happening in Europe up to the present. The gospel of international brotherhood and peace is constantly in conflict with nationalistic allegiances and ambitions, with the latter often reasserting themselves in explosive, colossally destructive ways. When Hitler appealed to the *Blut und Boden* instinct, he did so in the context of a bitter attack on the weakness and corruptibility of parliamentary democracies. The fact that millions of his cuntrymen heeded his call was a proof of the precarious hold of the universalistic humanistic ideology, which at least in the abstract dominated Western thought and flourished in Germany, the land of thinkers and poets. It is sobering to consider how difficult it seems to be to move the nations of Europe toward the concept of a United States of Europe – championed by Winston Churchill, but effectively opposed by Charles De Gaulle.

It is also thought-provoking to consider the apparent success of blending a universalistic ideology with particularistic parochialism in communist and fascist ideologies. They seem to embody characteristics attentively studied by Mann in the person of Leo Naphta. 'The little Jesuit terrorist' manages to combine a thoroughly articulated system of ideas with a programme for resolute action animated not by faith in reason but by a transparent zeal for power, for uprooting the present and revolutionising the future. The fact that his programme is motivated by his (questionable) conception of Christian religion is secondary. What was important and prophetic for the course of history after Mann's book saw the light of day was the rash of Messianic revolutionary movements dominated by the zeal to seize power and to use it resolutely and ruthlessly toward deliberately adopted ideological ends: Lenin's and Stalin's Russia, Hitler's Germany, Mussolini's Italy, Japan of the 1930s and 1940s, China under Mao Zedong. The particularism to which appeal is made by means of totalitarian propaganda may be nationalistic, as in the case of fascism, or internationalistic, as in the case of communism. The particularistic parochial element in communism is embodied in the theme of class warfare, of setting one segment of population against all others, who are represented in the darkest possible colours to justify their suppression and elimination, the practices of which the Soviet Gulag Archipelago is a telling example. In each case the emotions of adherents of the ideology are whipped up and the will manipulated by sharpening the contrast between 'us' and 'them'.

Hans Castorp's education consists in his introduction to the various themes which disturb or ought to disturb the calm of a complacent European man, a calm derived from unsuspecting assurance that everything is just fine with the rationally interpreted and humanistically organised world. That assurance was gained too quickly: much of our world, exterior and interior, is still dark and unexplored. We must not take it for granted that reason will triumph, Mann seems to be warning us. In the breast of men everywhere and anywhere impulses may stir that will lead to explosion, destruction, holocaust. Nature itself, conceived as benign and friendly by the optimistic centuries of enlightenment and faith in inevitable progress, shows its enigmatic, Sphinx-like, or at least Janus-like face.

All along in the book, Hans becomes increasingly aware, as is our entire Darwinised epoch, of the fragile, vulnerable status of the life process in the material universe dominated by inorganic laws. It is easy for living beings, man not excluded, to succumb to disease-dealing substances that convert health-producing cells into deadly chemical compounds. Ultimately the same process that results in life results in death, as Hans comes to discover when he studies the chemistry of living and dying cells. The ease with which healthy cells are transformed into cancerous ones baffles medical research even today.

The confidence that life, and human life in particular, is enjoying a privileged status in the universe is visibly undermined in the novel. And so is the expectation that in the areas subject to direct human control – the areas of social organisation and of moral management of our affairs – mankind is competent to find sensible solutions. The entire human experiment, over which Nietzsche was so excited, has come to a sort of impasse. The outcome of that experiment is in serious doubt. The novel places man not in the sunlight of affirmation, but, rather, in the twilight of uncertainty.

There is a moment in Mann's book when Hans *seems* to have worked his way to a kind of affirmative stance. In the 'Snow' chapter he finds the role of man to be that of the guardian of love perched precariously between the opposing forces cf light and darkness, reason the instinct. But that vision, the novel goes on to show, is difficult to maintain; it is constantly buffeted by forces that distract us from its appeal. Nevertheless, the fact that the vision came to Hans, our representative, is important. The possibility of the vision and of the resolve it is capable of producing – 'For the sake of goodness and love, man shall let death have no sovereignty over his thoughts' – precludes ultimate and irrevocable pessimism. Rather, Mann is showing us how difficult it is to maintain the vision and what are the various forces that keep us from being resolutely guided by it. There is no optimistic reassurance in Mann's book, as there is in Goethe's play (Faust is a good man, says the Lord) and in Dostoyevsky's novel ('Hurrah for Karamazov!' are its final words). Instead, the author asks the reader to ponder somberly the question, *Quo vadis, homine?*

Part III
NIGHT

As the twentieth century wore on, presenting mankind with new calamities and unexpected problematic situations, Western man increasingly became a question to himself. One philosophical movement in particular found man not only problematic but also absurd. Existentialism proclaimed that there is no human nature and that to be human means to put oneself perpetually in question. Many different conclusions were drawn from this new characterisation. Some saw it as an exhilarating liberation from all restraining shackles and welcomed the opportunity to celebrate the concomitant declaration of absolute human freedom, even though that freedom was bought at the price of living with constant anxiety about the meaning of one's actions. Some found that the non-dependence on any definite structures – social, psychological or moral – allowed human beings to rediscover their connection with the supernatural, as did Kierkegaard in the nineteenth century and his followers in ours. But there was also a growing realisation on the part of many influential writers that the detachment of human freedom both from nature and from the accumulated patterns of tradition and culture delivered mankind into the darkness of total uncertainty about everything.

The three works to be discussed here depict ways of facing this sense of uncertainty, of being in the dark as to what life is all about, of having lost one's moorings, of being alienated, estranged. The figures of the Underground Man, the Outsider, the Stranger, began to haunt contemporary consciousness. The Stranger was a puzzle to himself and to others, especially if the others desperately clung to some norms of a social or moral order. Not surprisingly, they found their values threatened and the stability of mores undermined. But our writers do not take the side of those who would prefer to live within the familiar frameworks of tradition. For that tradition looks to them stale, weak, diseased. Sartre moves even farther and projects a comprehensive metaphsical view according to which human beings cannot help being in each other's way, this condition being a logical consequence of absolute freedom each person possesses. *No Exit* is a telling illustration of how this metaphysical view works itself out in human life.

Beckett's perception, in *Waiting for Godot,* of how things stand with us is a dramatic presentation not just of a *fin de siècle* but of the complete demise of the positive, optimistic expectation projected into our culture by the exuberant prophets of the Renaissance and the Enlightenment. He gives us a picture not only of the mind at the end of its tether, but of *all* human faculties and capacities in the penultimate stage of disintegration and dissolution. It is *pen*ultimate, however, not ultimate, for even Beckett, simply in virtue of being an artist, depicts the pervasive mood of despair and absurdity with a touch of poignant sympathy. The characters he chooses to bear that profound calamity, so far unheard of in the annals of mankind's history, are experiencing that calamity with a passion that is at least remotely reminiscent of Golgotha. Nevertheless, for all the tenderness and subdued spiritual wailing in this enigmatic play, its pervading mood is that of gloom, abandonment, and a resigned waiting for the end of all things.

7 Alienation Embraced: Camus's *The Stranger*

Nietzsche claimed that Western man had killed the idea of God, and described the fateful consequences of this cultural murder. 'Whither are we moving now? Away from all suns? Are we not plunging continually? Backward, sideward, forward, in all directions? Is there any up or down left? Are we not straying as though through an infinite nothing?' Camus's Stranger is one of those men who, with the departure of God, are fluttering in the void. When deprived of firm and familiar guidance, man easily loses his bearings. He does not know what to do with himself or what gives his life meaning. In the character of Meursault Camus captures in a convincing way a phenomenon to which many representatives of our age have repeatedly called attention. When the spiritual and cultural fabric of a civilisation falls apart, it should not be surprising to find a vacuum in the soul of man. Indeed, the very presence of the soul may be put in doubt. When the prosecutor in Meursault's trial considers the defendant's soul, he finds a blank, 'literally nothing, gentlemen of the jury'. As Meursault reports, 'Really, he said, I have no soul, there was nothing human about me, not one of those moral qualities which normal men possess had any place in my mentality.'

Nietzsche was of the opinion that in the contemporary spiritual crisis the weak man, the 'last man', will prevail and then suffocate in his own nihilism. In the character of Meursault Camus gives us a less extreme and more believable portrait of a person who is thrown on his own resources, and who does not see his existence as related to some deeper source of meaning. It is not just the question of atheism, although Meursault's judges find it to be the main source of his wickedness. Meursault's alienation is more pervasive. Not only is he an atheist; he does not feel any *need* to see his life in relation to any kind of transcendent reality. He is estranged from members of his society precisely because their allegiance to some overarching moral truths and religious beliefs is incomprehensible to him. In turn, this trait in him makes him incomprehensible to them. The result is mutual estrangement.

But Meursault is not a wicked man. In fact, he seems a decent chap. He earns his living. He is a respectable, punctual, though not overly ambitious employee. It cannot be said that he is indifferent to the wellbeing of his old mother, although in the opinion of some people around him he should not have put her in the home for the aged. He enjoys the simple pleasures of life – going to the beach, watching the comings and goings of city life from his apartment window, catching a ride on a moving truck. He carries on an affair with a wholesome girl and stands in a friendly relation to several acquaintances. When asked for a favour he easily obliges without weighing any advantages for himself.

And, yet, even the small, simple pleasures he gets out of life do not engage him strongly. He takes things as they come; they do not arouse his interest in any firm and steady way. Things swim in and out of his consciousness, and he does not dwell on them with any degree of intensity. He enjoys making love to Marie, but he resists her attempts to interpret it as a sign of love for her. When she asks whether he wants to get married he is willing to do so, if it really is a matter of importance to her. To him it is not. But *not* marrying is not important to him either; as far as he is concerned, he could take it or leave it.

'I never have been able to regret anything at all in all my life. I've always been far too much absorbed in the present moment, or the immediate future, to think back.' This is Meursault's self-characterisation late in the novel when he listens to what is being said about him during his trial. The reader will agree with this characterisation, but he is not likely to be wholly satisfied with it. There is a strictly formal difficulty about understanding Meursault. Camus presents the story from the hero's point of view; Meursault is the speaker throughout. All other characters in the novel are presented as he sees or interprets them. He is a very perceptive observer, and much of what he says may be taken as expressing Camus's opinion and judgement. What we learn about Algiers between the two world wars – its people, it values, it style of life – must express Camus's own comments and criticism, moral and philosophical. But Meursault's views of things is certainly not Camus's, especially since the author does not work in black and white and does not appear to have a clear favourite in depicting his hero's conflict with society. Although he gives Meursault many admirable qualities, it is not easy to approve of him. Society has justifiable grievances against him, but its values and practices, as the author presents them in the novel, are far from admirable. Both the individual and society are problematic to the writer of this story, and a great deal of its interest for the reader is that he is called upon to react to its problematic nature.

Perhaps surprisingly, coupled with Meursault's indifference and unstudied nonchalance are strong powers of observation. He might be described as a generalised sort of voyeur; as Rilke observes in his *Duino Elegies,* one can always watch. Meursault is very responsive to the scenery around him; his gaze takes in things and events as they happen, and he absorbs them in a detached, spectator-like way. He is not a completely detached observer, for he briefly muses over what he sees, but his musing is short-lived and his observations pass unscrutinised. To be sure, he often finds things strange or stupid, but he is not really concerned or indignant. When some unwelcome things happen to him, he is annoyed and somewhat put off. But he does not dwell on such events: they do not touch him in a lasting way. Literally, he keeps his cool.

This receptiveness to stimuli operates not only on the intellectual level but also on the emotional and behavioural levels. Natural phenomena strongly impress themselves on his psyche. He is very conscious of the effects of the sun, sky, water. Bodily sensations seem to dominate his awareness. The weather, the time of day, dusk or dawn, affect the way he feels. Even the key events of his life seem to be almost determined by natural phenomena. The fateful shooting of the Arab is seen by him as the result of the sun's rays reflected in the blade of the knife.

The killing of the Arab is the turning-point in his life, and it is important to dwell on the way Meursault experiences it. Camus leaves no doubt in the reader's mind that Meursault never intended to kill the Arab. He is probably truthful and quite correct in telling the court when asked directly why he fired the first shot, 'It was because of the sun.' Here the reader, no matter how understanding, becomes uneasy. It is true that Meursault got drawn into the company of Raymond and his friends from understandable motives. But he is callously indifferent to the way in which Raymond treats his girlfriend. He is blind to obvious faults in his new friend's character, although he resists being regarded as his 'pal'. He shows no signs of sympathy with the young Arab who wants to attack Raymond out of loyalty to his sister. In short, Meursault allows himself to *drift* into a morally dubious affair and appears oblivious to its implications, especially to the danger which he and others are creating. Arabs too are strangers to him, even more remote than his French friends. In this regard, Meursault reflects the mores of the French colonial society. Camus represents the Arabs as somehow inhabiting a separate world, segregated from the French by a curtain of the shimmering sun. In other contexts of the story Camus makes clear that the attitude of the French in Algiers towards the Arabs was racist. Meursault labels Raymond's girlfriend as a Moor. Even more flagrantly racist, the interest of French officialdom in the murder of the Arab is at first only slight and becomes aroused only when the moral character of the killer becomes the almost exclusive and morbid centre of their interest.

Meursault's moral passivity is part and parcel of his basic estrangement. He is satisfied with living on the surface and is completely content to exist on an almost purely aesthetic level. But even that level lacks any activist note. A genuinely aesthetic response to experience normally includes a note of curiosity, an ambitious desire to seek a heightening experience, to enhance its quality, to explore its further horizons. There is no such ambition in Meursault. He is perfectly content with the simple life he is leading and rejects his boss's offer to become the firm's representative in Paris. Paris of all places! The centre of French life and culture, the dispenser of all kinds of pleasure, high and low. None of them has any pulling power for Meursault; he is fully satisfied where he is: working in his drab office, eating in Celeste's greasy-spoon restaurant or in his dingy apartment, 'off the pan', getting his kicks out of seeing Fernandel movies, and sleeping with Marie on weekends, after swimming in the sea and lazing on the beach. If one looks for an anti-Faust character in literature, Meursault is a good candidate. Nietzsche's Zarathustra would rail at him for his *Genügsamkeit*, his easy contentment.

Content with his apparent, almost fortuitous surface satisfactions, Meursault has an anaemic sense of life. On the other hand, he does not have any aggressive, destructive, rebellious impulses.

That is why the ascription of callous criminality and wickedness to him by the jury and the judges representing the 'upright' citizens of Algiers is incongruous. Meursault is surprised to find himself referred to as a criminal, and only gradually does it dawn on him that that label is not really inappropriate: after all, he killed a man. But, knowing Meursault's lukewarm motivation in anything he does, the reader is apt to sympathise with his puzzlement about whether he really fits the category of criminal. That category certainty is applicable to the bloody murder reported on the scrap of newspaper scrap he finds in the mattress in his cell, but, compared with that killing his act seems almost an unfortunate accident. Meursault shows no remorse about it. When he thinks about the killing he does not even regret that it took place; instead he feels 'a kind of vexation'. He had no malice toward the Arab, nor did he have reason to feel that the Arab harboured any feelings toward him. Both were estranged from the fatal encounter. Here we seem to have a classic example of what Hannah Arendt called 'the banality of evil'.

To call evil banal, however, is to cross incongruous concepts. This incogruity hovers over Meursault's life and behaviour. We do not object to banality as long as it is harmless. As long as Meursault moves through his customary round of existence, getting through one day after another, collecting his bits of simple pleasures, and absorbing a variety of sensory images and perceptions, he does not generate animosity or moral disapproval. One may wonder just what makes him so placid and easily satisfied, so uninterested in taking up challenges or in making waves, but who would feel entitled to register moral indignation just becasue of that? There is even a certain appeal in Meursault's unpretentiousness; his direct, almost innocent honesty with himself and with others is disarming. Because Camus makes the reader aware and responsive to this side of his hero's personality, he has a relatively easy time in arousing a dislike of Meursault's judges.

The judges, among whom Camus means to include public opinion, are unfair to Meursault. Their interest in the case is aroused only after the strange character of the defendant has come to light. The centre of attention is not the killing of a person, but the discovery of Meursault's disturbing character traits. These traits are seen as a threat to the received moral and religious convictions. Meursault's behaviour and 'lack of soul' create an alarm, a panic in his fellow citizens. A man who allows himself to smoke cigarettes and to drink *café au lait* while sitting by his mother's coffin must be an unfeeling monster. Only a callous wicked person would go to see a comic film and take a girl to bed the day after burying his mother. The magistrate's preliminary investigation takes a bad turn for Meursault when he reveals himself to be an atheist. When this fact comes to light it seems entirely to displace the question of the young man's guilt. His admission of atheism is seen as a personal attack on the magistrate and his cherished beliefs. '"Do you wish", he asked indignantly, "my life to have no meaning?"' Incredibly, instead of discharging his task to establish the truth in this case, the official converts the hearing into a frightened defence of his private religious beliefs. From that point on it is an established fact for the magistrate that Meursault is a hardened criminal.

The entire trial and the prosecutor's speech revolve around the question of Meursault's moral depravity. Every incident that can by any manner of means by converted into a sign of such depravity is represented as such, and in most cases falsely so, or at least misleadingly. Meursault's motives were hardly malicious, however ill considered they may have been. But even to say that they were ill considered is to say too much: it would be truer to say that they were not considered at all. True, Meursault often considers them in retrospect, and his appraisal of his motives is usually honest; a charge of self-deception would be out of place.

But even self-decpetion, one feels like saying, would have been preferable to this cool, dispassionate and purposeless self-analysis. A self-deceived person at least has a motive, which he *wants* to hide from himself. What does Meursault want? Nothing in particular. He *reacts* to things, events, people, when they come his way, but he is not seeking anything. He is lukewarm toward values that matter so much to others, such as loyalty and respect for the memory of one's mother. That is what irritates and frightens his fellow citizens. If he were rebellious and iconoclastic, if he pushed strongly some of his own values or vices, one could understand him and enter into some sort of dialogue, exchange, contest. Even a hostile dialogue is better than no dialogue at all. Silence isolates, claims Herr Settembrini in *The Magic Mountain*. A look of hatred is better than a shrug of shoulders. Herein lies Meursault's radical strangeness: one does not know what one is up against. Is he human at all? Does he have a soul? The prosecutor concludes that he does not.

The society depicted by Camus is nervous and insecure about its own values. No wonder that it is incapable of sympathy for such a value-free, independent being as Meursault. The total lack of sympathy for him and for his irreverence points to a certain hardness in the hearts of the upright citizens who insist that all trappings of conventional piety and decorum be observed. The procesutor's eagerness to deny any trace of humanity to the defendant is frightening. Yes, he can build his case on all these external signs of the defendant's immorality, but that eagerness looks indecent and self-righteous: there is no trace of compassion in it, no attempt to grant the defendant the least benefit of a doubt. One feels that, like the magistrate, the prosecutor believes himself personally offended by the very existence of such a man as Meursault. Hence the desire to punish does not stem from commitment to justice but from resentment of the affront suffered by each 'decent' member of society. The judgement is pronounced in the name of the French people, but that people Camus presents as paralysed by bigotry and morbidity.

Nevertheless, the mutually incomprehending confontation between the aberrant individual and the punishing, morally closed society brings about an inner transformation in the former. The high point, the *denouement,* of the novel is found in Meursault's reaction to that confrontation. The killing of the Arab puts him not only into a direct, active conflict with a society which has so far ignored him: it also forces him, for the first time in his life, to face himself. The special and perhaps uncanny feature of his mode of living prior to being arrested was precisely that total lack of concern with himself, with what or who he was. He liked himself, but he never judged, evaluated himself. Indeed, it seems as if he never asked himself whether he possessed an identity of his own. He drifted, for the most part pleasantly if evasively, through his daily routine. It takes him a while to take in the fact that *he* is the centre of attention. On several occasions during the interrogation and the trial he is surprised that it is he who is being referred to, identified, examined, charged, judged. He feels the eyes of people riveted on him, with great interest and intense curiosity. At first this realisation gives him an uneasy feeling. Why should he be singled out for attention? But then he remembers that he is the accused, a criminal, although even his labelling himself as such seems to be just an objective, dispassionate observation of one external fact among many, which just happens to explain why he is in jail. It is as if he found oneself uncomfortably warm and then discovered that he had inadvertently put on a warm coat.

But the confrontation with society is insistent and leads Meursault to the discovery of and confrontation with his own self. The outer confrontation is just the trigger, the occasion for the inner one. Given Meursault's easy-going character, one should not really call it a confrontation. Rather, it is a reluctant, and at first casual, self-examination. Having nothing to do in his prison cell, he returns in thought to incidents of his previous life and turns them over in his mind. He begins to wonder what various events *meant* to him, what he felt toward Marie, and what could have been her feelings. He wonders what his mother's life must have been like and what her friend in the old-folks home meant to her. In other words, the circumstances shake loose his paradoxically self-less self-centredness and bring home to him the realisation that deep down he does have a living, reactive identity.

Nevertheless, this reactiveness remains resigned, low-level, until the explosive incident with the priest who visits him in jail, in spite of the prisoner's repeated refusals to see him. That explosion could be seen as the climax of the novel and might be even read as signalling a radical transformation in Meursault. The torrent of words he utters on that occasion is almost out of character. It seems to contain a sudden release of a covertly articulated philosophical decision about the meaning of life. The transformation is startling because all of a sudden the passive, easy-going, inarticulate Meursault speaks out of the depths of his soul whose very existence has been questioned! The assertion is strong, confident, resolute, both in its defiance and in its affirmation. Both need examining. On the last few pages of the novel, Camus appears to be giving us Meursault's *apologia pro vita sua*.

The priest's mission is to save the condemned prisoner's soul. He is convinced that a person facing the loss of earthly existence is bound to turn his attention to forces which promise to rescue his being from oblivion. Believing that man's greatest possession is his eternal soul, he wants to awaken in Meursault, who is about to lose everything else, a desire to acknowledge his supernatural part. The necessary condition for this discovery is the recovery of his faith in God. Ultimately, God's justice is more important than that of Meursault's earthly peers who condemned him. Moreover, divine justice is also merciful and forgiving. All that is required is that Meursault acknowledge God's right and power to judge his sins. The priest urges him to prepare himself to see a divine face on the wall of his prison cell. Only if he surrenders himself to God's presence and power can be assure his survival after death.

But Meursault has no desire for an afterlife. To him the wish for it is like any other wish he had on earth. If there were an afterlife, he would wish it to contain only the memories of his life on earth. When the priest persists in his efforts and offers to pray for Meursault's hardened heart, the prisoner suddenly explodes in a torrent of abuse. He grabs the priest by the collar and hurls at him violent insults: he need not waste his rotten prayers, they are as worthless as the rest of his religious beliefs. To dedicate oneself to such beliefs is to live like a corpse, to turn one's back on life. On the verge of death, he has a more secure existence in his hands than the priest has, he tells him. Even the assurance that death is coming is solid and concrete. It is a certainty into which he can sink his teeth. Meursault now sees that every moment of his life has been as real and as solid as his present confrontation with death. The nearness of death brings home to him the realisation of his and everyone's inevitable mortality. From the vantage point of the present moment of this ultimate confrontation, every moment of his life appears just as inevitable and necessary. In the end it does not matter what course of life a person has chosen: in every case the final result is oblivion. The only important thing is to recognise this inevitability and at the moment of death to affirm the life which led up to it. Herein, in the power to choose one's fate, lies man's special distinction. In this way, every man is privilaged: 'there was only one class of men, the privileged class'. It so happens that he is to be executed for not weeping at his mother's funeral, but his death could come as a result of other happenings. It does not matter what leads up to one's death: in the end it comes to the same thing.

Meursault's reference to his execution as being due to his 'unacceptable' behaviour at his mother's funeral is significant. It calls attention to the absurdity of circumstances which may lead up to a person's death. All human choices and acts are permeated by this absurdity; there is no intelligible justification for *any* way of life. Everyone is as 'guilty' as everyone else for the choices he actually makes. Hence, there is no reason to regard any life, and its termination, as better than any other.

Having perceived this truth, Meursault now looks at all events of his life in a different light: they are all equally good and meaningful. Listening to the sounds of the city coming into his cell through the prison window, he sees them as ultimately unjustifiable yet ultimately good. The nearness of death has removed the scales from his eyes: every moment of life is self-justifying and carries in itself the basis for its affirmation. He now understands why his mother felt like starting all over again with death so near. And, since she felt like that, no one had the right to weep for her. Similarly, no one has the right to weep for him; he needs no one, no society and no priests, to teach him in what the meaning of life consists. He feels it now, surrounded by 'the benign indifference of the universe', and he can affirm the same acceptance, the same happiness about every past moment of his existence and about whatever moments are still left for him. To underscore this conviction that this is so, he wishes for a huge crowd of spectators to witness his execution and to greet it 'with howls of execration'.

B

Meursault's final judgment on himself is reminiscent of the judgement made by Kurtz on his death-bed in Conrad's *Heart of Darkness*. Marlow calls Kurtz's judgement a kind of victory. Is Meursault's judgement a victory as well? From one perspective it certainly seems so. Meursault is a transformed man. Up to this moment of insight he lived with scales on his eyes. He did not know that he was happy, that every moment of life mattered. Now he knows and is absolutely sure of it. The irony is that he has come to this knowledge only when he has no more time left. Like Faust's final insight into the truth of his condition, it comes too late to live in the light of it.

But the affirmation made by Goethe's and Conrad's heroes contains an element that Camus's hero seems to lack: a moral dimension. They pass judgement on a kind of life that is worth living or condemning. Faust recognises the need to use one's freedom in the service of free mankind. Kurtz pronounces a judgement on the horror of his own moral degradation. Meursault affirms life as such, without attaching *any* moral conditions. In fact, he appears to dismiss moral distinctions because, as in his own case, such distinctions are morally ambiguous. The contrast he wishes to draw is between concrete earthly human existence and the supposition of its supernatural counterpart. It is in the light of *that* contrast that he insists on being satisfied with the former alone.

The reader is bound to be puzzled by making this contrast exclusively relevant, as Camus appears to be doing. From one point of view it may look like an affirmation of the value of every life, no matter what its content. Camus makes it easy for us to be sympathetic toward Meursault because in an important way he is wrongly judged by his society. He is not a killer, a vicious person. On the contrary, he is likable and normal, like the rest of us. His honesty, his rejection of hypocrisy are impressive and refreshing. Moreover, we watch in him an awakening of the need to understand, to make sense of, to justify his existence, Undoubtedly, his stance is more heroic than that of the placidly believing priest. Camus presents his honesty and innocent openness as a foil to the frightened and cruel conformism of his fellow citizens.

And, yet, are we to overlook and excuse the obvious harm Meursault inflicts on people around him? In his self-absorption he appears indifferent to Marie's feelings, to Raymond's dubious motives and hurtful acts, to the murderous consequences of his own reactiveness to sensuous stimuli. At no time, and especially after experiencing the great metaphysical insight (if we are to call it that) does Meursault turn his attention to these factors of his experience. In this regard he appears completely amoral; he looks at his life from a purely aesthetic point of view. Even the happiness which he experiences is aesthetic, in a metaphysical sort of way. In that sense he remains, and dies, a stranger. He says that he 'understands' how his mother, Marie and Salamano may have felt about their problems. And, yet, this seems an external sort of understanding: he seems incapable of something like Alyosha's identification with others. It does not even occur to him that their interests and desires could become his as well, at least up to a point, in a small but genuine way. In this respect he remains a puzzle, a Stranger to the reader as well.

When Camus later, in a postscript to the novel, referred to its hero as 'the only Christ we deserve', he emphasised Meursault's honesty, his refusal to play the hypocritical game of his society, his desire to live in the truth. But Camus goes too far, it seems to me, when he says of his hero that 'Far from being bereft of all

feeling, he is animated by a passion that is deep because it is
stubborn, a passion for the absolute and for truth.' Conrad's
Marlow also has a passion for truth and believes that lying has in
it a taint of death. But he cannot bring himself to tell the truth
about Kurtz's final words to his intended, because he thinks that
such a disclosure would be 'too dark'. From what Camus tells us
about his hero we can conclude that Meursault's passion for truth
would have made him indifferent to Marlow's scruples. One
cannot help feeling uneasy about such an absolutising of one
value: it appears oblivious to all *other* values. Camus is right when
he goes on to describe his hero's passion as negative, but he is
mistaken, when he concludes that such a negative passion alone
'is a condition of a conquest of ourselves or of the world'. No
matter how important and admirable such a negative passion
may be, it nevertheless leaves Meursault without any appreciation
of qualities that give life positive meaning. 'This is may way.
What is yours?', asks Nietzsche's Zarathustra. Up to the dramatic
confrontation with the priest, Meursault had no way he could call
his. The one he articulates after the confrontation shows much
metaphysical pathos but no moral direction.

In the character of the Stranger Camus has captured a striking
phenomenon of the contemporary hollow man, stubbornly adrift
in his valueless solitariness. When Camus defends this levelling of
all values to the abstract affirmation of *any* kind of life, and of all
experiences regardless of their merit, he seems to present us with
a new revolutionary alternative answer to the question of life's
meaning. The question of good and evil, of better or worse, is
answered, he seems to be saying through this novel, by the mere
resolute affirmation of whatever is put in our path by the circumstances. The rejection of the supernatural dimension as possibly
entering into the human scheme leaves Meursault with the sense
of ultimate futility of what one does. Everything deserves to
perish, proclaims Mephistopheles, and everything does perish,
echoes Meursault. The effort to connect and to guide human
actions in the light of one's commitment to some values deemed
worthy of realisation would strike Meursault as futile, on the
grounds that the exertion required to give one's experience some
definite direction, some continuity, some consecutively unfolding
development is irksome and doomed to failure. Any experience is
just as good as any other experience. When Marie envisions the
possibility of transforming her affair into a richer relationship of

marriage and wonders whether Meursault would be attracted to the idea of building up their present casual relationship into something more stable, she finds him scoffingly indifferent. His reaction is in effect a squelching of her aspiration to give more substance and more challenge to her life. He is perfectly content to live on the surface of interpersonal relationships, uncommitted to the idea of permanence or long-range loyalty.

How can we explain his rejection of these values? One possibility is to surmise that he sees through the hollowness, deception and hypocrisy of interpersonal relationships around him. Although Camus does not show us Meursault thinking such critical thoughts, he nevertheless may expect the reader to conclude that, given the general hypocrisy and self-deception of bourgeois Algerian society, this is what Meursault must have been thinking and therefore found no attraction in Marie's half-hearted attempts to commit him to bourgeois values.

But there seems to be no argument in the novel on this question one way or another. Rather, we are given a sweeping philosophical conclusion expressed by Meursault as he appraises his own life as compared with the lives led by the members of his society or with an alternative life he might have embraced. The conclusion is, as we have seen, that the distinctions between the *qualities* of human lives and between the particular experiences in individual lives are invidious. This conclusion bears a strong resemblance to the classical Epicurean doctrine, according to which all experiences are to be judged in the light of their immediate character. Seek pleasure and avoid pain, proclaimed the Epicureans. Beside momentary satisfactions, life has nothing to offer; a wise person will therefore refrain from straining toward a cumulative personal career in which some actions are seen as means, as preparatory for more substantive achievements. Like the Epicureans, Meursault does not see any promise of some lasting patterning of values emerging from particular actions of human beings. Like them, he seems to accept a view of the universe governed by disconnected atomicity of chance events. Like them, he does not put much store by the ability of human freedom to assert itself significantly in the mindless march of atoms in the void.

That is why he can say that to the extent that he savoured some fleeting satisfactions – absorbing the sun on the beach, making love to Marie, watching the passing street scene beneath his balcony – he was genuinely happy. That is why he adds that he is happy still – reviewing in memory those pleasant moments and in making whatever use he can of the opportunities still afforded him by his life, just as absurdly deminished by his unfortunate shooting of the Arab as they were absurdly granted him in his just as fortuitously arranged life 'in freedom'. Following this line of thought, we must conclude that the Stranger was more profoundly estranged from his world than the initial, less penetrating reading of his story may suggest. He is estranged from the very possibility of seeing life as affording any kind of hierarchy of values. His extreme levelling of all experiences is in effect a declaration of the impossibility of judging some of them as better than others. In the light of this consideration, his final outburst at the end of the novel is incongruous, wholly out of character with the message that Camus is communicating through Meursault's conclusions and behaviour. The desire to see himself reviled by the crowd that came to witness his execution is a desire to lift that experience above the crowd of other experiences and to proclaim it as *worth having*. But his central and persistent tacit belief was that *nothing* is better than anything else. Hence, like the Epicurean injunction to seek simple pleasures and to avoid exertion toward more demanding goals, Meursault's final wish is useless and self-defeating, because incongruous.

As the darkness of the night precludes optical discriminations, so the moral opacity of our situation precludes the possibility of making valid discriminations in the realm of values. The night, therefore, is a fitting symbol for the way the human condition looks to Meursault. Camus's novel teaches us that the spaces through which Nietzsche's madman sees modern man aimlessly tumbling are not only cold, 'away from all suns': they are dark as well.

8 Freedom Frustrated: Sartre's *No Exit*

A

We seldom question the assumption that a mutually satisfying relationship between human beings is possible. This expectation seems mataphysically and morally grounded in our traditional view of man. When there is a failure in communication, or when people inflict harm on one another, we look for an explanation either in some wilful perversion, or in ignorance, or in unfortunate circumstances. The basic assumption is that a mutual accommodation of interests and desires is possible. Normally and normatively human nature is geared toward harmony and fulfilment.

Sartre's *No Exit*, along with his formally developed philosophy, questions this assumption. A case can be made for regarding this short play as embodying some of Sartre's central philosophical claims, and we shall turn our attention to this connection. But the best place to begin is the play itself. It *shows* what Sartre formulates systematically in his abstract work.

The key device is simple and ingenious at the same time. The action takes place in hell, unconventionally conceived. There is an undertone of satire in Sartre's image of hell. That image is far removed from the customary picture of fire, brimstone, and torture, given to us in our tradition religious mythologies. Hell, *à la* Sartre, is just an ordinary middle-class living-room, with sofas, mantlepieces and aesthetically pretentious decorations. There are also such modern conveniences as electric doorbells. And, yes, there is also a servant, who admits visitors, politely answers their questions, and bids them good evening before leaving. There are, of course, some special features. The room has no windows, and the doorbell is capricious. At times it works, but often it does not, especially when one *wants* it to work. The hallway from the door leads only to similar rooms in the building, and beyond the building there is nothing.

139

The living-room in which our action takes place contains three persons, who enter it successively. All three are, of course, dead. Upon entering they discover that whoever is responsible for the arrangements in hell has provided for them to spend their respective eternities in one another's company. The action, and the play's message, lies in their discovering the nature of this togetherness. What they find out, to let the cat out of the bag right away, is that they themselves are bringing hell into their existence. That is why external trappings are minimal and relatively harmless. Indeed, they secure even some degree of physical comfort: each permanent visitor has a personal sofa.

The sofas are arranged in a way that facilitates conversation. The setting is such that, with nothing else to do, our visitors can occupy their (eternal) time with attempts to get to know one another and to enter into desired relationships. And, as it turns out, the visitors have a good deal to talk about, many experiences to share. Once they, reluctantly, realise that they are dead, they feel the need to put their (past) lives in order. Each, in his or her own way, comes to offer an *apologia pro vita sua*, the way Meursault does, except, of course, that Camus's hero has an opportunity to do so before dying.

Different as the three characters are, none of them represents an exceptional person. The author sets before our eyes three people with individual personality traits, from different walks of life, and with different life histories behind them. In many ways they are ordinary people, everyman. In daily lives, this side of hell, people are also fortuitously thrown together with others. Each has his own projects and objectives, and pursues them according to personal dispositions, judgements and choices. In this respect what goes on in Sartre's hell is meant to be seen as a replica or a continuation of what happens this side of hell. But, if we realise that what we are to each other in hell is not much different from what we are to each other in life, we cannot escape the conclusion Sartre intends us to draw. Hell is other people, anywhere.

The radical conclusion is that this is not an unusual circumstance: it lies in the nature of the case. It is *normal* for people to to be hell to one another; it cannot be metaphysically or morally helped. At least, this is the conclusion we must draw if we look at the relationships that develop between Garcin, Inez and Estelle, the three inhabitants of Sartrian hell. Of course, if we regard their kind of relationship as idiosyncratic, abnormal, unusual, avoidable, then we are in the presence of something special, unrepresentative. But it seems that Sartre uses the play to illustrate what *all* human relationships must be, given certain inescapable facts about the human reality.

The play reveals a continuity between the life careers of each character and of the way each behaves in hell. Their basic projects, orientations and needs do not change after death. They are intelligible, to themselves, to one another and to us as readers, in terms of their actual life careers and of free decisions they had made and are still condemned to make, as long as the (omnipotent) author allows them to act, deliberate, judge, choose. What we are witnessing in the play is the inescapable need to make choices. And our characters make them.

Unfortunately, they discover that the choices they are making are mutually incompatible. They are so not because of some external circumstances, of some conditions beyond their control. Sartre endows his characters, even in hell, with the capacity to choose for themselves, to determine what they want and how they will go about getting it. Consequently, one cannot appeal to any sort of determinism, theological or natural, which could be blamed for what they do or what happens to them. They themselves are responsible for what they choose and how they act. They fully express they existential personalities, and each choice defines, step by step, what that personality is. We are what we do, and we do what we choose.

But that turns out to be precisely our problem. By our choices we frustrate other people's choices. The frustration occurs precisely because we are free to make choices. The Garcin-Inez-Estelle circle is hell because what each wants and chooses makes it impossible to satisfy their needs. This is, Sartre appears to be saying, the reality of the human condition. What he is giving us is simply a logical analysis of the consequences of what we are. Let us see how this conclusion is exemplified in the 'lives' of our three characters.

Inez needs Estelle. Estelle needs Garcin. Inez cannot get Estelle because Estelle needs Garcin. Estelle cannot get Garcin because he needs Inez. Garcin cannot get Inez because Estelle needs him. The respective needs are, of course, different. These needs cover a whole spectrum of what people may seek in life. The point is still that the satisfaction of these deliberately sought needs is mutually incompatible. It is as simple, or as complicated, as that.

What are the respective needs? To start with the least complex character, Estelle, we are shown that she needs just a man – and only one happens to be available. On earth, married to a man thrice her age, she had affairs with other men. One of the affairs resulted in pregnancy, which she hid from her husband by taking a long vacation, and wound up drowning her child. Her lover, the father of the child, took this development hard enough to blow his brains out. She got over it by starting a new affair with a baby-faced youngster who called her his 'glancing stream'. In general, her great need was to be loved, admired, seen. Even in her own eyes her existence was insecure if unconfirmed by some admiring eye. Her home was full of mirrors because without their confirming testimony she felt unreal, absent. Her main complaint about the hell in which Sartre put her is that the room has no mirrors and that even her pocket mirror is taken away.

Inez offers Estelle her eyes as a substitute mirror. Inez has a motive. She is attracted to Estelle. On earth a lesbian, she remains one in hell. Her life had its share of disappointments. Competing with her male cousin for the affection of a woman, she finally won, which drove the young man under the wheels of a tram. But the new relationship did not thrive, because Florence, the lady friend, in despondency turned on the gas in their bedroom, and they both died. Since Florence has apparently been assigned a different room in hell, Estelle is the only woman available, and Inez finds her strongly attractive.

Garcin's need is more subtle. As his cruel treatment of his wife on earth shows, he is not much given to tender romantic feeling. He loathed his masochistic wife. In his post-mortem situation, of the two available women he prefers Estelle. He would not mind distracting the hellish boredom in Estelle's arms, and she is quite willing and eager to oblige. But there is a hitch. Garcin is bothered by his self-image. He left life under somewhat ambiguous circumstances. He got shot escaping from the country, and his fellows in a cause for which he ran a newspaper regard his escape as the act of a coward. He is not sure he is one, but overhearing their conversations from hell makes him uneasy. (Sartre gives his condemned the capacity to observe what is happening on earth after their demise. They would have been better off without this capacity, for the things they learn about themselves and the consequences of their acts are not pretty. But, after all, they *are* in hell, and probably not without cause.)

We are, in part, what others say we are. Hence it is of interest and important to Garcin that he is regarded by his friends as a coward. Soon they will start saying of others, 'He is a coward, like that pig Garcin.' But Garcin does not quite agree with the verdict. His act of leaving the country might be viewed in a different light. That depends on the viewer. To justify, to set his life in order, for which task he appears to have a greater need than the other two inmates of hell, he is anxious to know how others will choose to interpret his crucial act. The others in his present situation are Estelle and Inez, and it is to them that he must turn with his problem.

At first, he hopes that both his needs, to have a woman and to have self-respect, can be satisfied by Estelle. When he asks her whether she thinks him a coward, she answers no, but then ruins his hopes by adding that she doesn't really care whether he is one or not. 'Coward or hero, it's all one – provided he kisses well.' Estelle's reaction indicates that she cannot give Garcin the kind of trust he needs. On earth he has left his fate and reputation in the hands of men who now proclaim him a coward. Since he is dead, he cannot protest to *them* that they may be mistaken, and so his only possibilities are the judgements of Estelle and Inez. Estelle simply does not understand what is at stake. She is too shallow, too egotistic, not sensitive to such a need. Of course, she is willing to love him whether he is a coward or a hero, but her incapacity to see his deep need for self-respect disgusts him. She strikes him as soft and slimy, and he turns away from her.

Repelled by both women, he makes a desperate attempt to leave the room, forgetting that the doorbell does not ring when you want it to ring. In rage, he drums on the door, and then, surprisingly, it flies open. He and the others are free to go. Estelle urges Garcin to leave with her. But he hesitates. It has dawned on him that Inez may have the solution to problem. Hard and cruel as she is, she nevertheless knows what wickedness and shame are, and hence she must know what it means to be a coward. She at least knows what evil *costs*. Hence, her judgement matters, and, if *she* has faith in him, he may be saved. Noticing his desperate need, Inez realises that he is in her power. It is up her to decide what he will think of himself. So she tells him, 'You are a coward, Garcin, because I wish it.' Weak and defenceless as she herself is, she nevertheless has control over him, and he cannot do anything about it, because it is her *thought* that determines what label he deserves. He is defenceless against her wish, because 'You can't throttle thoughts with hands.' He is at her mercy.

But then he realises that she is at his mercy as well; by offering himself to Estelle he can prevent Inez from establishing a contact with the only person *she* needs. And so they are inseparable in their frustrated interdependence. Condemned to remain together for all eternity, they will keep reminding one another that they are in each other's way.

B

Sartre's philosophical conclusion is that man is an inevitable victim of his own freedom. In contrast to beings lacking consciousness, man can constantly revise himself through acts of will. This capacity for radical choice shows that man has no essence. None of us *has* to be what he chooses to be. The paths of life chosen by Garcin, Inez and Estelle are of their own making. Born into a certain situation, they nevertheless used that situation to define their personalities, their characters, and their careers. Since from inside that self-definition is always fluid and revisable in terms of further choices, the person's character and qualities are *defined* by the judgements of others. We cannot control what others think or say of us. That is why Garcin is so wrought up by being dubbed a 'coward'. In his mind the question is far from settled. While others may say that he simply 'bolted' across the border in fear of danger, he would say that he simply 'went away' and that his motives were not necessarily despicable. Furthermore, he was conscious of the choices as he made them, and in his subjective judgement they were far from crystallised the way they appear to be crystallised in the objective judgement 'Garcin is a coward.' This discrepancy between the subjectively perceived reality and the objectification it receives through the free judgement of others puts us always at the mercy of the others. Unable to fix our personal essence because we are 'condemned to be free', we are nevertheless ascribed by others characteristics which we resent. And there is no way out of this dilemma.

Death especially is an affront to us. One always dies too soon, because one is never allowed enough time to exonerate oneself. At the moment of death life is complete, 'with a line drawn neatly under it, ready for the summing up'. Mercifully perhaps, the loss of consciousness in death terminates the futile effort to justify oneself. In that sense, oblivion is a 'consummation devoutly to be wished'. It is release, Nirvana, final peace of the Schopenhauerian will to live. Conversely, conscious existence on earth is a living hell where we humans are our own torturers.

This appears to be Sartre's message in *No Exit*. His analysis of the human condition relentlessly draws the logical conclusion from the fact of what we are: absolutely free, self-defining and self-revising creatures. The Schopenhauerian note is not incidental, it is dominant in this philosophy. Sartre's absolute freedom is another name for the restless will constantly renewing itself in a futile search for satisfaction. Since this will is individualised, it is wholly itself in each person; it cannot possibly change places with another manifestation of that will. In this sense, the Alyosha-like identification with the wishes and hopes of another person seems precluded: it is a metaphysical impossibility. And a metaphysical impossibility is *ipso facto* a moral impossibility. Metaphysical facts are unchangeable; they set the limit to what human beings can attempt. (This is the reason for an inconsistency in Schopenhauer's philosophy when he declares that the will can seek and attain its own *quiescence* in the acts of compassion with other suffering objectifications of the will or in the acts of aesthetic contemplation. Sartre's view, for better or for worse, does not suffer from this inconsistency.)

Camus's Stranger at least betrays the presence of some capacity to put himself in other people's place and sympathetically to absorb their desires, hopes and wishes. Up to a point, cerebrally, 'objectively', he can trace out what others may have been thinking and feeling, even though he cannot break through into being 'with them', willing with them the fulfilment of their desires. Occasionally, a glimmer of this possibility occurs to him after the prolonged idleness in prison has forced him to concentrate on the memories of his contacts with other people. When he finally 'affirms' the goodness of life, that affirmation also seems to be of that impersonal, 'objective', metaphysical sort. But, in contrast to Sartre's story, there is nothing in Camus's characterisation of human reality that prevents Meursault in principle from developing moral feelings of genuine identification with others. At times he comes close to that, when, for instance, he 'understands' how his mother could have experienced her new friendship or how Marie could be happy in someone's else's arms. Camus's novel induces in the reader a feeling of some acceptance for his hero not only because he insists on being absolutely honest with himself and others, but also because he finally recognises the *importance* of happiness, for himself and for others. He finally breaks out of his cool indifference, even though, as we have noted in the preceding chapter, such deliberate embracing of some values condtradicts his previous detached, estranged posture toward experience.

The tragedy of the characters in the Sartrian hell is due to their knowledge that their attempts to establish a satisfying, reliable relation to others are doomed to failure. That failure is, paradoxically, due to the *freedom* of others. For Sartre, the fact of human freedom has two faces. Seen from the direction of the individual, it opens up unlimited possibilities for choice, for unhindered selection of personal projects. But, seen as the freedom of others, it is a constant threat and potential obstacle to all our goals and projects. Because other people have their own intentions, form resolutions and pursue their own goals, it is natural to expect failure in interpersonal relations. I cannot get hold of another person's freedom, for I cannot control what he thinks, feels or intends to do. In order to retain his freedom, the other must not subordinate it to my freedom. And so it is precisely the freedom of others that is a perpetual outrage to us. Since in many situations the attainment of what we want depends on what others want, and, since what they want does not necessarily coincide with our desires, the result is frustration. That frustration is a natural, inevitable component of the human condition, which prompts Sartre to speak of man as 'futile passion'.

9 Meanings Exhausted: Beckett's *Waiting for Godot*

A

Beckett's play is both difficult and easy to interpret. It is difficult because we can never be sure what its minimal action and the four enigmatic characters represent. But it is also easy because the surface vagueness and indeterminacy of what is going on gives the reader a licence to supply his own interpretations. When some readers suggested that by Godot Beckett might have meant God, the author disclaimed any such intention and refused to provide any alternatives. All the same, throughout the play one has repeated 'recognition effects' – somehow one has the feeling that the reader knows what the author wants to be recognised.

One such recognition or repetition may be invoked to characterise the central action, or, to fall in with the contemporary tendency to negate all previous forms of discourse, non-action. The state of mind manifested by Vladimir and Estragon is reminiscent of the way Faust felt at the start of Goethe's poem. The state of mind of Beckett's characters is, however, decidedly more radical and persistent. Goethe has his hero break out of that state, in part through interaction with external forces – nature, world, people – and move toward some kind of resolution or overcoming. Beckett's heroes, or anti-heroes, never manage anything of the sort. They remain arrested in the initial state of suspense, resignation, stubborn scepticism. Whatever discourse and action take place in the play, Beckett's characters only furnish a further confirmation that no other alternatives to this state are possible. The characters do not move beyond the initial starting points. Both acts end with the stage direction 'They do not move.'

The setting within which the 'action' of the play develops is indeterminate. Any guess as to its time and place is hazardous.

The world around the characters is anonymous and possibly non-existent. One may speculate that we are dealing with fragments of scattered humanity after an atomic holocaust. On the other hand, the world and mankind may still be functioning in some shape or form beyond the desolate little plot of land on which we encounter our 'heroes'. One thing is sure about that world in the dark background: it isn't friendly. When Estragon moves out of Vladimir's sight or spends the night somewhere in the ditch, he is inevitably beaten up. By whom and for what reason we never learn; the characters do not tell us, possibly because they themselves do not know who their enemies are. We know that they are people, but what they are after, how they live, why they are hostile to our friends on the stage remains a mystery, like the rest of the connections to the 'outside world'.

The absence of hints as to what that world might be like justifies concentration on what Vladimir and Estragon, and later Pozzo and Lucky, seem to reveal. The four of them are a sad lot. Each pair reveals a very different sort of interpersonal relationship. Estragon and Vladimir cling to each other in their predicament. Pozzo and Lucky are tied to each other by a different kind of bond. The contrast calls for an examination, but, before it can be undertaken, each pair, and their relation one to the other, need to be discussed.

Estragon and Vladimir are waiting. For whom or for what? Supposedly they have an appointment with a personage they call Godot, who occasionally sends an enigmatic messenger in the person of a boy, whose identity, however, is also uncertain. Our friends are not sure whether it is the same boy each time, and his instructions as to when and where they are supposed to meet his master are hardly precise. While waiting, their chief difficulty appears to be in determining how they should pass the time. Nothing seems to them worth doing. Even the most ordinary and basic functions of life have lost whatever appeal they may have had in the past. Functions such as eating or urinating are still necessary, but they are accompanied by ennui, despair, discomfort, or pain. The most 'active' kind of activity we see is Estragon's taking off and putting on his boots, which he can hardly manage by himself and requires repeated help from Vladimir. What they eat is not much: turnips, radishes or, at best, carrots, provided in a disgruntled way from Vladimir's pocket. Vladimir has a serious problem with his bladder; the only kind of mild elation he experiences is when things work well in that department.

It is clear that the only kind of positive distraction or entertainment in their task of killing (pointless) time can come only from themselves. But they have little, if anything, to offer from that resource. It appears to be barren, wholly dried up. It is difficult to resist the temptation to interpret the laconic, almost monosyllabic 'non-conversation' between Estragon and Vladimir as allegorically taking note of the exhaustion of civilisation. Civilisation has reached not only its discontent but also, radically and irreversibly, its demise. Neither crying nor laughing has an adequate, justifiable target. 'One daren't even laugh anymore.' But to lower one's sights and be satisfied with smiling also strikes Vladimir as bitter: 'It is not the same thing. Nothing to be done.'

Haphazardly hitting on some subject of conversation, our helpless and hapless tramps are puzzled that even the texts used as sources of sense and value for human life are full of nonsense and contradiction. The Gospels, for example, do not agree about the fate of the thieves that were crucified together with our Saviour. They find it 'extraordinarily interesting' (an ironically used phrase) that of the four Evangelists only one speaks of a thief who was saved, two do not mention any thieves, and the fourth says that both thieves abused Jesus. In spite of such disagreements, the only version that people know and believe is the first. Estragon's comment on that is that 'People are bloody ignorant apes.'

But this remark, with many others like it, does not indicate that the tramps have a high regard for reason and thinking, either others' or their own. Rather, they are of the opinion that all efforts to make sense of life, to understand it, to arrange it in a sensible manner, have failed, and that nothing promising is to be expected from traditional sources of human pride and dignity. They are expecting, although they are not prepared for, the worst. They are not agents but patients. Of the two, Vladimir seems the more resigned and stoical. He says, 'I get used to the muck as I go along.' They both agree, however, that one is what one is. There is nothing one can do about it – no use struggling and wriggling.

They also agree that it is safer to do nothing rather than something. Even the thought of trying to commit suicide, briefly considered by them, strikes them as too strenuous and probably futile. Faust's paeans to striving would induce in them convulsive laughter. They have no tasks to perform, no heights to scale, no depths to explore. They are not tied to anything, and no one has a claim on their exertion or effort. Even the personage with whom they supposedly have an appointment is of interest to them only in a tenuous, ambiguous way. If Godot is not God, as Beckett assures us, then at least he is the residual remnant of the promise which the idea of God, in its heyday, represented. The waiting is justified if something can be found out at the end of it. So Vladimir says about Godot, 'I'm curious to hear what he has to offer. Then we'll take it or leave it.' The staccato 'dialoguising' in which the two tramps indulge at this point contains elements of a satire on the theological accounts of God's relation to man. What does man want from God? He does not himself know. Toward the Deity man projects a kind of prayer or vague supplication. And what does he get in return? Nothing definite either. He'll see. He cannot promise anything. He will have to think it over. It is tempting to read the following lines as a parody on the biblical story. God thinks 'in the quiet of his home' (heaven?). Before deciding, he will consult his family (Holy Trinity?), his friends, agents, correspondents (prophets, messiahs, disciples, evangelists?), his books (the Holy Scriptures?), his bank account (rewards of the afterlife?)

When Estragon remarks at this point, 'It's the normal thing', he appears to register the disillusionment of seeing through the customary mythological facades of such stories, familiar to all tribes and ages of mankind. When Vladimir, in answer to Estragon's question, says that we (mankind) must approach these vague promises on our hands and knees, he reminds us of the virtue of humility expected of all believers. We have no prerogatives nor rights. When Estragon asks whether we have lost our rights, Vladimir replies, distinctly, 'We got rid of them.' If one is tempted to speculate on this dark saying, one might come up with a Nietzschean thought that in declaring for blind faith we have opted out of our rights, or at least out of some of them, such as the right to understand. *Credo quia absurdum est.*

The hopelessly half-hearted banter of the two inseparable friends is interrupted by the appearance of Pozzo and Lucky. What *they* might symbolise or represent is another puzzle. Some features stand out distinctly. Pozzo is a master, Lucky his slave. The slave, led by a rope around his neck, carries the master's property – a food basket with chicken and wine, a stool for Pozzo to sit on when they rest. Lucky is treated by Pozzo in a cruelly abusive manner. Pozzo's interests and activities are elementary. He eats and drinks, smokes his pipe, uses a vaporiser to keep his throat in shape for brief speeches, in which he shows pomposity, arrogance and disdain for his audience. Curiously enough, he appears to *need* his audience's attention. Even such simple actions of his as sitting down are *performances* intended to place him in the limelight. He confesses, 'I have such a need of encouragement!' But at heart he is as disillusioned and cynical as the two tramps. The difference between them and him is that, while they have completely abandoned the hope of finding any meaningful activity, he hangs on to the brutish enjoyment of satisfactions derived from basic needs, bolstered by the sense of power stemming from his absolute control and cruel treatment of Lucky. His slave's name is an ironic remainder that éven being *used* as such an obedient tool introduces some meaning into the slave's life. In the Pozzo–Lucky relationship we see the extreme nakedly cruel form of the master–slave relationship. Perhaps this kind of relation will be the last surviving vestige of human presence on earth when it runs its course, either naturally or by self-inflicted destruction of the human race – a prospect far removed from the high hopes of the City of Man, not to speak of the City of God.

Lucky is a melancholy reminder of things of which human civilisation used to be proud. For the crass sneering entertainment of the tramps he is forced by Pozzo to dance and think, in that 'natural' order. Both activities are pathetic parodies. The dance is short, mechanical, repetitious. The 'thinking' entertainment is also a repetition of something long gone. Having put on his hat, without which he apparently cannot think (a suggestion perhaps that the hat is a dead repository of traditional forms of thought), he indulges in a long unpunctuated tirade which mixes words and phrases from miscellaneous dimensions of language: theology, philosophy, psychology, technology, commerce, education, science and sports, in incongruous juxtapositions. It is clearly a satire on the ambitious expectations of the human intellect, now reduced to meaningless twaddle. Curiously enough, as the thinking act put on by Lucky progresses, his three listeners change their responses to the show. Pozzo is dejected and disgusted from the start, and later begins to suffer and groan. Vladimir and Estragon are at first attentive but then begin to protest violently, so that Lucky has to shout his text. In the end all three listeners throw themselves on Lucky and seize his hat. That immediately stops his torrent of words, and silence ensues, punctuated by the pantings of the 'victors' in the mêlée. Estragon shouts, 'Avenged!', and Pozzo tramples on the hat, exclaiming, 'There's an end to his thinking!'

In spite of the apparent madness of the speech, there appears to be some hidden method in it. Snatches of juxtapositions seem meaningful. A degree of patience and ingenuity probably could produce a coherent *explication de texte* of this bizarre performance, although it would be hazardous to pin down definite meanings of symbolic allusions. Even behind the satirical coinages, such as 'anthropopopometry' or 'Essy-in-Possy', in spite of the vulgar and derisive overtones, the intentions of the author are not too well hidden. The whole peroration can be read as a recitation, ironically, satirically, debunkingly, outrageously presented, of the conceptual corpus of a dead civilisation. 'Corpus' here should be taken both as a collection and as a dead body (as in 'Corpus Christi'). Reminiscently reproduced in Lucky's deadened, worn out, oppressed, almost wholly destroyed mind (he himself comes close to being no more than a body, responsive only to jerks of the noose around his neck), the 'speech' is a painful reminder of items of language, once potent and promising but now reduced to fragments thrown off by agitated neurons in Lucky's brain. It belches forth a mixture of terms from geography and travel in the use of such names as Cunard or some London suburbs (appropriately denigrated by associations with venereal disease), from the world of industry and business (represented by such conjunctions as Puncher and Wattman), from the labours of unnamed disciplines associated with the Russian-sounding name of Fartov (Pavlov?) and its English counterpart Belcher. The reference to God is followed by 'quaquaquaqua', undoubtedly suggesting Latin verbal quackery of theology. The sequence 'dead loss her head since the death of Bishop Berkeley being to the tune of one inch per ounce per head approximately by and large more or less to the nearest decimal' is an obvious ridicule of philosophical obfuscating verbiage, not accidentally affiliated with the thinker who questioned the reality of material substance. Repetition of phrases such as 'for reasons unknown' and 'time will tell' calls attention to the inconclusiveness of the whole intellectual enterprise on which mankind pinned its lofty hopes. Toward the end a litany on tennis-balls and stones and skulls – round, battered dead objects – winds up the speech on an elegiac, lamenting note, and the final word is 'unfinished'.

One may wonder why the listeners find Lucky's peroration disturbing and in the end react violently to it. Although stupefied, mentally dumb and emotionally worn out, they still are stirred by it. Why? Perhaps they find that reminder of the vanished cultural aspirations painful and embarrassing. They are resentful and angry that civilisation has proved but a bitter disappointment, a teaser, a mirage, leaving them stranded in a physical and spiritual desert. The listeners' reaction to Lucky's ability to 'entertain' them by producing such reminders from mankind's past is, however, ambivalent. Hostile toward Lucky, they nevertheless struggle to put him back on his feet when he collapses after the speech. Even the hardened Pozzo finds it hard to depart from the tramps after the episode. Nevertheless, he does so, reinforced by the onslaught of a cruel emotion immediately translated into physical abuse of his slave.

With the departure of Pozzo and Lucky, Vladimir and Estragon lapse into their usual stupor, merely remarking that the visit has helped them to pass the time. They do not know what to do, but remember that they are supposed to be waiting for Godot. Vladimir's thought returns to the two departed visitors. He reminds the forgetful Estragon that they know them from the past and remarks on how they have changed. The suggestion seems to be that all human contacts either cease to be memorable or are unwelcome. Hence the apparent uncertainty or possibly repression of memory about personal encounters. 'I too pretended not to recognise them. And then, nobody recognises us,' says Vladimir. The last sentence may be taken as a comment on the loss or total unimportance of personal identity.

When the boy appeears with another vague message from Godot, we learn that he was also afraid of Pozzo's whip and roars, and that is why he is late. Quizzed by Vladimir, he assures him that the Pozzo – Lucky pair is native to those parts. They are at home there – not a comforting thought. But we also learn from the boy that, although Godot does not beat him, he does beat his brother. The boy does not know why he himself escapes beatings. The discrimination, we may suppose, is again, 'for reasons unknown'. When the boy asks the tramps what message *they* have for Godot, Vladimir replies, after a moment of hesitation, 'tell him that you saw us'. The request sounds like a plea, a prayer, a vague supplication. It is as if, from the recesses of a forgotten self, the voice whispered, asking for an acknowledgement, recognition, acceptance of one's personal reality, now in danger of total dissolution.

Yet it is dangerous to be around without taking cover for the night. Of course, the two friends do nothing of the kind. Although urging each other to go somewhere, they do not move. Before taking that 'non-decision' they reflect a moment on their relationship. They have been together a long time and there even exists between them a bond. Somewhere in the now forgotten past they were grape-harvesting together, and Vladimir fished Estragon out of the water. Estragon speaks an almost lyrical line: 'My clothes dried in the sun.' But he checks himself and, inexplicably, turns against Vladimir. 'I sometimes wonder if we wouldn't have been better off alone, each one for himself. We weren't made for the same road.' To that Vladimir, a sober if disillusioned realist, replies, without anger, 'It's not certain.' Nothing is, in their world.

The ambivalent relationship between Vladimir and Estragon comes to surface early in the second act when Gogo tells Didi: 'Don't touch me! Don't question! Don't speak to me! Stay with me!' It is clear that in the extremity of their hopeless situation they feel a strong need to stay together. Estragon's dependence need is stronger than that of Vladimir, and Vladimir seems to recognise and respect it, in spite of surface harshness and impatience. He says that he is happy in seeing Estragon again. His mood, however, is complex and not transparent even to himself. What is he happy about? Distinctions are in order, and Beckett makes them in three brief masterful phrases: '(*Joyous.*) There you are again . . . (*Indifferent.*) There we are again . . . (*Gloomy.*) There I am again.' The differences of mood accompanying each remark tell all. He is joyous to find the other again. When he thinks what their being together will amount to, his spirits fall: it will be disillusioning, indifferent. When he returns to himself, he comes back to his own, gloom-inducing emptiness.

In the ensuing exchange Vladimir shows a tender protectiveness toward his friend. He tells Estragon that if he were around he would stop him from doing things that led to his being beaten. When Estragon protests that he was not doing anything, Beckett puts a light, disarming note into Vladimir's paradoxical response: 'Perhaps you weren't. But it's the way of doing it that counts, the way of doing it, if you want to go on living.'

This light-hearted, almost fraternal exchange makes the tramps feel better, and they decide that they are happy, for no other reason that they simply say the words 'I am happy.' But their problem does not go away. 'What do we do now, now that we are happy?' asks Estragon. The ensuing period of waiting for Godot is filled with a number of fortuitous distractions. The tramps make observations on the changing scenery; they notice that the tree under which they sat yesterday began to ooze. They attempt to carry on a conversation, 'since we are incapable of keeping silent, "we're inexhaustible"'. Part of the conversation is a subdued poetic commentary on the transitoriness of things. Having quickly exhausted the poetic mood, the tramps decide to play the game of thinking and of contradicting one another. However, Vladimir, the realist, declares matter-of-factly, 'We're in no danger of thinking any more', and later adds, dejectedly, 'What is terrible is to *have* thought.' (It may be thought-provoking to note that Beckett's contemporary Martin Heidegger draws a very different conclusion from his analysis of our times: we have not yet *learned* to think.) At this point the reader is likely to flash back to Lucky's exercise of thinking. Estragon's suggestion that 'we should turn resolutely towards Nature' has a quick counter from Vladimir: 'We've tried that.' They remember the visit by Pozzo and Lucky, its reality being confirmed by the festering wound on Estragon's leg on which Lucky's kick landed yesterday. They notice that the boots Estragon left yesterday are still there, but their size is, inexplicably, different. They think about food, but, alas, the only thing Vladimir can produce from his pocket is a radish, and not even a pink one, to Estragon's disappointment. These distractions help to pass time, they give them, as Estragon says, the impression that they exist. They are even tired enough for sleep, and Estragon does fall asleep. The protective Vladimir puts his coat over the sleeping friend, and takes him in his arms when he wakes up from a nightmare.

They entertain themselves further when they find Lucky's hat and play a game of adjusting successively his and their own hats on their heads. The elaborate stage directions given for this ritual, and the time it takes, suggest that Beckett returns to the symbolic play with depositories of tradition. But the game ends on a sour note when Vladimir finally throws his hat to the ground. Since Lucky's hat does not irk or itch him, he decides to keep it. (Are we to take it as a suggestion that Vladimir feels a nostalgic attachment to the items which were produced yesterday by Lucky from his hat?) It occurs to them that they might play at being Pozzo and Lucky, and Vladimir orders Estragon to think and dance, but not much comes of it. Moreover, it seems that the game does not appeal to them, because it threatens their relationship. They *want* to remain close. Apparently they hear some noises and at first take them for the approach of Godot, but then decide they were mistaken. In one of Beckett's intentional moves to involve the audience, Vladimir gestures toward the auditorium saying, 'Not a soul in sight!' The tramps do not expect help from us, who sit in the audience.

The temporary alarm over an approaching unnamable danger subsides, and our anti-heroes are again at a loss as to how to kill time waiting. They decide to abuse each other. Starting with the mildest epithets 'moron' and 'vermin', they graduate to 'curate' and then, with finality, to 'crrritic!', giving Beckett a chance to express his opinion about that class of people. The abuse-hurling must make them feel good, because they embrace each other afterwards. They decide to indulge in a few half-hearted callisthenic exercises; the 'relaxations' and 'elongations' are expected 'To warm us up. To calm us down.' But they soon get tired, even of breathing. Estragon has a passing thought about Godot and demands, 'God have pity on me.' When Vladimir asks, vexed, 'and me?' Estragon childlishly insists, 'On me! On me!' (Is this Beckett's way of likening the believer's concern with getting personal attention from God to a spoiled child's insistence on not sharing his toys?)

But then they are joined by two people who are even more in need of pity. Pozzo and Lucky reappear. Not recognising them, Vladimir and Estragon experience a rush of hope. Estragon thinks Godot has come, and Vladimir thinks they will not be alone 'waiting for . . . waiting'. But then they recognise their visitors from yesterday. Considerations of gain and revenge cross their minds. Seeing Pozzo sprawled on the ground and needing help, they consider going after some material advantages. More-over, Estragon might have a chance to repay Lucky for the kick in the shins.

Realising that this is their chance to *do* something, Vladimir exhorts himself and his friend to action, and he does so in a long, heroically sounding speech, delivered with bombast and pathos – all this while Pozzo, now blind and helpless, is desperately struggling to get up. He is offering monetary award, and the tramps are bickering about the amount. Vladimir again has a truthful insight into himself. A diversion comes along, and what do we do? We let it go to waste. After further rather rambling discourse, they take a brief nap and upon waking up realise that they are still in Pozzo's presence, and Vladimir gives him a beating. But, with that outburst of violence gone, they wonder whether it really is Pozzo and try out on him various names, including Abel and Cain – to both of which Pozzo replies with a cry of 'Help!', leading Estragon to conclude that 'He's all humanity.' They still do not help Pozzo, because, as they justify their lack of interest in him, they are waiting for Godot. (Is Beckett telling us that a desperate need to recover a sense of meaning does not necessarily make us morally better, that we are *always* in danger of lapsing into cruelty and brutality?)

Finally, as if their insensitivity and harshness were but a passing, unaccountable spell, they realise that Pozzo *wants* to get up and they help him to his feet. Being blind, he of course does not know who they are and takes them for highwaymen. Sightless, he also does not know what time of the day it is, and has to rely on Vladimir's assurance that it is evening. When asked how he lost his sight, he answers, 'I woke up one fine day as blind as Fortune.' Now he no longer has any notion of time. But he has not lost his cruelty. His attitude to Lucky is as it was before. He encourages the tramps to wake up the exhausted slave by beating him, and Estragon kicks Lucky, hurting himself in the process. Pozzo does not remember having ever met the two tramps, and he is ready to proceed on his way, with Lucky as his guide, but without Lucky's other, more sophisticated services, because his slave is now dumb and therefore can neither sing nor think nor recite. Pozzo's blindness and the loss of the sense of time reinforce his savage bitterness. He does not want to be tormented with accursed questions *when* anything happened or will happen. 'When! When! One day, is that not enough for you, one day he went dumb, one day I went blind, one day we'll go deaf, one day we were born, one day we shall die, the same day, the same second, is that not enough for you?' These words spoken, he leaves, with Lucky leading, the rope around his neck. The dumb leading the blind. (Pozzo's final outburst brings again to mind Faust's deep disillusionment with life, with the passage of time – without a disclosure of any ultimate meaning, except that Pozzo's disillusionment is bitter and deeply resentful.)

For a moment Estragon returns to his suspicion that Pozzo might be Godot. At first Vladimir rejects the idea vehemently, but the assurance of his denial diminishes each time as he repeats thrice, 'Not at all!' In spite of his apparent ability to cope with the futility of the situation, Vladimir lacks assurance that there is any reality to what he and his friend are experiencing, remembering, interpreting. What truth is there in what we are undergoing? he asks. In asking this question he is looking at Estragon, who is now dozing again. By repeating Pozzo's horrendous characterisation of human existence, 'Astride a grave giving a difficult birth', he seems to want to protect Estragon in his innocence, his feebleness, his simple-minded ignorance of the ultimate horror of life. 'He is sleeping, he knows nothing, let him sleep on.'

When the boy appears again with the message that Godot will come tomorrow (we have heard that before), Vladimir asks him a few rather innocuous questions. When he learns that Godot probably has a white beard, Vladimir exclaims, 'Christ have mercy on us!' – suggesting, perhaps, that mankind has heard that before too; Yahveh's white beard was a common image. Nevertheless, he still has the same message for Godot, 'Tell him . . . that you saw me.' Suddenly distrustful of the boy's veracity, he tells him, with violence, 'You're sure you saw me, and you won't come and tell tomorrow that you never saw me!' He is afraid, as he tells the waking Estragon, that, if they drop Godot, he will punish them. The suggestion seems to be that the final motivating force in wanting to go on with life is fear.

The two friends remain, with nothing around but the dead tree, even though that tree has sprouted, mysteriously, one leaf overnight. The thought of suicide returns, to be discarded once more as unrealistic. Or, rather, it is postponed – till tomorrow, if they do not part, which they also regard as a possiblity. But it remains a mere possibility. When Estragon utters the final words of the play, 'Let's go', they do not move.

B

Waiting for Godot, like most of Beckett's plays, is a *tour de force,* a deliberate forcing of people into incredibly difficult situations. The situation of the four characters is so extreme as to be hardly credible. The degree of absurdity we see presented on the stage evokes puzzlement because it seems too difficult to contemplate even as a possibility. Beckett does not shy away from extremities of human predicament. On the contrary, he seems to cultivate them. But this always has been the prerogative of a dramatist. He needs to put his case as strongly and as starkly as his art permits.

Every single value of Western man is parodied in the play. The human beings we see on stage are refugees from humanity. They remember their home – civilised mankind – but the memories are bitter, painful, disabusing. The expectations we had of ourselves turn out to be illusory, and the promise of fulfilment fails to materialise. Our friends on the stage are not pleasant to look at: they are physical wrecks, aesthetically repelling and socially crude, even cruel to one another. Indeed, the indulgence in brutal cruelty has become the only motive power of Pozzo's existence. Vladimir and Estragon, although preoccupied with other matters, suffer onslaughts of beastliness and beat up the luckless Lucky. Their minimal existence is spent on wallowing – irreverently, with bitterness, and without hope – in the debris of the civilisation of which they still have fleeting but disconnected and disillusioned glimpses. Nothing evokes their admiration, everything is exhausted; nature and culture, like the lifeless tree, stand denuded of meaning. The only thing that the remnants of cultural heritage are good for is coarse and derisive humour; it makes the pain more bearable and distracts from the hopeless predicament.

The collapse of values in *Waiting for Godot* is more radical and more pervasive than it is in Camus's *The Stranger* or in Sartre's *No Exit*. Meursault is estranged from his society but at least he does not question the naked power of the culture he personally finds meaningless and rejects. His adversary relationship to his social environment still has an element of meaningful confrontation, and he derives some satisfaction from the battle he is forced to wage. The tragic frustration of the characters in Sartre's hell is at least mitigated by the characters' mutual awareness of the opposing egos that stand in each other's way. Human striving may be doomed to fail, but the clash of wills at least lends a dramatic albeit enervating excitement. Beckett's human wrecks are beyond any illusions of finding their existence meaningful even in such

minimal and negative ways. The night of absurdity has des-
cended on them with a vengeance; all escape routes appear to be
closed.

And, yet, even in *Godot* we discern a redeeming note. Perhaps
this is not surprising if we remember that in each case we are
dealing with a work of art. No matter how dark a situation is, an
artisitic portrayal of it is possible only if the writer can show us
something that can lead us beyond darkness. We can sympathise
with the author's characters only if we can discern in them the
possibility of awareness which the author wants to communicate
to the audience through their reactions. We can understand
Meursault's or Garcin's or Vladimir's problems and predicaments
because we can envisage these problems and predicaments
becoming ours. There, but for the grace of God, go I. The artist's
power lies in his ability to show us that nothing human is alien to
a human being. Although the wickedness or cruetly with which
the author endows his characters appals us, if these characters are
at all credible, we ascribe to them at least the possibility of
becoming conscious of the meaning of what they are doing. If this
condition is not met, if the characters are depicted as lacking any
insight into themselves and their actions, we do not find them
credible as human beings. Totally depraved, wholly unfeeling
monsters do not move us. They may evoke fear, terror, or dis-
quiet, but we do not see in them anything that can speak to us.

All of the characters of our three writers speak to us, and each
does so in a different way. They confront the darkness, the night,
in their own souls, and, because we sense their (often unex-
pressed) agony, we find them believable human beings, like
ourselves. Paradoxically perhaps, the darkest of the three works
we are examining contains a note that is responsible for its
positive aesthetic effect. The theme of the play is waiting.
Waiting is the only 'activity', the only 'project' that is left over for
Vladimir and Estragon, who are stranded among the debris of
destroyed civilisation. One may see this 'activity' as a remnant of
the characteristic celebrated by Goethe in his *Faust*: striving.
Goethe's hero was worthy of salvation because he remained faithful to this one, typically human, task. In Beckett's play waiting is
but an echo of striving. But waiting is still a form of striving,
albeit attenuated to a bare minimum. At the same time, it could
be regarded as striving in its purest form. It is relatively easy to
maintain an attitude, a stance of striving when the goals are

clearly there before you, unquestioned and unambiguous. Faust's problem is, in part, that there seems to be a superabundance, an infinity, of projects worth pursuing. But what can a human being do when he begins to question the very meaning and value of objectives in the service of which human energy might be enlisted? Is anything left over for us to do when the disillusion-ment with what we may undertake is extreme, as in the situation Beckett constructs for our imaginations?

What is left over, he seems to be concluding, is what Vladimir and Estragon are doing. They are still capable of *waiting*, of directing their devastated souls, or whatever is left of them, toward something that may at least contain a *possibility* of value, a promise of salvation or fulfilment. (In *Thus Spoke Zarathustra* Nietzsche berates the impatient ones who are *incapable* of waiting.) Despite their repeated frustrations, they keep faith. They do not give up waiting, even though they get no more than ambiguous and suspect signs from that desperately hoped-for source.

Despite the extreme pessimism about the human condition which the play presents on its surface, there is a powerful positive element in it. Indeed, that element may be the most important insight or message of the play. In their desparate situation Vladimir and Estragon have each other. The waiting is their *common* project. It joins their spirits and lends them whatever minimum of security, comfort or companionship are still possi-ble. They can go on hoping against hope because they derive a modicum of support from their mutual participation in this pure spiritual striving Beckett describes as waiting. It seems as if they are doing it not for their own sake – they have seen through the illusions of personal happiness a long time ago – but on behalf of humanity, which is so reluctant to accept the verdict of its ultimate failure. In that sense, paradoxically, Vladimir and Estragon may be seen as images of mankind's contemporary heroes, perpetuating the spirit of Prometheus, who resisted the overwhelming forces bent on subduing his spirit.

Camus said that his Meursault could be seen as the only Christ we deserve. Beckett seems to have felt that we still deserve some-thing better. The suffering that Vladimir and Estragon are undergoing is relentless and overwhelming. In that sense, the play is a passion play, in the Christian sense of the word. Neither Vladimir nor Estragon can be regarded as a Christ figure, but they nevertheless appear to be the bearers of burdens heaped upon the human psyche when things indeed are cosmically out of joint. Although they are not harbingers of good news, the faith, the loyalty of their waiting at least preserves the possibility that good news will be received, if and when it comes. Vladimir and Estragon are standing on the edge of the human world, fearful that they stand before the final abyss, and yet they place themselves as sentinels of this ultimate outpost, ready to receive a ray of light, should it penetrate the darkness.

The total spiritual immobility of the two friends, frightening and disheartening as it is, is at least redeemed by another kind of immobility. Thrown into ultimate predicament, Vladimir and Estragon remain loyal to one another – in spite of what they say to each other in despair or anger. There is a blind, stubborn trust in Estragon's behaviour toward Vladimir. Without question and without justification he throws himself on Vladimir's sympathy, kindness and goodwill. And Vladimir provides them, somehow aware of Estragon's need and weakness. Himself dispossessed of any hope or sense of meaning, he nevertheless lends whatever support and comfort he can muster. Beckett may be saying that even in such extremities love can still lighten our burdens and thus shine in the darkness, even total darkness. If so, more is dreamt in his philosophy than in that of Sartre and Camus.

It is significant that Beckett did not put the burden of waiting just on *one* person. He understood the importance of the need for intersubjective mutual support in crisis situations. He is careful to show us that mutuality need not necessarily involve similar, equally strong, or equally good persons. There are important personal differences between Vladimir and Estragon, as noted above. What they mean and can give to one another is very different. Their needs contrast with and complement one another. Estragon cannot exist without protection; Vladimir realises that his very self depends on his ability to provide protection. Vladimir is certainly a stronger and, therefore, more tragic character than his dependent, incompetent, forgetful, not very bright and easily discouraged friend. Vladimir knows Estragon's weaknesses, and yet he shows toward him a remarkable respect, tolerance and – one almost wants to use again that overused word 'love'. There is something incredibly powerful and at the same time tender in the final scene when Vladimir wants Estragon to sleep on without realising how dark and how hopeless their situation really is. The scene is reminiscent of the one in which Hamlet decides to exclude Ophelia from knowing and thus sharing the burden he is destined to carry. Vladimir, like Hamlet, stands alone in his terrible knowledge. And, yet, Vladimir's loneliness is softened, his burden made more bearable because he has Estragon to care for, and to stand with him through this wearying and inconclusive waiting. Man, Beckett seems to emend Aristotle, is a *spiritually* social animal.

We are also shown in the play how the intensely felt shared predicament can result in an occasional ability to transcend it. In spite of appearances to the contrary, there is cosmic laughter in the play. The destruction of foibles, illusions, blunders and insufficiencies, brought about with such force and finality in short laconic and ironic exchanges between the characters, strikes the reader at times as utterly funny. Through the tears there breaks out laughter. In this way the artist makes us immune to the blows of absurdity by enabling us to stand outside, beyond it, and hence liberated from its oppression. This is one way in which art may redeem life, and metaphysical darkness can lead to ethical light.

PART IV
DAWN

In the *Four Quartets* Eliot says that 'human kind/cannot bear very much reality'. But it can be also asked whether mankind can bear the prospect of total meaninglessness. It should not be surprising that the blasts of negation call forth a defensive reaction. Even the bleakest work in our collection, Beckett's *Waiting for Godot,* reaches out toward some respite, some relief from the oppressing darkness. Where can such relief be found? It is not surprising that some writers turn their attention to the time in history when we were not obsessed with the idea of creating, from our own resources, the Garden of Eden. Before being fascinated by our newly discovered or rediscovered toy, the secular reason, we believed ourselves to have other resources. Perhaps it was a mistake to turn away from them. Now that we have seen through the delusions of grandeur of our earthly dreams of glory, we may again be able to recall our connection with the super-temporal, super-historical power of God.

This was Auden's and Eliot's conclusion. They came to believe that our situation was not ultimately hopeless and that our hopes lie beyond the pain of admitting to and suffering from our sinfulness. They saw the trials of the delusive ambition to do without God as a necessary step toward recovering our spiritual sanity. They concluded that all of modern history, with its merely apparent triumphs and its all-too-palpable horrors, must be seen as included in God's plan for the recovery of mankind. Both poets see the dawn of hope in the return to religious faith.

Rilke's gaze does not rest on the special events of Christian revelation. His recommendation is different. He urges us to celebrate spiritual achievements of all races and of all human beings at all times of chequered human history. To be sure, with the other two poets he shares the recognition of basic flaws and imperfections of the human lot. He does not think that we can escape pain, suffering, disillusionment, lament. They are an inescapable part of our groping toward maturity, wisdom, completion. But he is also struck by the fruits borne by our endeavours to struggle against error, evil and tragedy. In an important sense, Rilke turns to Goethe's insight that, like Faust,

167

all of us must go through the trials and tribulations of boredom, blindness and hubris. In Goethe's drama, God knows about the unlovely traits of his favourite crerature, and yet he does give us up; in some crucial ways he finds us good.

Perhaps, wonders Rilke, this goodness consists precisely in our capacity to return to the endless quest to give life meaning even under the darkest conditions. In that endeavour the living are not altogether on their own. We can often lean on others, the way Elliot the poet could feel the support of those long-gone poets who walked with him, in dead patrol, along burning streets of London. Some of the struggles and achievements had heroic proportions, and it behoves us to pay homage to them and to take pride in them, whenever we are animated by the glorious effects of our cultural heritage. For this constitutes a very special, exceptional circumstance of earthly spaces: they are *still* animated by the spirit of human suffering and creation. Rilke's elegiac affirmation leads us toward hopes not limited either to our modern 'average Aristotelian city', nor to special theological patterns representing traditional religion. He bids us to fare forward without losing hope that we may fare well.

There is a special difficulty in interpreting poets. No one can presume to speak *for* the poet and to pretend to render 'in other words' what he gropes to express in his unique use of language. As Eliot remarked, anything which can be said as well in prose can be said better in prose. But to try to catch a poet's meaning in a neat statement is to run the risk of saying both more and less than is said in his work of art. In either case the result is distortion. Nevertheless, a poet who deals, in his own way, with deep human predicaments is bound to elicit a response expressible in prose. A reader of a poem, without claiming with any confidence to read the poet's mind, may at least be stimulated to formulate the thoughts to which the reading of the poem gave rise in his own mind. The discussion to follow expresses one such reader's reaction to the three poems, each of which no doubt intends to tell us something true and important about our human situation.

10   Faith Renewed: Auden's *For the Time Being*

A

Auden's poem contrasts the Time Being with the Fullness of Time. By the Time Being he means human existence in its many aspects: personal, social, historical, cultural. That existence he finds essentially flawed and definitely not sufficient unto itself. In saying that the Time Being can be redeemed only by the Fullness of Time, Auden claims that human life can be made ultimately meaningful only by ackowledging its relation to the timeless supernatural. He returns to the story of the birth of Christ in order to explicate its meaning for human life on earth. In that event, initiated by God, he finds the bridge to the supernatural. Only in Divine Love can human beings find ultimate peace and salvation from sinfulness that is unavoidable and inescapble in the Time Being.

The poem is in part a modern survey of human sinfulness. God's truth, of course, speaks to all times and all places, but every age has its own context within which the insufficiency and short-handedness of man can be discovered. Speaking for our epoch, Auden discerns in it some special features that are particularly powerful in calling us back to our connection with the super-natural. Auden's perception and characterisation of these features owe much to his sympathetic reading of Kierkegaard and Reinhold Niebuhr, but without a doubt they come from the depth of Auden's own religious experience and from his personal estimate of the course of our modern civilisation. The cast of his mind is both philosophical and poetic. It is philosophical in the sense that it seeks to understand and to assess the variety of significant human pursuits in our time, and poetic in that it seeks to capture this assessment in fitting images any symbols. There is no denying that the philosophical insight gains power and con-creteness in poetic utterance.

The catalogue of ills to which contemporary culture bears

witness is extensive. Indeed, the indictments come thick and fast, from many angles and directions. Our entire spiritual climate wears many faces of evil. The opening stanza is dominated by the lines, 'Darkness and snow descend on all personality.' These lines and their context generate a mood of defeat, disillusionment, hopelessness and boredom. 'The clock on the mantlepiece has nothing to recommend', and when we look in the mirror we do not discern that nobility which, delusively, we tend to ascribe to ourselves. Both the public and its leaders suffer from massive inertia and apathy. Probably referring to the outrages and cruelties to which the world was exposed on the eve of and during the Second World War, Auden remarks that 'Our angers do not increase', indicating thereby that situations that *should* provoke righteous anger and resistance to the horrors perpetrated in the name of political ideals leave us unmoved. We excuse ourselves by remarking, complacently, that 'Love is not what it used to be,' thus disclaiming any responsibility while piously resorting to external, 'sociological' explanations of our indolence.

Even a Hercules would be unequal to the task of morally reinvigorating our decadent culture. That culture is a ruined temple whose inhabitants, including their leaders, are oblivious to mortal dangers from fanatics threatening to invade and destroy all vestiges of civilisation. The falling snow levels everything and obliterates all symbols of vitality and resistance to evil. 'As winter completes an age', fear, doubt, and resignation dominate both the ruled and the rulers, whose power 'ebbs from the heavy signet ring'. Even the lanterns of potential prophets are out, and the distinctions between right and wrong, the boundaries between good and evil, are covered up. In the meantime, 'outside the civil garden', wild aggressive passions are getting ready to do their work of destruction and self-destruction. The disheartened poet despairs over the impossibility of comprehending such horrid urges to aggression and ends the stanza with a devastating image: 'Like wheat our souls are sifted and cast into the void.' The suggestion seems to be that what is retained in our souls is not the wheat, the good but the chaff, evil. No wonder that such souls must be scattered into the void. The future is laden with impending disasters: war, fear, hate and death, and no one, neither the people nor their leaders, is prepared or competent to prevent them.

The litany of shortcomings, evils and tribulations is expanded

by the peom's narrator, who depicts the disruptions and catastrophes accompanying strife and conflicts that characterise
human history. Moreover, the upheavals of our times are not
new, 'we have been through them all before, many many times'.
The round of life is always characterised by its formal opposites:
'from sword to ploughshare, coffin to cradle, war to work'. That
fluctuation is accepted by us with a callous indifference to the
difference between good and bad and 'is permanent in a general
average way'.

There is, however, a new note in the contemporary experience
of human sinfulness. That note is Nameless Horror. In its more
innocent ages mankind was erring in almost natural ways. Our
mutual aggressiveness was countered by unself-conscious opposition and by straightforward assertion of child-like wills. But
recently 'an outrageous novelty has been introduced into our
lives': we have come to experience the existential dread of not
knowing what threatens us and why. Sometimes we are struck by
the utter unreality of things, which, in Auden's account of it, is a
mirror image of our own unreality. We discover a vacuum, a void
at the inner core of our being, we become fictions in our own
eyes. Our evil tendencies receive an explanation in this act of self-
discovery; our lives and our history are what they are because we
are hollow men and women. And, if *we* are unreal, how can we
capture the true meaning of things? For this reason, the awareness of that Nameless Horror, of objectless anxiety, can be seen as
the most radical reminder of our insufficiency and shorthanded-
ness.

Such a reminder, in the form of absolute dread, can come only
from one source: namely, God. God's wrath is behind the realisation of our sinfulness and ultimate dependence. The scary
discovery of our ultimate emptiness, of the meaninglessness of
anything we undertake on our own, puts us before the Abyss.
Facing it, we realise our absolute incapacity to make sense of our
mortal lives. That incapacity also includes the intellectual impossibility of explaining how we could be saved. Hence, our
salvation must necessarily come to us in the form of the miraculous.

Anything less than the miraculous is not equal to the task,
because all our explanations come in forms of ordinary human
understanding, and that understanding, as long as it insists on
self-sufficiency, must be tinted by rebellion: it leaves God out of

the explanation. Hence the acceptance of his reality must entail the acceptance of the absurd. 'The Real will strike you as really absurd' – that is, not measurable by all the powers of our discursive intellect. The challenge to accept the Real Being is the greatest challenge for man precisely because, unlike inanimate beings and lower forms of life, he considers his mind, his intellect, as his most distinguished, glorious asset. His concern is always the desire to protect truth from illusion and to avoid the worship of idols. And yet, if he is to come into the light of the truth that is not confined to his circumscribed, temporal, mortal vision, he must open himself to that which will lead him beyond these radical limitations. He must find an experience with 'a magic secret of how to extemporalize life'. To extemporalise life means to move beyond its merely temporal limitations characterising the Time Being, and to respond to the call of the Fullness of Being.

The inner dividedness of human life is also perceptible in the mutual strife of man's four faculties: intuition, feeling, sensation and thought. Adverting to the doctrine of the Fall, Auden reminds us that before that dreadful event the four faculties were one. But now the radically split human personality expresses itself inharmoniously through each separate faculty, which Auden, following tradition, associates with some bodily aspect: intuition with the stomach, feeling with the heart, sensation with the entire body, and thought with the brain. Their respective functions are suspect in themselves: intuition works in the dark, the feeling is nymph-like, sensation is subservient to the contradictory demands of the body, and thought is dream-like, prone to fantasy. Each faculty is a partial and partisan spokesman, 'adopted to each individual humour', and the information they jointly produce is confused, ambiguous, uncertain. True, they enable us to have fleeting glimpses beyond our limiting condition, but the decision whether to move beyond that condition must transcend them; it must be a personal act of will.

In a personalised exchange between the four faculties Auden depicts their special provinces and their particular inadequacies. Sensation is buffeted by natural incitements of the moment, many of which are gross and coarse, yet enticing. Feeling is at the mercy of a variety of conflicting, unruly moods: rage, fear, pleasure, excitement, violence. Thought, conscious of the ghostly nature of its operations, is plagued by the awareness of its omissions, evasiveness, inconclusiveness, repetitiveness, inefficacy; on ultimate questions it has nothing to say. For thought, 'To Be was an archaic nuisance.' Intuition intimates possibilities but also presides over the demise of human plans and projects, 'each ruin of a will'. And, yet, it is intuition that can be a gate to transcendental awareness, and feeling can be alerted to a radical change in the garden of deeper human awareness. These two faculties sense the presence of the angel Gabriel, God's messenger.

Thus Incarnation, God's intervention in the course of human history, is accessible to men everywhere and at any time, provided they heed the hidden signs, obscured by earthly concerns. Auden's poem reviews the possible ways in which Incarnation, God becoming man, could have affected the chosen persons: Mary and, later, Joseph. Having been told by the angel Gabriel that 'Love's will on earth may be, through you, / No longer a pretend but true', Mary experiences a kind of joy which, although unearthly, spiritual, can be rendered poetically by resorting to earthly images. 'Light blazes out of the stone / the taciturn water / Bursts into music.' She realises that through the event she will command the course of history, and she knows that her body is commanded by a higher power. When Gabriel informs her that her affirmation of God's will will wipe out Eve's negation, Mary, in terror and fire, rejoices that she is to be 'Love's engagement ring'. God's decision to bestow this privilege on her does not, however, violate her dignity as a person. Chosen by God for his purposes, she still has the power to choose to conceive the Child. In this line Auden takes a stand on the philosophical issue with regard to the question of compatibility of human freedom with God's will. For Auden the two are not mutually exclusive.

The Annunciation section is completed by a rejoicing chorus which celebrates God's direct intervention in human affairs through Incarnation. The Good News transforms the whole material world, which now has 'The truth at the proper centre'. The great, the small, the young and the old break out into singing and dancing. The great now see through their arrogance, the small do not feel threatened by the powerful, the young lovers transcend that mutual betrayals, and the old do not feel abandoned. For everyone 'There's a Way. There's a Voice.'

The section entitled 'The Temptation of Joseph' uses the miracle of the virgin birth to bring to the surface the numerous ways in which the relation between the sexes can be and usually is distorted in our lives. First of all, the very idea of Mary's purity is likely to be doubted. This doubt is rooted in our unwillingness to admit the possibility that an act of pure Divine Love can occur at all. Used to cynicism, we question whether any being, including God, is capable of disinterested intervention on our behalf, not to speak of self-sacrifice. Any pure motive is automatically suspect, even if that motive has divine origin. Used to our sinfulness, and expecting all events to be prompted by self-interested desires and pleasures, we tend to reject out of court honourable explanations. Hence, Mary's claim that she is to conceive a child, with Joseph playing no role in it, can be explained only by adultery. 'But, Joseph, are you sure? . . . you know what / Your world, of course, will say / About you anyway.'

Auden depicts Joseph as a trusting and loving husband who believes in Mary's innocence, and yet he is confused by the stupid remarks and insinuations directed at him. He trusts God, but would like to have an explanation that would convince the sceptics. How does he know that the Father is just? 'Give me one reason', he asks. To which Gabriel responds with a flat no. Although Joseph would love to have just one 'Important and elegant proof', he is told, 'No, you must believe; / Be silent, and sit still.' This injunction is quite consistent with what we were told earlier. In wishing to comprehend God's ways, man wants to measure God by his own limited, earth-bound intellect. But the intrusion of the Timeless into time cannot be fathomed by temporal thought.

The idea of virgin birth prompts Auden to reflect on the idea of womanhood as such and on the relation between the sexes. He notes 'the perpetual excuse' men use for their wrongdoings by blaming it on their women. 'My little Eve, / God bless her, did beguile me and I ate.' Not content with exploiting women and regarding them as personal servants and providers of comforts, men tend to ascribe to them a variety of unflattering traits. They speak of *femmes fatales,* liken love to warlike contests, prattle about spirituality while bent on sexual conquest, pretend to be charming while meaning harm, boast of conquests in sexist club rooms and on toilet walls, and cynically scoff at purity and innocence. Joseph is now challenged to atone for these various forms of male chauvinism. The miraculous event, which lifts the woman to the heights of personal dignity, reverses the traditional conception; now man must be 'The weaker sex whose passion is passivity'. It may be difficult for him to resist these age-old undeserved imputations and to accept the role demanded of him by the Exceptional, but, if he is to live up to what is best in him, he must keep his faith.

Joined in the task of celebrating the spiritual mission which they are privileged to fulfil, Many and Joseph are now fit to intercede for all those who do not quite manage to establish a mutual relationship worthy of the highest human calling. Among those needing intercession and prayer are lovers whose romantic dreams displace their real awarness of each other as persons, and those who mistake lust for love. Auden perceives the tendency to sin in the very possibility of deep sensual encounter, which deludes into thinking that simultaneous passion purifies our lusts. That possibility he sees not only in mature persons but also foreshadowed in the 'germ-cell's primary division', leaning in this radical comment in the direction of the Manichaean view of the human body. Sin, present in the natural tendencies of living bodies as a fact, is perpetuated in the act of sexual encounter.

Interpersonal relations can go wrong in other ways. From romantic infatuation we may pass into its opposite: conventional routine, dullness, 'indolent fidelity', when domestic hatred becomes 'a habit-forming drug'. Our timid prudence appeases our resentments and suppressed rebellions. Auden's depiction of such relationships is also supplemented by a deeper psychological analysis. Almost in a Freudian fashion, he connects the formation of individuality with the emergence of libidinal forces in our early childhood. The roots of our mature dicontents lie already in our sexual infancy. The significance of the event occurring through virgin birth and Incarnation lies in its miraculous ability to tear us away from this normal average distortion of our ultimate calling and to turn us toward perfection.

The section entitled 'The Summons' describes the impact of the Incarnation on the attempts to build a City of Man. The Star of Nativity warns of the trials and tribulations that must be faced in the transition from following mere human intelligence to accepting God's will and wisdom. Men will have to discard this preoccupation with 'minor tasks' and schemes to impose secular order on human destiny, represented by such practical inventions as 'money, picnics, beer, and sanitation'. The abandonment of the ambition to order life in the light of puny human reason will of course lead to confusion, loss of confidence, vertigo and dread.

With no footholds for logic, lost without guidance in twisting lanes of solitary consciousness, bewildered human beings are exposed to nameless terrors and dangers, personified by the poet as 'cripples, tigers, thunder, pain'.

Each of the three Wise Men represents a province of our modern culture. The first one is the servant of science who begins to see that the attempts to put nature through the hoops of theoretical inquisition does not really produce firm, conclusive answers. Science constantly has to revise itself, because in the end nature is cagey and does not yield its secrets. 'She is just a big liar, in fact, as we are.' The attraction of the Star is its promise of leading to real truth, not to fickle verdicts produced by science.

The Second Wise Man is stumped by the elusive nature of time. Auden's reference here seems to be to the theory of relativity and its bewildering effects on the customary ways of thinking about time. The new conceptions of physics and the strange facts underlying the subatomic structure of matter seem to dissolve what we up to Einstein believed to be constant and solid. The vastness of the time–space continuum seems to rob *our* present of all its 'inherited self-importance'. What human life amounts to in such a context is a puzzle; hence, the Wise Man follows the Star in order to discover 'how to be living now'.

The problem for the Third Wise Man comes from his disappointment over the inability to organise human affairs in a rational manner by resorting to various forms of social enginee-ring. He and other like-minded leaders of mankind have thought that the mere introduction of the abstract concept of 'ought' would make people's passions philanthopic, and that the greatest good of the greatest number can be discerned by introspection. But such cerebral schemes fail to yield satisfactory results and disillusion the masses about the learned. So, to 'discover how to be loving now', we must follow the Star.

The journey toward a new spiritual source is not easy and is marked by dreariness, derision and discomfort. Dispiritedness, disgruntlement and disillusionment ensue, leading to uncertainty and loss of resoluteness. There is always a temptation to return to the familiar, conventional, customary. But somehow the Wise Men sense that their deeper humanity is at stake in this journey, and they continue. The Star does not offer direct encouragement and does not conceal the requirement of taking 'the cold hand of Terror for a guide' in this difficult journey toward true self-discovery. If the rose-garden is to be reached, a resolute 'I will' is required.

While our deeper selves strain toward our ultimate destiny, secular powers are not likely to cease exerting themselves to gain our full allegiance. Indeed, Caesar, who represents secular authority, will continue to distract us from our chief mission. He will not stop issuing commands which we will have to obey on pain of punishment. Of course, his henchmen, politicians, bureaucrats and journalists will do their best to glorify his achievements and will demand grateful praise from the subjects. Auden, in undisguised satire, gives a detailed account of the ways in which the earthly powers of our civilisation pat themselves on the back. Caesar is great because he has conquered seven impressive kingdoms. The conquest of these kingdoms is, of course, a prolonged historical affair and includes much on what human beings tend to pride themselves.

First, over a span of time, mankind has developed sophisticated powers of abstraction. Our language, instead of dealing clumsily with separate particulars, one by one, has found ways of referring to general classes and universals, invoking complex grammatical and logical categories for our thought. Philosophers have even come up with the widest possible category: Being.

Second, in inventing the idea of 'natural cause', we can subsume all events under impersonal laws and use them efficiently for prediction and control. Laboratory experiments and pointer-readings have replaced rites and prayers. 'Our lives are no longer erratic but efficient.'

The impressive powers of mathematics inhabit the third kingdom. From primitive counting we have moved to precise calculations that enable us to give speedily definite answers to all our questions involving numbers. At higher levels of expertise some of our experts have established personal friendships with infinite numbers and transcendentals.

The fourth kingdom is that of scientific economics, money and banking. The intricate movement of goods across markets is controlled by adjusting supply to demand, surplus to deficit. With conveniences such as COD and time payments, all transactions are smooth and efficient. We may no longer be neighbours, but we are all customers.

Technology inhabits the fifth kingdom. Inorganic giants stand at our disposal, transporting us, producing and moving things for us, providing arms for our armies whenever they are needed, for defence or attack. Any want is instantly satisfied, for all matter is controlled by our free mind.

Medicine, the sixth kingdom, not only strikes dead all diseases but also gives us substances that keep us in any condition we desire: tranquility, elation, excitement or peace of mind. 'When we feel like sheep, They make us lions; / When we feel like geldings, They make us stallions.'

The seventh kingdom is the realm of the Popular Soul, created by mass culture and mass media. We need not be ordered about by harsh governments because it is much easier to control us by manipulating our values – through advertising, fashion and creating the desired climate of opinion. Advanced techniqes of mass communication have no difficulty in giving us a Brave New World or creating the one-dimensional man.

The very fact that these impressive, spectacular kingdoms are in existence is proof positive, claims the secular mind, that Caesar is great and that God must be with him. But the bombastic self-assurance cannot maintain itself for long. No matter how diligently the official propaganda may try to lull us with its promises to solve all our problems – economic, ecological, social or political – it is not difficult to see through its sham facades. Some events palpably show that mortal dangers and chaos are constantly threatening us, as the world was threatened by the aggressive politics of the Axis Powers in the advent of the Second World War. We fail to read ominous signs because 'we are never alone and always busy'. But in the long run we cannot be taken in, and in a sudden moment of unexpected dread we realise that problems and tribulations visit us not because we are unlucky but because we are evil. Our utopian dreams of a secular perfect state or of no state at all are mere evasions, 'a part of our punishment'.

At such moments of contrite self-realisation, of truthful insight into our situation, we may acknowledge that 'Powers and Times are not gods but mortal gifts from God', and that 'all societies and epochs are transient details'. Behind these details is the Ever-lasting Present of the Fullness of Time, toward which the only proper attitude is prayer. The section ends in a supplication that the occasions of our distress teach us to put our trust in God's infinite goodness.

The section titled 'The Vision of the Shepherds' is a reminder that not all of humanity is irrestistibly attracted to the inflated promises of intellectuals, ideologues and politicians. The Three Shepherds, representing simple folk, unaffected by and healthily sceptical of the hurly-burly of progressivist busybodiness, are, nevertheless, or precisely for that reason, better attuned to deeper spiritual stirrings than are their self-appointed leaders. Performing their daily tasks, which provide the necessities of life for the whole society, they are conscious of the fact that their centreless, unself-conscious simplicity is envied by the condescending movers and shakers. The patronising upper classes may deem the simple folk incapable of appreciating education and the uses of money, but their access to surplus amenities does not make them necessarily happier. There is here also a tone of disillusionment with Auden's previous belief that leftist causes are fair to the masses. The leaders of such causes incite the underprivileged to resistance against the oppressive classes, but then show callous disregard of sacrifices and injuries sustained by the rebelling proletariat. The Second Shepherd pinpoints the callousness of leaders toward the masses they contrive to control: 'It is only our numbers that count.' In this low-key indictment stand condemned all movements that accept the principle that the ends justify the means, when these means entail trampling on lives and liberties of individuals.

The special virtue of simple folk is that they are not wholly swayed by false promises of those who desperately and impatiently try to establish the City of Man. Themselves in the dark, they nevertheless see through the darkness of self-deluded power-seekers. They sense that some other alternative is available to mankind, provided we open ourselves to it. 'What is real / about us is that each of us is waiting', says a shepherd. Although confused and uncertain about their grasp of wordly ways, and amusing themselves with song and unpretentious conversations, the simple people know that something of unusual human interest is about to happen. Their unspoiled souls are prepared to receive the Good News, which they know will differ radically from a reporter's item.

Their resolute hope is not disappointed, even though they too are frequently given to disheartening, suicidal thoughts. They trust in the Unknown 'Who answers for our fear / As if it were His own'. They become conscious of their souls' higher destiny. The section ends with the chorus of angels proclaiming 'The ingression of Love' which will replace the frigid silence of the world by God's forgiveness, and the authoritarian constraint by his Covenant. All creatures will rejoice, and the human souls – dead, living and still unborn – will experience the affectionateness of Father Abyss. The word 'Abyss' has previously been used to describe the experience of seeing through the sinfulness and self-deception of the over-weening human intellect. But now the terror of God's wrath reveals itself to be just one side of the coin, and Abyss shows itself to be *Father* Abyss. The Shepherds, and all other still uncorrupted souls, will heed God's invitation to meet him in Bethlehem.

'At the Manger' provides the setting for the statement of the ways in which Divine Love affects human existence. The section starts with a tender lullaby Mary sings to baby Jesus, in which she expresses her consciousness of the contrast between the human and the divine. The Incarnation is a union of the incorruptible with the corruptible, the perfect peace of God with the anxiety of man. She has a premonition of sorrows the child she has brought into the world will have to bear. She asks, 'Why was I chosen to teach His Son to weep? and 'How soon will he start on the Sorrowful Way?'

The meeting of the Wise Men with the Shepherds at the manger provides another contrast, that between two kinds of human experience. The Wise Men represent the restless journey of mankind through the ages in search of meaning. The history of this journey is symbolically condensed in the images of stifling gorges, level lakes, intense tundras and unresponsive seas. All of them represent the futile attempts to find meaning within the confines of earthly existence. The domains of civilisation are captured in brief references to ruined arches and modern shops, and the social experience is characterised by a mention of 'vacant crowds and humming silences'. The road which mankind has travelled has been long and weary, covering countless miles and absurd mistakes. Even wise men have been plagued by 'doubts, reproaches, boredom, the unknown'. In contrast, the Shepherds, representing simple untravelled people of all epochs and nations, have, although often lonely, never felt alone, because the poor are closer to each other's problems and needs. Confined to the prison of routine and habit, they have not needed to move from their customary habitat to hear the call from on high, signalising the beginning of their endless journey to perfection.

The two contrasting types of human experience have corresponding basic delusions. The wise are driven by their 'arrogant longing to attain the tomb', representing a glorification of the sort sought by Egyptian pharaohs; the unambitious Shepherds harbour the 'sullen wish to go back to the womb'. The Good News calls them back from these vices and rejects their denial both of the past and of the future, for even human weakness can be used by God 'as a guard and guide'. Recognising their mutual humanity, the gifted and the ordinary 'bless each other's sin': the impatience and conceit of the former, the laziness and 'average fear' of the latter. Divine Love releases them from their particular bondage, accepting from each 'his gift according to his kind'.

The Wise Men recognise that divine perfection is not to be compared with any human talents, which are always prone to error and distortion. Possibly referring to Socrates's claim that he who knows that he does not know is wiser than the one who does not know it, Auden points to the ironic nature of this sort of 'wisdom'. Alternating between sheep-like submission and drinking bouts to escape the voice of conscience, the Shepherds turn to the Child so that he can redeem their childish ways. The presence of the Child, representing 'an Otherness that can say *I*', makes all men conscious of their shortcomings; they can now see that Love's energy is not *in* the Time Being but *with* it. At all times and in all places it is still possible to turn to God: 'The choice to love is open till we die.' Having made that choice, we shall feel the joy of life 'revealed in Love's creation'.

The two contrasting attitudes, spiritual humility and secular arrogance, are explored in depth in the following two sections: 'The Meditation of Simeon' and 'The Massacre of the Innocents'. In a telling image, Simeon compares the entire historical experience of the human race to the period during which 'the apple had not been entirely digested', referring, of course, to the biblical account of Adam's expulsion from Paradise. Human sinfulness is coextensive with all attempts to proclaim mankind sufficient unto itself – that is, capable of establishing for itself ultimate values.

The search for such values was extensive, relentless, and covers all of human history. As long as anything was left unexplored in the realm of sensation and action, the hope could be maintained that the search for ultimate meaning within human experience alone could succeed. As long as some experiments were not tried, in any sphere open to our control – aesthetic, social, political, scientific, philosophical – a possibility could be entertained that man could save himself, that the Fall was not really radical and that a City of Man could be built. This is why it was necessary for man to 'reach the ultimate frontier of consciousness', through pursuit of science, philosophy, secular art and political aims, before he could test his presumptions. But, as each of man's multiple and tenacious attempts to lift himself by his bootstraps ended in failure, 'there remained but one thing for him to know, his Original Sin'. Indeed, he realised that it is precisely that sin that conditions his will to knowledge', and that 'he could only eat of the Tree of the Knowledge of Good and Evil by forgetting that its existence was a fiction of the Evil One, that there is only the Tree of Life'.

With the Incarnation become explicit in the birth of Christ, we can now recognise our utlimate sinfulness and weakness and can be 'bold to say that we have seen our salvation. In contrast to the intrinsic reality of the Child, all other events in human history, whether in the lives of great or ordinary people, show their ultimate insignificance. 'Every tea-table is a battlefield littered with old catastrophes and haunted by the vague ghosts of vast issues, every martyrdom an occasion for flip cracks and sententious oratory.' Only in faith is the darkness of sin dispelled. With faith the perpetual recurrence of art and the continuous development of science assured. Reason is freed 'from incestuous fixation on her own Logic' and finds refuge from its self-inflicted quandaries and contradictions. The anxious pursuit of partial meanings ends in a wholehearted 'surrender to Him who is always and everywhere present'.

'The Massacre of the Innocents' introduces us to an up-to-date, modern, civilised, liberal Herod. He is bewildered because the course of events has imposed on him a most difficult decision: how to deal with the news brought to him by the trio 'with an ecstatic grin on their scholarly faces' that 'God has been born'. To the modern Herod this piece of news is another nuisance, symptomatic of the troublesome tendencies of his subjects. Herod is a rationalist, a believer in the possibility of transforming human beings into well-behaved, orderly, sensible, peace-lovig subjects. Up to a point he has been successful in bringing about a good and just society. 'It is a long time since anyone stole the park benches or murdered the swans. There are children in this province who have never seen a louse, shopkeepers who have never handled a counterfeit coin, women of forty who have never hidden in a ditch, except for fun.' In other words, there is progress, a change for the better in economic, social, and moral affairs. True, outside the Empire, and even within it, there are still plenty of irrational and superstitious practices, beliefs in witches and ouija-boards. The appeal of the occult is still strong and difficult to eradicate, even in the palace guard. There is idol worship and a blatant demotion of divinities to the human level. The public shuns stern demands of excellence hidden behind the myths of higher religions, because it senses in them 'a reproach to its own baseness'.

In short, Herod is despairing over the difficulty of imposing a rational order on society and is deeply concerned over the destructive tendencies of non-rational religious appeal. He is alarmed by many forms of religious worship, and fervour which encourages the abandoment of intellectual discipline and results in objective knowledge degenerating 'into a riot of subjective visions'. His suspicions of such tendencies of religion dispose him to be hostile to *any* forms of religion; thus he closes himself off from the possibility of discovering the genuine article. Hence he sees himself forced to stamp out the rumours that 'God has been born'. He is loath to resort to force, and yet he sees no other alternative. He deems it unfair of history to saddle him with this unplesant task. He registers a peevish complaint: 'I've tried to be good. I brush my teeth every night. I haven't had sex for a month. I object. I'm a liberal. I want everyone to be happy. I wish I had never been born.'

Herod's mild humanitarian misgivings about ordering the massacre are absent from the ensuing coarse bantering of professional soldiers charged with the task. Calloused and hardened by activities of this sort, in their songs they express mindless bravado, cruelty, aggressiveness and obscene humour. For them it is just another business assignment, promising drinking bouts and sexual exploits. The section ends with Rachel summing up the situation. Somewhere 'in these unending wastes', between the sensible sheep and upright citizens, between grinning dogs and professional killers, 'is a lost / child, speaking of Long Ago in the language of / wounds'.

Thrown among sinning mankind, the Child is now exposed to the dangers of temporarily being a human among humans. It is

Mary's and Joseph's task to protect the baby Jesus from the threats and dangers to which his humanity exposes him. 'The Flight into Egypt' carries them across the deadly desert, strewn with skulls and surveyed by the jackal's eye. The desert is a setting for thoughtless and devil-may-care pursuits of mankind that has lost its moral moorings. A repentant recitative urges the Holy Family to 'Fly from our death with our new life.'

The final speech of the Narrator puts the reader back into his familiar surroundings. Christmas is over, it is time to dismantle the tree and put away the decorations. Ordinary, normal life will begin tomorrow. Adults will go back to work, the children to school. The spiritual meaning of the holiday will probably be soon forgotten or covered over by the daily cares of living in our 'moderate Aristotelian city'. But 'To those who have seen / the Child, however dimly, however incredulously, / the Time Being is, in a sense, the most trying time of all.' Still, those who were touched by the vision will try, in small tasks and daily routine existence, to redeem to Time Being from insignificance. For he is the Way, the Truth, and the Life.

B

Auden sees the contemporary period as winter completing an age, and his poem can be understood as describing the winter of our discontents. The age that Auden has in mind is the modern age, the time span from the Renaissance onward, when Western man turned his back on the supernatural and attempted to build a City of Man rather than keepig his eyes on the City of God. The results of that endeavour, several centuries later, are now apparent. Appraising what has been accomplished, we can hardly say that we have succeeded. Neither natural nor human sciences have managed to bring us lasting, unambiguous satisfactions. We have discovered that our scientific theories about the nature of the universe do not stick, and that in trying to attain knowledge we can trust neither ourselves nor nature: 'She is just a big liar, in fact, as we are.' Drastic revisions or, more accurately, revolutions rock the scientific endeavour, and, as Thomas Kuhn's arguments attempt to show, there are no *rational* transitions from paradigm to paradigm, successively adopted and abandoned by modern science. Although Einstein refused to accept the conclusion that in arranging and running the world God may be resorting to throwing dice, other physicists are not so sure.

Given the radical inconclusiveness of scientific conclusions about the world, it should not be surprising that the application of scientific methods to the human order yields but ambiguous results. True, through technology science has transformed the modes of our living, giving us modern economy with its complicated commerce and banking, with spectacular enlargement of physical energy that can now move us with great rapidity all over the remote corners of the globe. Modern methods of agriculture and medicine have affected the ways in which we manage nutrition and health, but somehow they have not made us happier. Instead, we have been given more means to introduce more misery into our lives, both on the individual and the collective levels. By enabling us to forge devastating arms, technology has also created opportunities for ruthless or misguided power-seekers to wage, in the name of tribal–national or politico-ideological objectives, ruthless and cruel wars and to impose despotic totalitarian rule over the citizens. Instead of moving toward peace, the modern era has seen mankind live among wars and rumours of wars.

What conclusions can we draw from this fantastic misuse of power which the discoveries and inventions of the modern age have put into our hands? For Auden, the conclusions seem clear. The trials and tribulations are constant companions of our lives not because we are unlucky but because we are evil. True, we have become masters at rationalisation and self-decepetion. Our up-to-date Herods claim that their motives are pure but inevitably misunderstood. 'I tried to be good', says a Stalin, a Mussolini, a Hitler. We have not done anything wrong, we just followed orders, say masses of people. We did not mean to profit by shady deals, we did them for the good of the party or in the national interest. Whether in public or private affairs, we can find a hundred excuses for our crimes, misdeeds and mistakes.

The fact of the matter is, concludes Auden, that we are rediscovering the truth proclaimed a long time ago in the Bible: we are sinful creatures. The reason why we do not and cannot succeed in building a perfect City of Man is not to be sought in methods, in tactical or strategic mistakes, in unfortunate circumstances, in preventable miscalculations, but in the very nature of what we are: sinful and evil. As long as we rely on our own power, no matter how much enhanced by science and secular learning, our attempts to achieve a spiritually and morally healthy state of affairs on earth are bound to fail. But for those who acknowledge the word of the Scriptures and humbly accept the charge of sinfulness, there is another message in store: namely, the promise of redemption and salvation. That which strikes down our self-pride and hubris at the same time calls us back to a connection not to be discovered among earthly goods and projects. We cannot reach the connection by relying on earth-bound reason or on any other human powers. We can reach it only by surrendering our intellects and wills to a power that transcends them: the power of God.

Nevertheless, such a surrender has to be an act of *our* will. Auden interprets Christian theology in the manner of St Augustine and Kierkegaard; as our sinfulness is an exercise of our freedom, so our turning away from sinfulness is a genuine option for that freedom. Thus, Joseph is told that he must reject insinuations and doubts about Mary's purity by a resolute affirmation of faith – he cannot be given even one elegant proof for the validity of his religious belief. Similarly, it was not enough for Mary to be chosen by God to be his instrument for bringing about the Incarnation. She was called upon to *choose* the Child that chose her. Both Mary and Joseph, as human beings, are models for other Christians to follow. Faith is possible for human beings, and in choosing belief they choose the possibility of salvation. The possibility of turning toward our true, supernatural destiny is also demonstrated by the action of other, less than saintly, people. In their different ways, the Wise Men and the Shepherds are capable of responding to the call of the Star of Nativity. Both the learned and the humble can tune in to the message revealed in the Holy Scriptures, if only they suspend their secular rationalistic ambitions and fall back on their deepest intuitions and feelings. Those feelings can transform their life projects away from the temporal and transitory, toward the eternal and supernatural. Our response to the Love that knows no bounds can also become the basis for a new kind of relationship to other human beings, a relationship based on forgiveness and goodwill. By turning toward the City of God we shall perceive the vanity and the presumption of trying to build, self-aggrandisingly, the City of Man.

The return to the central message of Christianity will enable us to see through our delusions of self-sufficiency. We shall not seek salvation in secular endeavours because all societies and epochs are transient details, and because 'Powers and Times are not gods but mortal gifts from God.' Beyond the Time Being there is the Fullness of Time. Of course, our lives take their course 'in moderate Aristotelian cities', but, once we are reminded of that other connection, even if fleetingly and intermittently, there will exist a new option for our freedom: namely, the option to respond to the message of the Child in small and large tasks of daily existence. Auden's poem is an earnest personal attempt to remind us of that possibility. Having found for himself the ultimate answer to the question of the meaning of life in the Christian Gospel, he uses his poetic gifts to describe the way in which he was touched by the vision. That vision provided for him also a new perspective in which he understands our epoch. The self-imposed agonies and anxieties of the modern age are not the only options, nor the final word about human existence. By returning to Christian faith we can see dimensions that have been obscured by the pretensions of human arrogance. As T. S. Eliot will tell us in his poem, humility is endless. Auden's poem calls us back to the virtue of humility in the age of overweenig secular pride and to the reward reserved for the spiritually born-again or awakened.

11 Time Transcended: Eliot's *Four Quartets*

'BURNT NORTON'

'Burnt Norton' introduces Eliot's main theme and states his basic problem. The theme is the essential temporality of human exist-ence, and the problem 'Can time be transcended?' In several different ways Eliot calls attention to the concatenation of the three time-dimensions: past, present and future. Every passing moment contains in itself, or points to, its past and its future. There is even a hint of determinism in this view; what might have been belongs only to the world of speculation, says Eliot. Of course, that world too is a part of the real world, in the sense that our unfilfilled dreams are a part of what we are. Thus, glancing back to our past, we recall the poignancy of unfulfilled longing, which is just as much a part of ourselves as consummated satis-factions. Eilot sounds a theological note in saying that 'If all time is eternally present / All time is unredeemable.' That conclusion is logical enough. From the point of view of eternity the world must be seen as completed, and, if so, unchangeable. So, if the timeless substance of the world is essentially unsatisfactory, there is no way it could be made better or redeemed. Eliot's stumbling, hesitant soul-searching in this poem reveals his profound mis-givings about our ability to find the world satisfactory. But the poem also contains his confessional appraisal of situations in which the possibility of affirmation is fleetingly glimpsed.

Even if the world with all its history may be seen timelessly by an eternal being, every point of the world has a temporal location and any point may be chosen for examination. Examination calls for a reflective detachment, which can be attained either in introspection or in memory. In reflection or memory, when 'We move above the moving tree', we can appraise the meaning of our life's experiences. Some of them may strike us as special and truly memorable. After describing such a memory in detail, Eliot characterises features that make it stand out from the rest of life:

> The inner freedom from the practical desire,
> The release from action and suffering, release from the inner
> And the outer compulsion, yet surrounded
> By a grace of sense, a white light still moving,
> *Erhebung* without motion, concentration
> Without elimination, both a new world
> And the old made explicit, understood
> In the completion of its partial ecstasy,
> The resolution of its partial horror.

This characterisation fits all moments that bring together, in a harmonious whole, both the present and the future, 'both a new world and the old'. When the integration of past and future is explicit, the result is partial ecstasy. Because all three time-dimensions are integrated in such a heightened experience, it cannot be easily located *on* the temporal scale, or placed *in* time; it bursts its temporal frame. To insist on placing such an experience in time would be to divert attention from the elements that come into it both from the past and from the future. Because we want to include these elements, we must take an over-arching, time-transcending standpoint, otherwise we shall not capture the meaning of such moments.

However, even the linguistic means at our disposal are not quite equal or adequate to this task. As Eliot says, 'I can only say *there* we have been: but I cannot say where.' The referents of 'there' and 'where' are not to be understood spatially or temporally. The understanding has to move from the dance to 'the still point of the dance', from movement to pattern. Furthermore, the opposite of 'movement' in this context should not be called 'fixity' because at the still point the past and the future are *gathered* and stand in a dynamic, meaningful, vibrating correspondence to one another. The absence of either ascent or decline does not connote nothingness but fulfilment, completion. Ascent and decline are ascribable only to non-completions, to situations in which movement is still needed, but at the still point the movement has ceased and only the pattern, the meaning of the dance *is*, timelessly.

The particular experience which the poet conjures up from his past is, of course, something personal, although the images are universal. Words and voices echo in his memory, and the eye-beam of the soul rests briefly on the rose-garden, empty alley, box circle, the drained pool illusively filled with water by sunlight, the shrubbery, sunflowers, clematis, fingers of yew. The scene also includes people: Eliot as a young man, in the company of some-one who mattered much and might have been more, and in the background children playing in the apple tree. The emotion generated by 'unheard music' is intense, a happening, its signifi-cance and poignancy caught by an 'unseen eyebeam'. Eliot personalises the impersonal scene by a beautiful image: 'the roses had the look of flowers that are looked at'. Much is packed into that image. The poet is calling attention to the *animating* effect that perception has on its surroundings. Flowers looked at are different from flowers hidden from view; they are the object of an *interested* attention, and being such an object transforms them. Metaphorically, an experience on which our attention is focused may be described as the object of the *soul's* eyes, if the soul can be said to be equipped with an organ of vision. The poet resorts to natural vision in order to describe an inner, mental and emotional vision, where the still point, the pattern, is discerned within the movement, within the temporal unfolding of an event.

Alas, we do not have much talent for remaining faithful to such concentrated inward awareness: 'human kind / Cannot bear very much reality', 'reality' in this context meaning the contact with the meaning–bestowing still point, which easily goes out of focus for creatures dominated by the urgencies and distractions of time. The moments of possible fulfilment that in fact eluded us achieve an aura of poignancy precisely because of that fact. They leave scars, but, as long as the blood is moving below those scars, it keeps the faded memory of their promise intact. An entire human life is an accumulation of such partial ecstasies, of partly fulfilled longings, of what might have been. That life, in turn, fits into a larger pattern of events in the world and is concatenated with them.

The private and the cosmic world are intertwined. This thought seems to be communicated in Eliot's enigmatic lines

'Garlic and sapphires in the mud / Clot the bedded axle-tree.' Our aspirations and hopes get mired in the course of events, in the relentless march of historical time, containing in its mud both the glittering jewels of fulfilment and glory and the deflating smell of earth-bound garlic calling us back to mundane, uninspired nature. None of us has full control of our destiny, for through our historical embodiment in the world the circulation of our personal blood and lymph is interconnected with the impersonal drift of the stars, which in turn symbolises the larger course of events of world and cosmos. Eliot also reminds us that the constellations include both the hunter and the hunted, the boarhound and the boar. Transferred to the personal level, these images recognise the active and the passive aspects of man, and show him as aggressor and victim, partly in charge of his life, and yet often thrown into uncontrollable, threatening situations.

The ambivalence of the human condition is inescapable. But it is not necessarily to be deplored. For our embodiment protects us both 'from heaven and from damnation / Which flesh cannot endure'. Eliot's statement here is a brilliant understatement, disguising a weighty philosophical point. We are given to understand, almost casually, that our embodiment may be seen as a special favour given to our souls; the obtuseness and opacity of our bodies protect us from being consumed by either the fire of hell or the radiance of heaven. Plato had reminded us that, as looking directly at the sun would blind us, so in our embodied state we could not endure Truth itself. If the essential feature of embodiment is temporality, then 'the enchainment of past and future / Woven in the weakness of the changing body' is a protective device against the devastating action of pure powers of evil or good. On the other hand, if we were *just* creatures of flesh and blood, we could not endure, in that state, either heaven or damnation. One or the other would consume us without remainder.

Although as mortal flesh we are separated from perfection, we are nevertheless capable of glimpsing the possibility of breaking through our temporal limitation. Preoccupied either by the past alone or by the future alone, we cannot rise to a concentrated awareness of what we are. Such a heightened awareness, represented by remembered rose-gardens, would lift us out of the three-dimensional temporal framework. As we have seen, because such moments are simultaneously involved with past and future', when we have them we are not at the mercy of the partial dimension of time. Nevertheless, we are still *in* time: 'Only through time time is conquered.'

The image of the London underground is most effectively used by Eliot to symbolise a way of existing that is farthest removed from the possibility of conquering time. What characterises the riders on underground trains is the state of indeterminateness, uncollectedness, dividedness, ambiguity. Even the physical lighting is indicative of the state of the soul: neither daylight nor darkness. Suspended in the unclear air of petty preoccupation, we are neither hot nor cold but lukewarm, and, as such, worth spitting out. Apathy and distraction make us resemble bits of paper blown by underground fans. The gusts of wind blow either 'before or after time', thus catching us off-guard, unconcentratedly losing the meaning of the present.

This non-descript, uncommitted state of being is far removed from the darkness of despair experienced by some saints who saw through the limitations of the world of sense, turned their backs on possessions, real or imagined, and accepted internal darkness – deprivation and destitution. Their disconnection from the world, the descent into the darkness, is a deliberate act of will. The saints' abstention from movement, from being driven along the metalled ways of desire, is an alternative way of conquering time; it makes time irrelevant, as does the moment of partial ecstasy, when the past and the future are integrated into the present, thus achieving timelessness.

The brief fourth movement of *Burnt Norton* evokes the mood of the airy nothing and the transitoriness of life, of tacit expectation of inevitable death, coupled with nostalgic review of all that might have been a part of our total destiny. A human life, in the immensity of cosmic daylight, is just a passing phenomenon, to be likened to the flashing of a kingfisher's wing as it moves through sunlit space. But now we know that all passing, all temporality, *has* a still point, and that the passing light of our lives does not exhaust *all* light; the light of the world remains still, at *every* still point.

The final movement celebrates the reconciliation of temporality and timelessness. The pattern, the melody, the meaning of a verbal statement are not found in the partial components, but transcend them, lie beyond them. This applies to each human life as well. Eliot recalls us to the previously indicated concatenation of the three dimensions of time: 'And the end and the beginning were always there / Before the beginning and after the end.' 'Were', 'before' and 'after' are, of course, used timelessly in these two lines. The helplessness of death is unmasked in the suprising-sounding observation that 'that which is only living / Can only die'. The force of the first 'only' differs in import from the second. The first suggests that human beings are not *only* living, not confined to the temporal realm. The second 'only' defuses the threat of death, removes its sting. Being temporal, what else can we do but die? But, if we are not *just* temporal, our death is less of a calamity, perhaps no calamity at all.

A part of living in time consists in the attempts to capture its meaning in words, the vocation of a poet. Here we are unequal to the task, most of the time. Words strain, crack and break, slip, slide, perish, decay with imprecision. The reasons for this may be found in the motivation behind our uses of language. Instead of allowing it to reveal things as they are, we impose on it our aggressive subjective distortions. The result is shrieking, scolding, mocking or chattering. And the living Word of the scriptures is attacked by the voices of temptation in the desert, by egotistical, self-concerned lamentations, or by insistent pursuit of illusions.

In the final stanza the image of the still point, which renders dance possible, is assimilated to Love, which, itself unmoving, causes all movement, all temporal projects. Caught between unbeing and being, we perceive our true vocation in guessing the import of the shaft of sunlight left by timelessly meaningful moments, once again symbolised by the 'hidden laughter / Of children in the folliage'. Quickly catching further connotation of such moments, we manage to conquer time, which then appears ridiculous, wastefully and sadly 'stretching before and after'.

'EAST COKER'

'East Coker' deals with the temporality of the whole human race, with the transitoriness of all life. 'In my beginning is my end.' This line can be read in many ways. It may indicate a frightful compression of time. Barely begun, life is rolling toward its demise. Or so it seems, when we do stand near the end. But Eliot means more. He also wants to pack into this deceptively instantaneous, perishing span the entire *content* of experience, both a person's experience and the experience of the whole race rooted in the earth of our whirling planet. History is the succession of crumbling houses and factories, the old replacing the new, from age to age, from century to century. Even the mementos of royal glory, embroidered on silk in gold, in time become tatters delivered to mice and destined to rot.

The poet thinks of his beginnings, his ancestry. The round of English peasant life, filling successive spans of time centuries ago, is pictured in various scenes of village life. The road into the ancestral village, taken by the poet at some point of his middle age, can also lead backward into time when men and women, 'Rustically solemn or in rustic laughter', went through the rituals of marriage, baptism, funeral, and celebrated in dance and song the comings and goings of the seasons, milking and harvesting, moving from day to day, from year to year, from generation to generation. The dancing movements of their loam-laden feet, shod in clumsy shoes, are used by the poet as a symbol of ways in which they kept time and enacted the pattern of their lives. 'Keeping time' is a pun in this context. It means preserving the rhythm, the pattern, but also being true to the demands of the span of time in their charge. Dancing, copulating, eating and drinking, whether by men and women or by their domesticated beasts, all terminate in dung and death, in bodies under the earth, nourishing the corn. Everyone everywhere has this sort of ultimately decaying heritage. For everyone, the beginning fore-shadows, anticipates – and not just in a temporal sense – the end.

The succession of human or cosmic episodes is not always clear-cut. The interpenetration of successive phases is often confusing, less than orderly or predictable. At times even seasons overlap. It is as if nature were sometimes in conflict with itself. In the onrush of time, hardly finished processes get overtaken by hostile events: 'Late roses filled with early snow'. Even the heavens carry signs of conflict and war, with constellations whirling 'in a vortex'. More-over, ultimately that vortex 'shall bring / The world to that des-tructive fire / Which burns before the ice-cap reigns'. The final image brings home the radical unpredictability and uncertainty of cosmic forces. We cannot tell whether life on earth will die by freezing or by solar conflagration.

Not wishing to appear as a seer or an oracle, the poet, in a switch to a colloquial, almost prosaic speech, warns himself and the reader that his way of putting all those weighty things is, as always, not very satisfactory. No one can escape 'the intolerable wrestle / With words and meanings'. No doubt conscious of his own aging, Eliot asks himself about the reputed wisdom of old, experienced men. His sobering conclusion is that there is 'only a limited value / In the knowledge derived from experience'. All that promise to acquire deeper wisdom with advancing years turns out to be a fraud, a mere 'receipt for deceit'. All men, ultimately and always, peer into impenetrable darkness. Eliot's train of thought in this territory of his explorations contains even a hint of an irreducible relativity of all human knowledge. Knowledge is obtained by imposing a preconceived structure, an arbitrary pattern, which is bound to falsify, distort reality. In addition, every new experience may bring a surprise, a shock, a discovery that new data do not fit the old theories. By the time we have corrected the theory we are no longer in a position to correct errors based on the application of that theory, previously assumed to be correct. And that seems to be our permanent condition in pursuit of knowledge. We are always in danger of being bewitched and enchanted by our fancies and disenchanted by nasty discoveries. Not the wisdom but the folly of old men is to be noted. Chained to their narrow, earth-bound explorations, they become disillusioned and too timid to take any risks. They become persons of little faith, afraid to commit themselves unconditionally either to others or to God, whose knowledge transcends worldly wisdom. Consequently, the only wisdom human beings can acquire is humility, endless humility. The houses that had gone under the sea, and the dancers that are under the hill, are the dead reminders of that central truth.

Whither go all those lived-out human destinies, lives of captains, bankers, writers, statesmen, rulers, of important and unimportant contributors to human history? They go into the dark and vacant interstellar spaces, into nowhere. And, if their substance and essence is no longer, if it is scattered into endless cosmic spaces, can *they* have a funeral? If human life ends with the death of the body, and the body is all there is, then there is 'Nobody's funeral, for there is no one to bury'. But from the depth of this darkness the soul can come upon the stillness already adumbrated in 'Burnt Norton', the stillness of the timeless still point, around which and only because of which there is dance, temporal existence. The still soul can come face to face with another kind of darkness: the darkness of God.

The poet can only come up with hints or guesses about the nature of divine darkness. His images are taken from life, familiar life. Sitting in a darkened theatre, between the acts, we are aware that the whole scenery of the just completed act is being rolled away and that when the stage lights go on a completely new scenery will confront us, even though we do not know what it will be like. In the hushed silence of a stopped underground train between stations all sounds subside and passengers sink deeper into troubled thoughts, yet with expectation of imminent movement toward their destination. Even more effective is Eliot's image of a person's consciousness under ether: it is consciousness with no content, as if one's mind were a wrung-out sponge ready to be filled. But there is a radical difference between these, after all familiar, situations and the stillness of the soul prepared to receive the darkness of God. If our hopes, loves and thoughts in this radically new situation were to be based on hopes, loves and thoughts derived from earthly experience, we should not be ready to receive God: we should be projecting him in our own image – that is, not fit to receive him. Now Eliot returns to the echo of the ecstasy from the rose-garden in *Burnt Norton.* That ecstasy and the laughter in the garden were not self-justifying but only pointed to and required the agony described in *East Coker,* the agony of facing the utlimate meaninglessness of *all* life in time, of the entire temporal succession 'Of death and birth'.

Eliot acknowledges that he is repeating what he said before. But he adds that it needs to be said again and again. Relentlessly, we must reject all our connection with temporality with all its perishing delusive goods. For, if at the end of the journey we are naked souls in the presence of God, then we must acknowledge the ultimate importance of this new encounter by rejecting all *known* ecstasy, all claims to possessions, all claims to knowledge.

The mystery, the darkness of God is dispelled in the symbols of the next movement. These symbols clearly involve a Christian interpretation. The mortal disease from which we are suffering can be healed by the compassionate art of the healer, the Christ, who, although a competent–divine–surgeon, was himself wounded, embodied in human mortal flesh. Even though the Church is herself infirm, her task is to nurse us to health by reminding us of our sinfulness. The Church is not here to comfort and please us but to prepare us to accept our ultimate unworthiness in the face of God. The absolute paternal care of the physician will bring about our recovery by first preparing us for death – the death of our wordly dependence. God's preventing love is at the same time enabling love. By preventing us from remaining in our sinfulness, he enables us to rise to our ultimate salvation. Hence, before we can be warmed by divine fire, we must freeze, and die, in fear and trembling. Hence, the gruesome events of divine self-sacrifice, of which we are reminded by partaking of Christ's body and blood, are the means of our redemption, and this is why 'we call this Friday good'.

In the final movement the poet again returns to himself. He refers to the two inter-war decades of his life as wasted. He points to the failure of his poetic raids 'on the inarticulate', and to his inability to discipline the 'Undisciplined squads of emotion'. In other words, he is disillusioned with his own creative efforts and no longer thinks that he can say anything really fresh and new, because of the repeated discoveries that there have been others who said what he wished to say and said it much better. But, then, he accepts his shortcomings and limitations. It is not a matter of success. 'For us, there is only the trying. The rest is not our business.'

Old age does not give us wisdom; on the contrary, as Conrad observes in *Heart of Darkness,* it shows us that the world is stranger than we thought, that the pattern of the dead and the living is more complicated. Returning to the ecstasy of the rose-garden, the poet sees that it cannot be isolated from the rest of one's life, and that it is but a messenger of love burning not only in every moment of a lifetime, but in all lifetimes, including those mourned by indecipherable words on gravestones. The universality of that love becomes evident 'When here and now cease to matter'. That is why, from the spiritual point of view, there is no such thing as old age, and that is why 'Old men ought to be explorers.' For to their dying day they may still be moving into 'another intensity, / For a further union, a deeper communion'. Returning to the key thought of 'Burnt Norton', the three-dimensionality of time, Eliot now reverses the first lines of this quartet and completes the thought by proclaiming, 'In my end is my beginning.' The darkness of God in 'East Coker' becomes light.

'THE DRY SALVAGES'

Water is not just one of the primordial elements: it is also a fitting
symbol both for time and for eternity. It is natural for us to speak
of the 'river of time'. Time flows, like a river; it conveys things
from their origins to their destinations. Rivers, like time, are
intimately close to human beings. In the poet's own experience,
the Mississippi, likened to a strong brown god, was a dominant
factor in the life of the new nation settling the new land. At first
recognised as a frontier, a barrier, in time it became a conveyor of
commerce, a provider of sites for bustling cities. Almost fogotten
by them, it nevertheless reminds the city-dwellers of its ultimately
untamed power by periodic floods and storms. The watery
rhythms are too much a part of us; as a necessary ingredient of
our sustenance, they cannot be left out of account for long. The
river is always with us and within us.

But the river also connects with the sea, and Eliot uses the sea
to represent the vast, timeless depository of all life. It may be that
life originated in the sea. When life moved inland it never lost its
connection with its original home – 'the sea is all about us', and it
is 'the land's edge also'. Inhabitants of the land are persistently
reminded of earlier forms of life washed ashore: 'The starfish, the
horseshoe crab, the whale's backbone'. But the sea also 'tosses up
our losses', torn parts of fishing nets, broken oars, and other
belongings of dead seamen.

When Eliot observes that 'The sea has many voices, / Many
gods and many voices', he refers to it as an encompassing repository of both life and death: it contains both our origins and
our history. The human race, to survive and to propagate itself,
had to venture out onto the dangerous, hostile seas of the world.
The battle between the human will and the menacing watery elements had death and destruction as its constant companions. It is
as if the realm of waves and of the deep imposed its own rhythm
on the daring voyagers' survival and submergence. That rhythm
has been well known to countless women, anxiously waiting for
their seafaring husbands, fathers and sons to return from perilous
journeys. That rhythm plays havoc with the normal rhythm of
customary time. It is difficult to unravel the meaning of one's
life's time when, owing to upheavals created by shipwrecks and
drownings, the past is made 'all deception' and the future future-
less. The battle against the hostility of the watery elements makes

death a regular visitor, vividly reminding us of our mortality.

There is no end to the drifting wreckage of used-up life. Eliot uses the image of the life-dissolving and death-dealing sea to remind us of 'Years of living among the breakage / Of what was believed in us the most reliable'. There is no accumulation of meaning in human history; there is only addition, of life to life, of generation to generation, each ending in death and oblivion. Delusively clinging to perishable life as the most reliable reality, we should see it instead as 'the fittest for renunciation'. Ocean and time are intertwined for human beings, both historically and symbolically.

> We cannot think of a time that is oceanless
> Or of an ocean not littered with wastage
> Or of a future that is not liable
> Like the past, to have no destination.

These four lines sum up Eliot's argument against considering mere mortality, so relentless and so ubiquitous, as providing the source of meaning. This truth dawns on us with a particularly devastating force when, in old age, all our vital powers are failing, when we suddenly perceive ourselves as 'In a drifting boat with a slow leakage' and dimly sense the approaching annunciation of death. The daily round, in the endless procession of ultimately futile tasks, amounts to no more than 'forever bailing', leading in the end to death – a haul 'that will not bear examination'. Amidst the drifting wreckage of human mortality there may be heard, nevertheless, 'the hardly, barely prayable / Prayer of the one Annunciation'.

The Annunciation, mentioned here in the context of inescapable annunications of death, reminds us of the previously noted transition from human darkness to the darkness of God. The movement from one darkness to the other, from annunications to the one Annunciation, involves a full realisation that agony is unavoidable; 'we come to discover that the moments of agony . . . are likewise permanent / With such permanence as time has'. But Eliot's observation here seems to contain a deliberate ambiguity. As the moments of happiness cannot provide complete fulfilment – something else is needed – so the moments of agony do not say the last word on the human condition.

The remarks about agony are preceded by another aside on the advantages of growing older. One begins to see through the delusions of the promise of development or evolutionary growth. The notion of evolution is superficial because it disowns the past, makes it irrelevant. But, mindful of what we owe to our both personal and racial past ('In my beginning is my end'), we may see ourselves as inextricably united to all men and to all life. Even the moments of happiness conceived as 'the sudden illumination' and not just as a raw, unarticulated experience of satisfaction, when examined for their meaning (which is missed when we concentrate on the bare, immediate experience), lead us to perceive our connectedness to many generations, including the most remote and primitive ones, those pervaded by animal terror. Once more Eliot acknowledges our capacity to be affected by the experience of others. He is not pointing to some innate tendency to be sympathetic, but merely to the objective weight that the suffering of others may exert on our psyches. That weight is experienced more directly than our own agonies, because ours are usually covered 'by the currents of action', by our tendency to try to cope with them, while 'the torment of others remains an experience / Unqualified'.

To explain our connectedness with the past, *all* past, the poet produces another version of his previously developed notion of the unity of all time-dimensions: 'Time the destroyer is time the preserver.' Once more reminding us of events and actions testifying to human sinfulness, which, like a rock hidden in restless waters, is always there to founder the ships of our voyage, Eliot reinforces his repeated judgement that we cannot disown our past.

As we cannot deny the three-dimensionality of time by escaping from the past, so we cannot deny it by escaping into the future. Interpreting Krishna's message in the *Bhagavad-Gita*, Eliot suggests that 'the future is a faded song'. The paradoxicality of the expression did not deter other sages from resorting to it, and Eliot also cites the claim of Heraclitus that 'the way up is the way down' and amplifies it in the light of his own view of time by saying that 'the way forward is the way back'. To some extent the paradox is relieved by the reminder that our gaze into the future is often motivated by the desire to disavow or obliterate the present, but this is self-deceiving because, by the time the future arrives, we shall not be what we are now: 'time is no healer: the patient is no longer here'. Again, Eliot is urging us to come to terms with our past and to accept responsibility for it. His image is a compartment of train passengers, surrendering themselves to the motion along the metalled ways — that is, becoming mere spectators of their existence, not exerting their wills but allowing themselves to be carried, deterministically, by the current of events around them.

Thus, the poet's injunction 'Fare forward, travellers!' uses the word 'forward' not in a spatial or temporal sense, but in a time-transcending sense, 'not escaping from the past / Into different lives, or into any future'. 'You shall not think "the past is finished" / Or "the future is before us".' Instead, following Krishna's advice, we should 'consider the future / And the past with an equal mind', 'While time is withdrawn'. As at the moment of death we are forced to think in the direction of possible realities not dominated by time (for we are about to leave the realm of temporality), so at *any* moment we may gather into it *all* our past and *all* our future, thus raising the possibility of delivering ourselves into the care of a transcendent power. Since human actions always aim at some result in time, 'do not think of the fruit of action', but 'Fare forward' to 'your real destination'.

Since, as indicated, the 'forward' is to be interpreted trans-temporally, the invocation of that dimension is properly followed by a prayerful mood. The image of the Virgin Mary is invoked, since her shrines, in the lands of the believers, are the loci of prayers for those who perished 'in the sea's lips' or on the beaches, and for whom the sea bells ring a 'Perpetual angelus'.

In contrast to *this* kind of accepting one's past and one's future, the poet depicts the anxious, manipulative, often superstitious ways of interpreting these two time-dimensions. He ridicules the palm-readers and fortune-tellers and those who undertake to 'divine' the course of events from omens and signs, the explorers of 'womb, or tomb, or dreams'. These activities are no more than 'Pastimes and drugs', darlings of the sensationalist press and of gullible readers who are always on the lookout for stories to satisfy their boundless but idle curiosity. Enslaved to the mere fragments of time — past and future — they differ from the occasional saint who is able 'to apprehend / That point of intersection of the timeless / With time', in 'Ardour and selflessness and self-surrender'. For the rest of us, the unsaintly ones, there are only those fleeting messangers of the timeless, the moments of ecstasy descending upon us 'in a shaft of sunlight', like the one described in 'Burnt Norton'. But even these are 'only hints and guesses / Hints followed by guesses; and the rest / Is prayer, observance, discipline, thought and action'.

What is hinted at is the event already proclaimed by the one Annunciation – namely, Incarnation – in which the past and the future 'Are conquered and reconciled', and delivered from 'daemonic, chthonic / Powers'. This deliverance is beyond our powers; the most we can say is that we are undefeated 'Because we have gone on trying', a necessary condition to meet if our turning away from time is to nourish 'The life of significant soil'.

'LITTLE GIDDING'

From the very start, 'Little Gidding' celebrates the startling presence of an element that symbolises the supernatural in the natural. Fire, the most refined of the four elements, can also preside over their destruction, consuming air, earth, and water. While itself one of the basic components of nature, fire can also symbolise that which transcends them all. Its destructive power makes room for the constructive power of the supernatural, pentecostal fire. That fire is the Holy Spirit itself, whose essence is love, and whose presence permeates the world of time. Thus the opening movement shows, symbolically, the wintry scene of human life, flamed by spiritual fire. 'This is the spring time / But not in time's covenant.' And behind this unearthly spring there is promise of an equally otherworldly 'Zero summer', 'Summer beyond sense, the inapprehensible'.

The poet revisits the chapel in Little Gidding, site of the activity of a saintly man of the seventeenth century, Nicholas Ferrar, and visited by the 'broken king', Charles, when seeking refuge after his final defeat. The chapel is a place where all human purposes are transformed in prayer. Those who come here discover that all their earthly purposes are radically changed: 'the purpose is beyond the end you figured / And is altered in fulfilment'. No matter where one starts from, to arrive at such a place is to recognise the need 'to put off / Sense and notion'. All intellectual quest, all guesses, end here. 'You are here to kneel / Where prayer has been valid.' Prayer is not just its outward attire, nor is it articulable in speech derived from the order of living; it is a vehicle by means of which one crosses from time into its intersection with the timeless, an event which can occur anywhere, at any point of history, if the heart is right.

The second movement begins with a lyrical recapitulation of ways in which all mortal beings composed of the four elements undergo their demise in the face of eternal fire, which reveals itself at the intersection of time and eternity. In the light of the inevitability of this ultimate transformation, the poet once more asks himself what from his activity on earth is salvageable for the other side of living. This he does by a device of introducing a stranger emerging in a dream-like scene within the context of an air-raid alert.

The stranger is a composite figure of venerable poets, long dead, whose influence Eliot felt throughout his development as a poet and who, therefore, in part represent his own beliefs and theories about the poet's tasks. The stranger's advice, (which in a sense is Eliot's own insight into himself, since in this conversation he 'assumed a double part' is truthworthy because disinterested. It comes from the humility of the one who, being dead to time, has learned to put aside his human pride. Every view and every theory may be good enough for its time and place, but it is no use hanging on to it as if it were a timeless oracle; no human wisdom can attain that. 'Last season's fruit is eaten / And the fullfed beast shall kick the empty pail.' But those who speak from beyond the grave, being detached from the limiting purposes of their own, may disclose 'the gifts reserved for age'. First advice (reminiscent of Marlow's view in Conrad's *Heart of Darkness*) urges us not to expect revealing truths from the moments of dying. Secondly, there is no point in raging at human folly: it is unavoidable. And, lastly, one should accept the pain of admitting the repeated harm one has done to others and the suspect nature even of one's best motives, 'Which once you took for exercise of virtue.' There is no way to remove on one's own the wrongs one committed except by submitting oneself to the 'refining fire' of non-human, transcendent origin.

The third movement distinguishes between three conditions open to us: attachment to ourselves and the world, detachment from ourselves and the world, and indifference – with the last differing from the other two as death differs from life. Indifference is a terrible condition because it is a total cessation of the love impulse, toward either the world or the Beyond. What is required is not cessation, but the *expansion* of love beyond desire, which in turn entails 'liberation / From the future as well as the

past'. The task is not to do away with the love of the particular –
say, the love of one's country – but, rather, to transform it into a
pattern that includes but also moves beyond history. Drawing on
the writings of Dame Julian, a fourteenth-century English mystic,
the poet describes the necessity of accepting one's sinfulness while
retaining the hope for the now inapprehensible redemption to
come. All men, at all times, great and small, those who fought
and opposed each other, those who have already died and those
still living but are equally facing death, are 'folded into a single
party' and capable of receiving salvation 'By the purification of
the motive / In the ground of our beseeching.'

Once more contrasting the two kinds of fire – the earthly and
the divine, the self-concerned and the universally valid – the poet
points to the possibility of choice of the latter over the former. For
the torment of self-denial is devised by Love, in order to lead us
toward our true destination, at the intersection of time and
eternity.

Returning to his chosen task as a poet, Eliot points to an
analogy. The life of a successful poem begins when the process of
perfecting it has ended. In making this point Eliot also mentions
some characteristics of a well-made poem: 'Every phrase and
every sentence is an end and a beginning, / Every poem an epi-
taph.' So, too, with a human life: its completion can be seen as a
beginning of its new life; not only the *final* completion, but also
the completion of each meaningful moment, is a birth into timelessness. Even history is nothing that exists wholesale, 'for history
is a pattern / Of timeless moments'. That is why the return, in
memory, to this historical moment in the chapel of Little Gidding
can be a response to 'the voice of this Calling'.

Every moment returns us to whole of our life, which we explore
and re-explore as long as we live, seeing the old past ever with new
eyes. The river of life contains all the moments, including the one
with which the poet started his journey of exploration: the rose-
garden of 'Burnt Norton', with the hidden waterfall and children
in the apple tree. Such events point to and are ultimately taken
up in the pentecostal fire of the Holy Spirit.

B

Although Eliot, like Auden, leads modern disillusioned Western man back to the insights of Christianty, he does so on a much broader front. Auden's return to the promise of the Christian Gospel is clearly a response to the particular historical context of his time. In his descriptions we can easily discern the events leading up to and culminating in the Second World War. Our historical period is characterised by the emergence of new Herods and by the slaughter of millions of innocents. These calamitous events are taking place against the background of claims made for scientific and technological progress and in contrast to the hopes of liberal political and social progressives, among whom Auden once counted himself. Both science and morality have failed us, and the original sinfulness has once more surfaced with a vengeance, lealding to destruction and death. Auden's return to Christianity is at least in part prompted by his disillusionment with the actual course of historical events.

Eliot's analysis goes deeper. Even though he too finds the message of Christianity to be essential to the correct appraisal of the human reality, and, even though he invokes Christian theological concepts, such as Annunication, Incarnation and pentecostal fire, his religious point of view appears to move beyond these concepts and represents them as having a more general, Christianity-transcending validity. In this regard there is a degree of affinity between him and Goethe, who also used Christian symbolism to express what in his view were universal truths. Of course, the differencess between the two poets must not be forgotten: Eliot was a believing Christian, Goethe deemed himself a pagan. But this difference is less important, it seems to me, than the similarity of their attempts to move beyond the boundaries of traditional religion. Eliot did so while remaining a believer, utlimately subordinating reason to faith; Goethe, on the other hand, was still sufficiently infected by the rationalist spirit of the Enlightenment to think that an insight into ultimate truth about the human situation need not involve the separation of faith from reason. In this regard Auden was clearly influenced by contemporary Neo-Orthodox trends in theology, and Eliot brought to bear on his analysis some central conclusions of F. H. Bradley's Idealism, which on ultimate matters called for suicide of the intellect.

The unreality of time was a common theme of all Absolute Idealists. That theme receives a more concrete treatment in Eliot's poem. Time, or rather our enslavement to it, is the

destroyer. Unless we learn to see beyond time, unless we come to
think of ourselves as capable of transcending the time of our
lives, we too are slated for spiritual destruction. Ecstatic moments, which gather into themselves all three time dimensions,
thus giving these moments poignancy and meaning, are clues to
the possibility of transcending time, *all* time. As the meaning of
a moment calls for such time-transcendence, so does the meaning of the whole life, and not only of individual lives but of all
lives, of the entire human phenomenon on earth. That phenomenon, while having a temporal historical career, has, to borrow
Kant's terminology, also a noumenal side. For Kant that side was
glimpsed in moral experience, only indirectly pointing to central
claims of religion – immortality and God. For Eliot, the intersection of time and the timeless, of the phenomenal and the noumenal, occurs at moments of heightened awareness, triggered by
all significant personal experiences.

It is the task and the prerogative of the poet to make us attentive to such experiences. Moreoever, a deeply philosophical poet,
such as Eliot, will also invite us to reflect on some universal
features of human existence. He will make use of history, both
retail and wholesale, to tell us some important things about the
human condition. Thus Eliot, reflecting on his own ancestral
roots, makes us think of the history of England and of the Mis-
sissippi-dominated New World and its history, especially as it
connects with the landing sites of the Pilgrim settlers. But then
the reader's train of thought is eased along the watery passages
between the Old World and the New, stimulating us to reflect on
the relationship human history has to the oceans that divide and
connect continents. The poet is always forcing us to move from
the impersonal objective level to the personal, intimate experiences of human beings that make up the actual *content* of
history. We are made to think not about the numbers of ships or
of geographical locations, but of what it was like for seafarers to
battle the stormy seas, and for their wives and children to await
anxiously, often in vain, their return.

The focus of the poet's interest is always the state of mind and
the spiritual posture of human beings. Explaining his experience,
he throws light on ours. His rose-gardens become our rose-
gardens. Echoes of his memories trigger echoes in our memories.
We become conscious of the ways in which past events have left
permanent scars on our psyches, and how what we are today is

coloured by our past and conditioned by our expectations. The truths Eliot discovers in his own experience we find discoverable in ours. Conscious of failing to achieve the hoped-for degree of wisdom with the advent of maturity or aging, we perceive the justice of Eliot's scepticism about the wisdom of old age and of his conclusion that 'old men ought to be explorers'. Similarly, we recognise the futility of our repeated attempts to manipùlate, self-deceivingly, our future, by looking for omens and signs, thus escaping responsibility for what we need to do or face.

It is also not difficult to share Eliot's admiration for those who are capable of selflessness and self-surrender, the known and the unknown saintly figures who were able to see through their own weaknesses and mistakes, and yet 'have gone on trying', thus conquering and reconciling their past and future with the present. They were able to perceive that the need for humility is endless, and that the surrender of personal willfulness may radically transform our purposes. Seeing that the source of their lives' meaning lies beyond time, at the still point of the temporal world, they were not devastated by the need 'to put off sense and notion' but were moving in the direction of Love through prayer. Among models for us to emulate in this kind of self-surrender Eliot finds such admirable and memorable figures as Nicholas Ferrar, and such tragical, defeated figures as Charles I. Eliot surmises that the prayers of these two persons, in the chapel of Little Gidding, must have been valid, and that both men must have experienced the peace that passes understanding.

Eliot's relationship to his craft, poetry, as expressed in this poem, is also worth pondering. He acknowledges its difficulty and his failures. The difficulty stems in part from the impossibility of seeing beyond the horizon of one's time and of transcending the limitation of the categories of thought, which are always relative to the period of history in which one lives: no human thought is timeless. The failures are often due to the suspect nature of the motives that go into creating poetry, or, even more generally, using language to articulate distorted perceptions and merely subjective, egotistical purposes. According to Eliot, religious believers are not immune to this disease; frequently they too distort the living Word in pursuit of illusions.

The *Four Quartets* does not find the human world – both in its personal and in its historical dimensions – sufficient unto itself. The poem spells out the multiple ways in which our world bears the marks of human sinfulness. But the poet has also glimpsed the possibility of peeping through the curtain of our mortality at points where time and timelessness intersect. Such points consist in moments of deeply intense personal experiences, which then can serve as pointers toward the larger and deeper meaning, merely adumbrated in experiences of ecstasy and tragedy. For Eliot himself the connection of momentary love to Universal Love confirms the truth of Christianity, but his vision, as illustrated, of instance, by his use of Western philosophies and Eastern religions, has wider sympathies and is compatible with alternative patterns of seeing the world religiously.

12   Death Defused: Rilke's *Duino Elegies*

A

Rainer Maria Rilke's *Duino Elegies* has been long recognised as a profound philosophical poem. It has been said that Rilke translated Nietzsche into poetry and that Heidegger translated Rilke into prose. This remark alerts us to the likelihood of finding common elements in all three thinkers, and we may indeed conclude that Rilke's views are reminiscent of Nietzsche and anticipate Heidegger. But an examination of Rilke's thought will disclose that he pursued his own course and did so in a unique manner.

Our interpretation of the poem will be in the light of what Rilke himself, metaphorically, expresses. To concentrate on the philosophical import of what a poet says is, of course, a risky undertaking; as in the case of Auden and Eliot, one always runs the danger of failing to understand, or managing only to half-understand, what the poet conveys in his carefully chosen language. But, as in the case of the other two poets, the risks involved in interpreting Rilke are worth taking. His conclusions, in my opinion, add up to an inclusive, coherent philosophical statement about the nature of human existence. An attempt to capture this coherence and inclusiveness need not involve a diminution of aesthetic appreciation. On the contrary, this appreciation may be enhanced, if one also manages to capture the philosophy of life the poem expresses. There is such a philosophy in the *Duino Elegies*. Our attempt to unveil it, in contrast to the two preceding interpretations, will disregard the sequence of thoughts the poet expressed in his work, in order to bring out more sharply his two contrasting evaluations of life—one negative, one positive. In the end, I shall claim, the positive swallows up the negative; from the background of sorrow and sadness there bursts forth a song of celebration. Let us examine both sides of the coin, remembering, with Rilke, that the value of the coin embraces both.

The forms in which we come to experience disappointment and disillusionment with our lives are many. Every day we are reminded of our transitoriness. Every moment passes, not to return again. As Rilke says, 'we live our lives, for ever taking leave'.* There is no permanence to anything we do, anything we undertake. And there is that constantly recurring reminder of our inevitable death. 'Staying is nowhere.'

The very fact of existing may appear a burden. The etymological root of the word 'existence' itself offers a clue as to why we may feel that way. To exist (*ex-istere*) is to stand *out*, outside, not to belong, to be a stranger. Rilke captures this sense of separateness in two melancholy lines in the Eighth Elegy: 'That's what destiny means: being opposite / and nothing else, and always opposite.' In this regard we may feel a contrast between ourselves and other animals. Unlike us, they do not seem to experience the sense of oppositeness, separation. They are not *facing* Creation, the way we are. Lacking *self*-consciousness, they mirror the Creation and move freely and openly within it. They do not distinguish the self from the not-self, and hence are free of crises of identity. For them their own being is unintrospective, and therefore inapprehensible and infinite.

Animals are not dominated by the urgencies of the passing time; its future dimension does not absorb them the way it absorbs us. Where we see the future, or the past, or the present, the animal sees Everything, and itself in Everything, and in this unity it is 'for ever healed'. Confronting the gaze of a dumb brute, we may feel as if it were looking *through* us and moved immediately beyond us – to the surrounding world. We are not capable of such a perceiving of the openness of the world, because our self-consciousness separates us from the world, and our conscious attention to separable particulars in the world destroys its unity. For us, 'here all is distance'. We do not have the sense of being in the womb of Creation, the way a tiny gnat leaps *within* it. 'Oh bliss of tiny creatures that *remain* forever in the womb that brought them forth.' But even within the animal kingdom we

---

*This and all subsequent quotations from the *Duino Elegies* are taken from the translation by J. B. Leishman and Stephen Spender (London: Hogarth Press; New York: W. W. Norton, 1939).

may sometimes discern a germ of anxiety that is our permanent condition. A young bird learning to fly seems dismayed, afraid of its own self; its flight 'zigzags through the air like crack through cup'.

The double anxiety of transitoriness and separateness Rilke captures in four devastating lines:

> And we, spectators always, everywhere,
> looking at, never out of, everything!
> It fills us. We arrange it. It decays.
> We rearrange it, and decay ourselves.

The lines repeat, 'All is vanity!' This cry has been echoed and re-echoed throughout human history, by deep thinkers and by ordinary minds thrown against the wall of despair by hard and tragic circumstances.

That we are playthings of the overwhelmingly large and powerful cosmos is disclosed to us in the experience of our sexuality. That experience has a terrifying aspect. The overpowering ancestral urge asserts itself early, even in the dreams of the adolescent who feels 'the floods of origin flowing within him'. Rilke's Third Elegy is a phenomenological commentary on what Freud called 'the libido'. Its concrete, physical dominance is explained by Rilke in evolutionary terms. Sexuality is a fact not about individuals but about the entire human race. Every person is a carrier of the procreative instinct of nature, and we must acknowledge the physiological underpinnings of our romantic love. In singing the beloved we are also in the service of 'that hidden guilty river-god of the blood'. Mixed with our romantic attraction to a specific person there is also the procreative urge which reaches through an unbroken chain to all our ancestors who bestowed life on us by paying homage to that river-god within our blood. Rilke points to this connection as accounting for the power, intensity, and irresistible attraction of the sexual impulse.

> Look, we don't love like flowers, with only a single
> season behind us; immemorial sap
> mounts in our arms when we love.

To see oneself as a carrier of this immemorial biological energy is potentially destructive to our fragile psyche. For the essence of romantic love is concentrated on the *individuality* of the beloved. The lover believes that it is *she*, her looks, her beauty, that mobilises in him the sexual desire. But the presence of the ancient urge is always there to create a sense of doubt: do I really want her or just her body? This unpoetic, vulgar way of putting the question does not diminish its relevance, and Rilke perceives that it may lead to a sense of guilt. The lover wants to single out, to sing, to celebrate his beloved, and yet he also knows that he is at the services of this 'Neptune within our blood with his horrible trident.' The guilt may follow from the uncertainty as to which force is the dominant one in the encounters of two lovers. The deflation and disillusionment are reinforced when the romantic attraction passes. Alternatively, when the attraction to another person is explicitly and exclusively physical, the guilt takes another form: it is the guilt of *using* the person, of not appreciating personal qualities of the individual. (The guilt about prostitution, affecting both the prostitute and her client, stems from this realisation.)

Human sexuality, since it calls for a *personalised* expression, separates the individuals from the overwhelming ancestral biological stream. But the personalisation is only tentative and temporary. A sense of guilt is generated by a suppressed anxiety that we do not manage to reconcile the claims of the race with the expression of devotion to particular individuals we profess to love. Here we have a potent source of disillusionment with the human condition.

Repeatedly we discover that we are not equal to life's challenges. Dependent on a constant flow of psychic–physical energy, we often experience its absence, its lack. Exhaustion follows exertion. In moments of more pervasive melancholy all of life may appear to us a 'useless passion', to borrow Sartre's expression. Rilke captures this mood of exhaustion in the picture of circus acrobats in the Fifth Elegy. That elegy is a picture of still life – in more than one sense of the phrase. Inspired by Picasso's painting *Les Saltimbanques*, Rilke asks us to look at a group of circus performers. At the conclusion of their act, the energy, the potency of their skills has departed – and they stand there, used up. There is something melancholy about the loss of vitality; and yet, inevitably, this *is* our fate, always. Whether we are trapeze acrobats, carpenters, painters, poets or philosophers, the time comes when our act is over.

Rilke likens the acrobats' performance to a human life. Life's energy tosses and slings us through situations, projects, careers, and, when it is all over, we stand there, worn out and tired, on a threadbare capret. Placed as they are in Picasso's painting, the acrobats form in Rilke's eyes 'the great initial of thereness', the latter signifying *Dasein*, the German word for human existence. The threadbare carpet, on which we stand at the end of our journey, is the desolate universe, unfeeling, uncaring, indifferent to our fate. The emotion which Rilke discerns in the faces of the performers is not just exhaustion, tiredness: it is also disappointment, disenchantment, disillusionment. It is as if they felt themselves cheated by life's promise. The sadness is particularly touching, even heart-rending, in the faces of youthful performers – a small lad, a young girl, in whom the demands and the hardships of life manage to kill child-like enjoyment and innocent pleasure. Their wistful smile is the only value salvageable from this melancholy scene. There is, though, a sort of tiny victory in this smile, and Rilke suggests that the inscription 'Subrisio Saltat', 'a smile leaps', should be placed on a graceful urn, in praise of the youthful actors' self-conquest: a smile, in spite.

Rilke is musing over the fleetingness of our achievements, over the quickness of the transition from gain to loss, from attainment to satiation, from triumph to emptiness, from 'pure too-little' to 'empty too-much'. We hardly ever experience the *stasis* of satisfaction, because, as long as the curve of enjoyment is upward, we are attentive to the energy which secures its upward movement. And, when the climax, the zenith, is reached, we suffer an energy loss, and quickly the too-little becomes too-much.

That is why Rilke calls us back to Nietzsche's affirmation of potency, of the will to power, as characterising what is most distinctive about human reality. Potency is energy on the rise, bent on achievement, exertion, creative effort. He wants us to imagine the acrobats at the incipient moments of the acts they performed, when they were still able to manage 'their daring lofty figures of heart-flight', when they were still like quivering arrows before being released. But we give such moments little heed. Instead, we are preoccupied with 'the restless ways of the world', and produce endless ribbons of useless ornamentation, like the seamstress in Paris, whom Rilke calls Madame Lamort, symbolising Death, the ultimate tiredness.

Acrobats, at least, *respond* to life's possibilities. Like

Nietzsche's tightrope-walker in *Thus Spoke Zarathustra*, they choose a dangerous profession. Although buffeted by the hard tasks demanded by it, they are giving themselves to these demands. They perform, they answer the call of challenge. But what about us, can we say this of ourselves?

Already in the First Elegy Rilke has called attention to our inertia. Waves of values may rise toward us, but we are not equal to them. Somewhere the sound of a violin is heard, but is anyone listening? All too often we fail to notice what life around us is offering to us, because we are distracted by egocentric expectations. Preoccupied by preconceived goals and objectives, we are oblivious to values that offer themselves to us. We pass them by, in pursuit of something else. We do not see the person in front of us, because we are thinking of another.

Consider how often even lovers pass each other by. Even in the act of embrace we are beyond it. Our feelings are not co-ordinated. We sink 'because the other has so completely emerged'. After the first kiss, a tryst in the garden, the lovers are no longer the same. In the midst of such encounters we are ready to escape. We touch each other, but the touch does not generate loyalty. There is something fleeting, volatile about all human commitments and emotions. They do not exist the way trees and houses do. Impermanence characterises all our relations. 'We only pass everything by like a transposition of air.'

For these reasons Rilke discerns a certain wisdom in the sculptors' work an Attic steles, who managed to show how lightly, insubstantially, human figures touch one another: 'Remember the hands, / how they rest without pressure, though power is there in the torsos'. Gods may press more strongly upon us, but we are not gods; our emotions, feelings and loyalties are made out of impermanent, perishable stuff.

No matter how hopeful we are about the next personal encounter, the person we meet is likely to disappoint us. Initially intriguing or enticing, upon closer acquaintance he or she turns out to be just a groundling, a bourgeois, disguised for the sake of conquest. For the most part we are hollow men, with no substance inside us. Faced with such disappointing presentations of self in daily life we might be more at peace in dealing with a lifeless doll, which is at least not a half-filled mask – what it is is wholly outside, undisguised. A natural response to repeated disillusionments and disappointments in personal relationships is withdrawal; 'for one can always watch'.

The ability to distance oneself from others is acquired early in life and invades even the most intimate relationships. A father is disappointed with the path chosen by his son. Envisioning a certain course for his child's future, the parent is disheartened when he sees a quite different project emerge from the child's stubbornly self-determining will. Inevitably there comes a time when a child's love for his parents as distinct and unique individuals changes into something more abstract and distant, when he sees *beyond* them to other loves, other relationships. All sides suffer from this separation anxiety. The change is no easier for the children; for them the very sense of time takes on a different chararcter. For a child neither the past nor the future is easily separable from the present. All three time-dimensions are absorbed into a solid, certain present. But then suddenly we are old enough to see our past *as* past, as an object of a backward glance, and our future full of uncertainty and foreboding. Impatient to grow up, we are not prepared for the shock that the adults can give us nothing but their grown-upness. Then we shall miss the pure event, 'within the gap left between world and toy'. Rilke's image here manages to capture the essence of the child-like ability to immerse oneself wholly in a given experience. The toy and the world are one, not separated by circumspection, hesitation, questioning, or doubt.

But the child's life is not immune from dangers the world presents to all living beings. Ignorance of such dangers intensifies the poignancy of innocence. A death before life has begun, brought on by a combination of adverse circumstances and unsuspecting innocence is most difficult to comprehend and to accept. Such a death provides an ultimate challenge to those who perceive purpose and goodness at the heart of the universe.

Thoughts on death, however, may take an unexpected turn. Surprisingly, they may lead us from elegy to affirmation, for we are creatures 'for whom sorrow is so often source of blessedest progress'. This is the key insight of the poem, and Rilke first reports it in the First Elegy, where he observes that 'all of the living make the mistake of drawing too sharp distinctions'. This includes the distinction between life and death. We are invited to reflect upon it.

We should try to resist the ingrained picture of two realms, carved into us by our conceptual tradition. If death means obliteration, then there cannot be a realm of death. And yet reality *is* affected by the demise of the living. The substance of the world includes its history. The world is also what it has been. It is transformed by every life lived in it. Every life adds to the substance of the world in its own unique way. Rilke makes this point in a roundabout way, by a *tour de force* of poetic imagery. He asks us to imagine what we might think shortly after dying, if we were somehow able to retain consciousness. Separated from actuality, we should find no employment for our powers of perception, thought, feeling. It would seem strange not to follow the habits we acquired while inhabiting the world. All our relations to things and to people would be severed, would seem to flutter in the void. Used to being part of the actual world, to being engaged with it in multiple ways, we would be 'full of retrieving', wishing to reattach ourselves to the world from which death ejected us.

But all this exercise is a fantasy, a delusion, because there is no separate realm of death. And, if there is no such realm, then we should recognise that death transforms our being into a permanent, eternal feature of the world as it has been and continues to be, now enriched by all the relations we have contributed to it while living. This is the point behind Rilke's recommendation not to make such a sharp distinction between the living and the dead.

To help us break the hold of the old picture the poet puts forward an alternate one. Think of the life–death dyad as one *space*. Within this one space both the living and the dead can be located. Since change is a permanent feature of this space – all things come into and out of existence – it is just a matter of time before every living being is absorbed into the space from which it emerged. At one moment or another he no longer will be an active part of it, but he will still be a part of its substance, taken up into its eternal, timeless, changeless being. There is no way to obliterate any life, any event, from the world's history. It is embalmed there. But the value of the world as a whole is a sum total of what was put into it by living, finite beings. As George Santayana has put it, 'If time bred nothing, eternity would have nothing to embalm.'

Rilke uses the idea of space as a metaphor to encompass the living and the dead, time and eternity. (Plato's picture of time as the moving image of eternity comes to mind here.) If we think of them as a unity, then there is no ultimate oblivion of anything or of anyone. The timeless spaces of the universe are transformed by each intensely felt moment of life. This insight leads Rilke to make, early in the poem, this recommendation:

> Fling the emptiness out of your arms
> into the spaces we breathe—maybe that the birds
> will feel the extended air in more intimate flight.

The two words 'extended' and 'intimate' are to be taken almost literally. Even a homely example will provide a clue to what Rilke means to say. Suppose you are going to look up your friend in his room. The door is open, you enter. The room is empty; the friend is not there. If you are fond of the friend, need him, the room will look cheerless, desolate. The space which could contain him does not. With him absent, the space is deprived, robbed of a possible value. This kind of phenomenon has countless manifestations. How cold and lifeless is a room, a concert hall, a village, a city, when the occupants or inhabitants desert it. The film *On the Beach* shows the empty streets and buildings of San Francisco after an atomic-bomb attack. The sight provokes an eerie feeling of desolation, a loss beyond description.

Or consider Rilke's saying that the *spring* needs us, that stars are *waiting* to be espied by us. Spring is not fully spring if there are no creatures to celebrate its spring-like character. Nature comes into her own only when someone can respond to what she has to offer. Stars have no mysteries, except for their observers – astronomers and all others fascinated by the origins, dimensions, and destinies of heavenly bodies. How much poorer would be the universe without Newton and Einstein to discern and formulate the laws and relations that govern them. To remove physics from nature is to impoverish the universe. By ascertaining the laws and patterns that govern nature the physicist reveals otherwise unmanifest intelligible character.

In other words, cosmic spaces are transformed by man's presence, by human activity. The universe is literally animated by the human spirit. When Rilke begins to pursue this idea, its implications proliferate endlessly, and they point to the very special status of man on earth. It becomes clear to us *what man is for*. We discover wherein lie our tasks, our objectives, our hopes, possibilities and values.

We can do something that nothing else in the universe can: make the visible invisible. This is Rilke's metaphor for the capacity of consciousness to light up the universe from within, in the minds and hearts of persons. The material, concrete, visible world is transformed into spiritual human experience – the invisible, most perishing, epiphenomenal reality. Here Rilke can begin the praise of all the ways in which this spiritualising of the cosmos is brought about – in child-like wonderment and playful absorption, in the fascination of love, in heroic devotion. Art, music, poetry, science call attention to the importance of these values.

Remembering the terrifying, demanding Angel, Rilke after all can point out to him things of which man can be proud. Even the Angel should be impressed by them.

> So, after all, we have *not*
> failed to make use of the spaces, these generous spaces, these
> *our* spaces.

Surveying the world and its history we come upon remarkable monuments to human creativity and achievement: towers, pillars, pyramids, cathedrals, the Sphinx, the Parthenon, Chartres Cathedral, the Taj Mahal: all show forth what man was capable of producing. The course of civilisation is determined by the ingenuity, wit and will of conquerors and creators, lawgivers, judges, artists, artisans, music-lovers and composers, statesmen and citizens, philosophers and poets, doers and thinkers. Their contributions are not altogether scattered to the winds. Actual and palpable in their respective times, they still remain as heritage and influence, in statues, documents, monuments and memories, in institutions and practices, in oral and written traditions, in libraries, archives and concert halls. The volume and intensity of feeling generated in these human enterprises across the ages should impress even an angel. It is a wonder that the cosmic spaces are not overcrowded 'with thousands of years of feeling'. Rilke resorts here once more to his image of cosmic space inhabited by the values infused into them through human effort. These spaces must be immense to absorb all that we have created.

> Nay, even when one survives,
> one single thing once prayed or tended or knelt to,
> it's reaching, just as it is, into the unseen world.

Even a solitary person responding to beauty around or within him transforms the visible into the invisible, the physical, material, into immaterial, spiritual.

'Nowhere', says Rilke, 'can world exist but within.' The character of beauty and value is such that it cannot be confined to one experience. As Plato's Socrates observes in the *Symposium*, the particular leads us to a knowledge of the universal. At first discerned in one single thing, the character of beauty unsuspectingly turns up in other things. It echoes and re-echoes in the landscape of our experience. The love call can be answered by a multitude of persons, for, as Rilke asks, 'how could I limit the call I had called?' Even the most intense concentration of a lover is not confinable to the object of adoration. In Goethe's *Faust* Gretchen is more than a single tormented but triumphant spirit: she stands for the Eternally Feminine. And there is no reason why Faust should not stand for the Eternally Masculine. '. . . a single thing comprehended here is as good as a thousand.'

This train of thought leads Rilke to affirm what could be called the Principle of Concentration. There are blissful moments in every life, in childhood, maturity and old age, when we have 'veins full of existence', when the span of time between two moments is packed with meaning and fulfilment, when we declare life and world to be good. Of course, as Rilke reminds us, we are often distracted from appreciating such moments by watching instead the reaction of our neighbours to what *we* should be experiencing. When our experience is neither confirmed nor envied by others, we ourselves may fail to give such heightened moments their due.

Happiness, Rilke tells us in the Ninth Elegy, is not the main reason why life is important. Because it is inconstant and fleeting, he calls happiness 'that premature profit of imminent loss'. But sometimes we may see beyond the call of happiness and recognise that life is meaningful.

> because being here amounts to so much, because all
> this Here and Now, so fleeting, seems to require us and strangely
> concerns us. Us the most fleeting of all.

In these lines Rilke strikes a deeply religious note, a note which is repeated in Martin Heidegger's later notion of the 'call of Being' and in Paul Tillich's notion of 'ultimate concern'. Rilke's affirma-

tion is more radical than theirs because he proclaims the autonomous glory of finitude.

>   Just once,
> everything, and only once. Once and no more. And we, too
> once. And never again. But this
> having been once, though only once,
> having been once on earth—can it ever be cancelled?

The answer, as we have seen, is no. This answer is made possible
through the previous shift away from the picture of life and death
as inhabiting two separate realms. By replacing the two-realm
image with an image of space containing the living *and* the dead,
the cancellation of any existence is impossible. This realisation, in
turn, may show how important it is to fill life, one's own included,
with meaning and value.

How is this done? By tending lovingly, caringly to our tasks and
opportunities. By adding to the beauty of the world around us.
By facing up to problems which call for solutions. By turning our
attention to those features which absorb our energies as lovers,
parents, citizens. By naming and respecting values which lend
poignancy and intensity to our existence. By perpetuating our
traditions in celebration and ritual. The materials of this earth
hope to be intensely. And they achieve this intensity and meaning
through us. When the shapeless physical energies of the world are
transformed into such entities as house, bridge, fountain, gate,
window, pillar, tower, something new has been added to these
energies. All of the images are Rilke's, and he chose them as
symbols of human achievements and values. Each represents an
aspect of civilised existence and symbolises activities and forms of
life so characteristic of our longings and aspirations. We are
invited to exert our imaginations in trying to understand and
appreciate the familiar situations connected with the use of these
words. When Rilke tells us that we are here, on earth, for *saying*
these words, he packs a multitude of meanings into the simple
word 'saying'. Of course, it is primarily the poet who can show us
how bridges and fountains and windows can be connected with
various rites of passage, with striving and aspiration, with
opening new vistas, with love and wooing. But the poet differs
from us only in perceiving more sensitively and intensely what all
of us are capable of acknowledging and recognising in our own
experience. In other words, the poet can lead us to ourselves, to

our more deeply felt emotions. In saying after him what he says originally and revealingly, we are coming into our own, as beings who humanise the cosmic spaces, who make the earth alive with human meaning.

> Is not the secret purpose
> of this sly earth, in urging a pair of lovers,
> just to make everything leap with ecstasy in them?

From this point on the Ninth Elegy turns into a resounding affirmation of the ultimate importance of human existence. Even an angel, told what a human life can be, will stand astonished.

In the light of this ultimate affirmation the previously named features of human existence – childhood, love, herosim – stand out even more as targets of praise. The Sixth Elegy not only pays homage to heroism but also expresses wonder, astonishment, at the very possibility of heroic phenomena. It is difficult not be impressed by the display of heroic courage. Whether one's model is Samson or some other figure that stands out in our tradition and history, the hero's wholehearted, unreserved self-abandonment to his cause cannot help stirring up in us admiration and pride. The singlemindedness of the hero has its counterpart in the mutual devotion of lovers and in the total absorption of a child lost in the 'gap between toy and world'.

There are also tasks that call for very different sorts of character traits and dispositions. Returning to the 'river god of the blood' of the Third Elegy, we see Rilke suggesting that there is a human way of coping with ancestral biological evolutionary forces that come to the surface in sexuality. That way is understanding, compassion, tenderness. It is found in the caring, fear-dissolving countenance of the mother leaning over the bed of a child who is stirred by overpowering nightmares. It is also found in the gentleness of the lovers who counterbalance the animal aggressiveness of primordial instincts by channelling a part of the libido into the comfort of companionship and daily confidence.

Even sorrows may be seen in a new light when human life is seen as redeeming the silent, speechless cosmos. Our sorrows are but our 'winter foliage' – and winter belongs to the round of seasons. Instead of *wasting* sorrows, we should surrender ourselves to them, as reminders of values whose absence or violation we have reason to lament.

One consequence of suffering and disillusionment may be

despair and alienation. Having lost the more delicate resources of sensitivity, we may throw ourselves into cynical exploitation of power and pleasure and try to forget our humanity in sheer pursuit of physical or material comfort. Rilke resorts to sexual imagery to show the degradation of naked pursuit of pleasure and power, which creates a tinny, plastic, crass, aggressive, bombastic, vulgar culture, and offers nothing but constant distraction and empty entertainment. The frantic self-forgetfulness of sheer pleasure-seeking may take on obscene, pornographic, shallow, exploitative forms. 'Anatomy made amusing! Money's organs on view!' This section of the Tenth Elegy is a warning against the danger of dehumanisation when man abdicates his aesthetic and spiritual sensibilities. When we live only for pleasure we are doomed to disillusionment and to aimless, endless wandering along the 'streets of the City of Pain'.

Even if we manage to prevent the deterioration of broader sympathies and deeper sensibilities, we cannot avoid *all* suffering. For suffering is a part of life, and not an ignoble part of it. On the contrary, it can heighten our sense of the importance life has here on earth, for us its bearers, and for the earth its beneficiary. Lament may bring us to the wellsprings of Joy. Those afflicted by Primal Pain may be still aware of what the dead wish to retrieve. The thought of the endlessly departed may remind us of values whose absence induces pain and sorrow – the catkins hanging from empty hazels or the rain falling on the dark leaves in the early spring. There is a kind of happiness that is associated not with rising but with falling, not with anticipation but with regret – when we celebrate life by mourning. Rilke suggests that, by reversing the customary images connected with the idea of happiness, we may help to integrate the dark and the light sides of life, the up and the down of the Heraclitean cosmos, into a single indivisible whole.

> And we, who always thought
> of happiness climbing, would feel
> the emotion that almost startles
> when happiness falls.

B

Although Rilke's poem was composed decades before Auden and

Eliot published theirs, he was just as fully aware of the features of human existence that make it puzzling and problematic. Like Auden and Eliot, Rilke no longer accepts the optimistic appraisal of man bequeathed on the Western tradition by the Renaissance and the Enlightenment. All three perceive the irony of Hamlet's declamation 'What a piece of work is a man! how noble in reason! how infinite in faculties! in form and moving how express and admirable! in action how like an angel! in apprehension how like a god! the beauty of the world, the paragon of animals!' All three poets doubt that the label 'rational animal' is applicable to the species *Homo sapiens*. Or, at least, they add endless qualifications. The need to add these qualifications leads Auden and Eliot to return to the biblical verdict of original and pervasive human sinfulness. The positive, affirmative aspect of man is not inherently his but is due to the divine spark undeservedly bestowed on him by Divine Love. Thus life on earth, for Auden and Eliot, centres around hints and guesses that can lead us beyond the natural and the temporal to the eternal and supernatural. Perhaps Rilke too would have moved in their direction had he lived long enough to experience both the horrors of the Second World War and to be exposed to the revival of Augustinian Christianity in the garb of theological Neo-Orthodoxy.

But Rilke manages to transcend the basically elegiac mood, common to him and to Auden and Eliot as well, in terms of a decidedly this-worldly affirmation. His images and metaphors are not derived from the Christian tradition, as is the case with Goethe and Eliot. Rilke sees the possibility of celebrating existence without falling back on the notions of redemption and salvation. This does not put him into the category either of rationalistic optimists or of pessimists. It would be simply incorrect to claim that he closes his eyes to crucial flaws and imperfections that characterise human nature. He is no less saddened and disheartened by human weaknesses, insufficiencies and tragic flaws. He does not fail to perceive that all too often life is a vale of tears. Suffering and pain are unavoidable, and to a very great extent they are self-inflicted — through ignorance, perversity or weakness of will. But, while for Auden and Eliot redemption can come only from the outside, from the beyond, Rilke does not slight the achievements of the human spirit. He is anxious to recognise them and be fair to them, *alongside* a realistic facing up to our sinfulness, if that notion is taken in a broader sense than the theological.

We have noted that, while Eliot falls back on the central message of Christianity to appraise our total spiritual situation, he manages to make only a minimal use of theological concepts and he does so in a way that enables us to see the Christian point of view as merging with more universal philosophically defensible perspectives. When Eliot speaks of the intersection of time and timelessness he falls back on the tradition whose progenitor, or at least godfather, is Plato, who spoke of time as the moving image of eternity. Eliot's objective is similar to Plato's, or perhaps even more so to that of a brilliant Platonist, F. H. Bradley, whose version of the Platonic Form of the Good was represented by the Absolute. Like Bradley, Eliot seeks to collect the shattered fragments of experience and bring them before the healing, whole-making altar of the Absolute, which for him is equivalent to the God of Christianity. Unless and until the fragments of partial ecstasies and agonies are taken up by God's love, they are unredeemable in any other way and fall into the void.

Rilke saw another possibility. He too was trying to solve the problem of temporality and transitoriness. He too was oppressed by the spectre of death and ultimate oblivion. But he was apparently not attracted by the idea of resolving the issue by making the leap of faith into the miraculous intervention of a personal Saviour, to whom the believer, *de profundis,* surrenders his heart, mind, and soul. Such a surrender need not and should not be scoffed at. It is an understandable move of a soul *in extremis,* brought up against the limits of moral and spiritual endurance. The vision of the loving Father Abyss who is capable of taking up and redeeming all our agonies and anxieties, personal and cosmic, is touching and beautiful and has given meaning to many millions of lives.

But suppose we take another look at the situation. Suppose we ask what happens in and to the world that witnesses the ongoing dramas of human lives and history. Without slighting the heroic representatives of mankind, among whom prophets and founders of great religions certainly must be counted, Rilke attaches supreme importance to *every* human life as illuminating the cosmic spaces from within. He envisages the possibility for every one of us to declare solidarity with all achievements of the human spirit, in all the creations of art, science, morality, statemanship. There *are* reasons why we also should be proud of our membership in the human race, as well, of course, as there are ample reasons for being ashamed of it. But Rilke invites us to balance shame and pride, suffering and happiness. Even shame and suffering testify to our ability to recognise and appreciate values which are violated when we have cause to be ashamed or to suffer. To the extent that we can experience our lot as tragic and not just pathetic, we are bearing witness to our capacity to recognise the importance of spiritual values in the otherwise value-less cosmos.

Rilke solves the problem of death, as we have seen, by suggesting that we shift around our basic images. Think of life and death not as following one another but as two sides of the same coin. Cosmic spaces accommodate both the living *and* the dead, the existent and the non-existent, including those still to come. And think of yourself as an occupant of that generous all-accommodating cosmic space. Someday you will be dead, of course; that's inevitable. But it is also inevitable that you will become a permanent part of all that has been, and in that sense you cannot be eradicated, you are immortal, just as are all those who went before you and will come and go after you.

There is a connection between private rose-gardens, partial personal ecstasies, and the overarching cosmic human meaning, and the relationship is not altogether different from the way Auden and Eliot saw it. For Eliot these private ecstasies are hinted at by the one Annunciation of the ever-present reality of Divine Love that is discerned in all moments of temporal creative love. For Rilke, on the other hand, such moments of ecstasy connect us with the whole stream of creative endeavour, enshrined for us in potent universal symbols celebrated by poets: house, bridge, window, gate, pillar, tower. These symbols are meant to recall us to our bond with the inner content of deep human experiences, scattered through all human history, which have transformed the visible into the invisible, thus making the earth and the spaces around it intimate with spirituality.

Rilke's failure to single out any specific persons from human history as representing epitomies of spiritual achievement may be his way of paying homage to *all* humanity. By speaking anonymously of all of us and by crediting us with the possibility of identifying ourselves with the highest and best creations of the human race ('But wasn't Chartres great?'), Rilke's spiritual ideology is truly democratic, non-elitist, and thoroughly compassionate. No one is excluded from the realm of values, for all of us, at one time or another, are capable of having 'veins full of existence'.

Is Rilke's world view religious? That depends on how generously one conceives the word. No living word is static; in time it takes on new connotations and overtones. During the modern period, from the Renaissance up to the present, mankind has continued to engage in serious soul-searching about itself. It has definitely moved beyond the initial one-sided, over-optimistic and unrealistic conception of humanity. Its expectations to create, by means of science and technology, a perfect City of Man, has foundered on many intractable problems, both internal and external. To conquer nature and to make it our servant has turned out to be harder than we supposed. The pressure of life itself has created an unmanageable population explosion, and aggressive schemes and overambitious ideologies have kept transforming the globe into a warring camp. We have also learned that our inner life is not as easily mappable as was dreamt in rationalistic philosophies and psychologies.

But the discovery of complexities lurking in the depths of our psyches is not necessarily a loss. As Dostoyevsky observed, man is wide indeed, but who would have him narrower? Rilke refused to be psychoanalysed, on the grounds that in the process of eliminating his foibles all his creative talent would be analysed away as well. Rilke's fears may have been unfounded, but we know by now that the schemes to 'streamline' human beings, to make them amenable to a hidden persuasion by narrow-minded social engineers or power-hungry ideologues are anti-human in the most concrete sense of the term. Human beings are still too deep a mystery to fit any reductionist pattern. Our great modern writers have tried to respond in a fair-minded, reverent way to the unfathomableness human beings often display. This reverence toward the human enterprise in the cosmos permeates the work of the three poets we have just discussed. All of them have moved beyond the shallow promises and simple-minded hopes of the Age of Reason. They showed that our self-conception need be neither shallow nor simple-minded. If it is realistic and fair to the total scope of our capabilities, it may enlarge our vision, ecourage our hopes, and inspire our actions.

Conclusion

Man is also what he *thinks* he is. What we make of our human condition is itself a part of that condition. As sensitive observers of our situation, great writers are not just commenting on what they see happening in their world. They are not impartial observers, giving us clinical, merely factual reports in a fictional garb: they share with us their evaluations as well. In reading their works, we sense that they are not indifferent to the question of whether we succeed or fail in formulating and implementing our objectives. They reorient and redirect our consciousness by showing us the consequences and implications of embracing certain values or of flaunting them. In that sense, great artists also play a normative role and contribute to the *making* of our cultural climate. They are not only meteorologists but also weather-makers.

In shaping his art the writer is formulating – in character and plot or in poetic images – his own personal conception of human possibilities, but in doing so he often speaks for all mankind. He loves his imagined characters because, in one way or another, he sees himself in them. He does not necessary approve of what they do and say in his work, but, if he is a sympathetic observer of the human psyche, which a good artist always is, he understands even a criminal mind. Nothing human is alien to such a sympathetic student of the human lot. Even his villains he sees as aberrations into wich any one of us, at least in part, inadvertently or inexplicably may fall.

The twelve works discussed in this book manage to put before us scenes from life that force us to look more deeply into ourselves. In musing about their characters, the authors ponder their lives – and ours. They interest us in Faust's exuberant pursuit of experience, in Hamlet's agonised reaction to his shattering discovery, in Kurtz's response to his own degradation, in Billy Budd's self-sacrificial martyrdom, in Ivan Karamazov's instructive failure to solve the problem of evil and in Alyosha's more realistic approach to it, in Hans Castorp's delicate talent for

227

learning from his mentors, in Meursault's estrangement from his culture, in Garcin's frustration with himself and others, in Vladimir's and Estragon's attempts to rescue some meaning from the depths of despair, in Auden's and Eliot's return to religious roots, in Rilke's call to marry life and death. Following the twists and turns in the lives of fictional characters, pondering with them their dilemmas and their efforts to come to terms with them, we are alerted to analogous problems and options that enter, in some shape or form, our own experience. Likewise, in absorbing the poetically and metaphorically rendered crisis situations, we recognise in them our own moods, feelings, and thoughts. These are ways in which art can sometimes speak to us.

The temporal drama of individual and collective existences, imaginatively embodied in great writings, calls us back to ourselves. That is why we are spellbound by genius, recognising its echo in our spiritually starved egos. In great works of art we are sharing their authors' excitement and anguish, condemnation and praise, pain and exultation. Like them, we bask in amazement and wonder over the heights and depths of human existence, its misery and its glory, its degrading stumblings and mighty achievements, its inescapable juggling of evil and good.

Great fictional and poetic works are often journeys toward self-discovery. As we have noted, it is never just a matter of reporting on something pre-existing. Rather, it is a matter of creating an imaginary context which can throw light on what we are up against, confused and bewildered in our inconclusive quest. As the writers realise, our problem in crossroad or crisis situations is not that we do not know what our possibilities are, but rather the superabundance of models and options that come our way from the past and the present, from our traditions and from contemporary surroundings. A person's task is to find his way among multiple possibilities, often tantalisingly attractive and yet harbouring dangers, unexpectedly trying and demanding, but also challenging and exhilarating. Artists are especially sensitive to the ways in which the human drama of self-discovery may lead to self-realisation or self-alienation, to fulfilment or frustration.

A successful literary work speaks to the reader directly. The author knows and respects the tendency of every person to think of himself as different from all others. No person thinks of himself as a replica. But the consciousness of not being a replica does not automatically lead to a sense of self-worth. Rather it is experienced as a challenge. We ask, 'What *is* different about me?' The force of the question is not to invite a search for what one already is but to initiate a quest for what one can become. Here is the origin of the myth of the Holy Grail. We are a mystery to ourselves not because something already existing is hidden from us, but because we are tantalised by the problem as to which possibilities and potentialities open to us we can, want to, or should realise. This is the unique and the constant task of being human, and in this task the function of art is indispensable.

It does not take us long to realise that there is no easy answer to the question of what we want to or should become. We find ourselves equipped with capacities, talents, proclivities and bents which even in incipient exercise seem to be largely open-ended. In putting before us imaginatively constructed human possibilities, a writer, to be sure, complicates and intensifies the problem of self-discovery, or, more accurately, of self-formation. But, in learning what other individuals, real or fictional, could do with their lives, what they accomplished or created, how they faced various kinds of obstacles and problems, what visions they entertained, what schemes they concocted, what crimes they committed, what heinous or heroic deeds they performed, what they thought of their societies or religions, we construct a background against which we can see our own possibilities. The more models and examples we have for our perpetual self-definition, the greater the chances that we can find among them feasible or acceptable leads for our choices.

While thinking of our possibilities, our options, our destinies, the artist is also thinking about the world into which we are born and of which we are a part. What does *it* amount to? Does it make sense? What is it worth? Does it have some deep secrets, some ultimate meaning? The answers to such questions are bound to affect what we think of ourselves, of the meaning of our lives. Metaphysical speculation quickly connects with the question of how we are to translate it into action. In showing us, fictionally, how this connection can occur, great artists act as our vanguard.

As we have seen, the self-perception of the modern man has been undergoing significant changes. Locating the origins of Western modernity in the Renaissance, we have been looking at questions raised about its subsequent course. Has the affirmative momentum generated in the Renaissance spent itself? Are we at the end of an era? That the estimates as to where we stand on the rise–decline scale should vary from age to age and from thinker to thinker should not be surprising. It is not easy to determine the moral health of a civilisation, because, as Toynbee noted and other writers confirm, a culture is not completely subject to external causal determination but may gather inner responses to threatening challenges. Whether a culture will produce adequate responses is an open question and may depend on regenerative individual resources within it. There seems to be a parallel here to William James's claim that, when on an important issue the objective evidence is inconclusive either way, the rightness of the solution is in part determined by the nature of our response. When the spiritual health and prospects of a culture are being considered, the estimates of how deeply we have sunk and what are the prospects of recovery depend in part on the perceivers' vision. This includes the vision of creative writers as well. We have noted that they are not just commentators or prophets: they are also evaluators and as such are capable of stimulating us to translate our perceptions into active attitudes. They may point a way toward a possible regeneration while not denying the depth of our predicaments.

The artists remind us that what we make of the world includes the way we choose to relate ourselves to it – by taking our stand in it, by adding our voice, by registering our protest, by setting ourselves against it, by trying to correct its mistakes. This applies even to situations of extreme crisis. Even if our philosophical reflections convince us that ultimately the world is too much of a riddle, or that the promise of some deeper meaning is in fact an impostor, teasing us with possibilities of eternal grace, glory or salvation while mindlessly obeying the second law of thermodynamics, the verdict is not all in. It is fully in only after we have registered our *reaction* to this, supposedly unredeemable, state of affairs. And then, surprisingly perhaps, we may be struck by the thought that, since we are a part of that allegedly meaningless world, what *we* introduce into the world by means of our reaction makes a difference to that verdict. The ability to introduce revisions into the state of affairs by taking a stand on them may be perceived as man's calling on earth. Indeed, our special distinction and dignity may consist in our ability to shape our lives and destinies in ways *we* deem worthy and desirable, even under the most trying of circumstances. If the ethical light of our response can enter the metaphysical darkness, that darkness is not impenetrable.

The works we have examined abound in striking examples of how the metaphysical quest may merge into ethical insight. Moral considerations in *Hamlet* are prominent and specific. Whatever we learn from this play about the status of man in the universe must include the prince's moral stance with regard to that status. Through his reaction to his difficult personal circumstances Hamlet transforms them into something special – tragic, but awe-inspiring. A timeless universe that contains Hamlet is in incomparably richer than the one that does not. Even Rilke's Angel would be astonished to encounter such a noble figure. A similar conclusion can be drawn about Billy Budd. His innocent and willing martyrdom raises the moral stature of man. Captain Vere's agonised conscience, imposing on him a hellishly difficult decision and leaving him with a moral burden that surpasses guilt and remorse, is an awesome crucible in which the human spirit is tried. Even if we have doubts about the rightness of Vere's decision, we cannot quarrel with the motives which lead him to it: the sense of responsibility for persons in his charge and the unquestioned desire to do the right thing by the cause to which he and others are committed. Even when evil is unavoidable and when we must be its instruments, the *way* in which we act in such circumstances may be a kind of victory over evil.

As Marlow tells us, Kurtz was capable of such a victory. When he looked into himself he rejected what he saw. The struggle in his soul produced a truthful, undeceived judgement, a self-condemnation that was prompted by a desire for honest self-appraisal. It is no mean achievement to be thus ruthlessly honest with oneself and to retrieve the painful truth about one's moral downfall. All the cruelties and stupidites Marlow observed in the Congo are somehow put in a different light when at least one talented and clear-headed person is capable of cutting through his self-deceiving rationalisations and of facing his own unspeakable degradation. Marlow, who witnessed Kurtz's inner struggle and suffering, was profoundly moved by it and honoured it in his subsequent behaviour. Even if we compare the human soul to a jungle, we still must not ignore the flickering of conscience so masterfully portrayed in Conrad's story. Is the world dark? Yes, but there are ways in which human beings sometimes can prevent it from being *too* dark, from falling into utter darkness.

Alyosha Karamazov is particularly talented in turning on the light in human souls, thus helping fellow human beings to be better than they otherwise would have been. He does so out of the conviction that each person has the source of light within him and that our task in life should be to help it emerge. How important is the role of Alyosha in *The Brothers Karamazov*? Well, try to imagine the novel without him.

Although Hans Castorp is not such an effective Alyosha-like catalyst that helps people's better side to emerge, he at least has the talent to allow the delicate promptings of reason, goodness, and love to rise from beneath the crust of his own inertia, ennui, insensibility. He manages to stay receptive to stimuli that keep the divine spark from being extinguished. He responds to influences that concern his status as *homo Dei* and slowly but steadily works his way out of confusion generated by human and natural forces in and around him. To the alternatives presented to him in the dream during the snow scene he does not respond with a mere intellectual judgement but with a moral decision not to let the forces of death have sovereignty over him. In that scene Mann makes it clear that it is man's task to resolve metaphysical perspectives by ethical decisions. This is man's special way of making a difference in the universe.

Interestingly enough, this is precisely the way in which such disparate characters as Faust and Meursault find their way to clarity. Faust's final wisdom lies in rededicating himself to what is truly divine in him: the inexhaustible potential for growth. Meursault's 'conversion' consists in the transition from apathy to affirmation, from passivity to resoluteness. In the exchange with the priest he suddenly discovers that he was happy before but did not know it. Now he knows that his life is good, good absolutely, and he resolves to live out its remaining moments in full conviction of its positive meaning. His self-alienation is overcome in his decision to rededicate himself to life and to affirm its unquestionable value.

Likewise, Vladimir and Estragon retain dominance over despair and despondency by not giving up their waiting; hoping against hope, they refuse to budge from the stage of life. It is significant that in their stubborn persistence to hold Godot to his word they keep their capacity for mutual attachment, their minimal but tender love for one another. This tenderness is a moral force that lightens their metaphysical burden and physical pain. Auden's, Eliot's, and Rilke's poems also manifest this spiritual tenaciousness in the face of the tenuousness and fragility of human existence. Only *through* time and human actions *in* time can time be redeemed, concluded Eliot. Although, according to Rilke, we live our lives forever taking leave, the leave-taking is in the nature of a call. 'Who, if I cried, would hear me among the angelic orders?' asks Rilke in the first lines of his poem. Not sure whether the Angel will respond to our call, we nevertheless keep calling because *through* this call the visible is transformed into invisible. The dark earth comes into the light of the spirit.

Unlike Beckett, Rilke did not believe that the human call remains minimal and limited. The difference between them lies in their respective estimates of the ultimate efficacy of the call. Beckett's notion of time led him to think that all past human achievements have dissolved into nothingness, or at most have their lame fragmented traces in Lucky's battered hat. Rilke's notion of time allows him to treat values brought into the universe through human striving as objectively immortal, as indestructible elements of the cosmos. Ultimately this is not a difference in intellectual interpretation but a difference in evaluation; even the timeless Angel must be impressed when he contemplates what the human spirit has brought into 'these generous spaces', crowded 'with thousands of years of feeling'. Among the permanent inhabitants of these spaces we must count the thoughts and feelings that gave rise to the works examined in this study.

Index